Whispers
in the
Windstorm

Whispers in the Windstorm

A JOURNAL OF GOD'S BLESSED ASSURANCE DURING MY YEAR WITH BREAST CANCER

KATHRYN DANYLKO

PEREGRINE
PRODUCTIONS

Cover by Adazing Design

Publisher's Cataloging-in-Publication data

Names: Danylko, Kathryn.
Title: Whispers in the windstorm : a journal of God's blessed assurance during my year with breast cancer / Kathryn Danylko.
Description: Rochester, New York: Peregrine Productions, 2016.
Identifiers: ISBN 978-0-9973983-9-7 | LCCN 2016937929.
Subjects: LCSH Danylko, Kathryn --Health. | Cancer patients. | Breast--Cancer--Patients--United States--Biography. | Christian biography. | BISAC BIOGRAPHY & AUTOBIOGRAPHY / Personal Memoirs | RELIGION / Christian Life / General | HEALTH & FITNESS / Diseases / Cancer.
Classification: LCC RC280.B8 D36 2016 | DDC 362.19699/4490092--dc23

Printed in the United States of America

For the Lord of lords.

Someday I hope to hear,
"Well done, good and faithful servant!"

Listen to the inward whisper of His Spirit and follow it—that is enough; but to listen, one must be silent, and to follow, one must yield.

François Fénelon (1651 – 1715)

Contents

A word from the author vii

Preface ix

Foreshadowing 1

December 5

January 23

February 129

March 171

April 199

May 223

June 233

July 255

August 287

September 317

October 331

November 353

Epilogue 359

Appendix 363

A word from the author

This book is based on handwritten journals that I kept in small spiral-bound notebooks from December 2010 until November 2011. When I transcribed my handwritten notes, I ended up with seven hundred typed pages. In this book, I have expanded some entries, condensed and omitted many others.

The conversations are written from memory, usually the day of the dialogue. Oftentimes I shortened the conversations. However, the words prophesied by Pastor Michael, Brother Paul, and Rev. Ted Shuttlesworth are written exactly as they were spoken; they were transcribed from digital recordings that I took of Pastor Michael and Brother Paul, and a DVD of the Faith Temple service with Rev. Ted Shuttlesworth. The recordings of Pastor Michael and Brother Paul were translated from Ukrainian, the language that I speak at home and that I spoke with these men.

While the events I describe are accurate, I have changed the names of some people in the book for the sake of their privacy.

I write about my medical treatments (and refusal of treatments) not as medical advice, but as record of my own thought processes and decisions. These may not be the right decisions for you. Please consult your own physicians and seek the advice of professionals, and get down on your knees. God is the best advisor and healer.

Cancer is a difficult journey. Each patient walks that path alone on a solitary trek even when surrounded by loved ones. During my illness, I felt fortunate to have my husband and children with me.

Although family and friends provided tremendous support and lifted my spirits with touching acts of kindness, my primary encouragement came from my Christian faith. I was reassured that the Holy Spirit lives in me, and at times felt an unearthly peace. I took great comfort knowing that I will be with Jesus when my stay on earth is through. However, there were also times I felt empty and gave in to fear and panic and tears. I'm human.

I start almost every journal entry with a Bible verse because I found solace in these verses. As I read the Bible, I jotted down verses that touched me, lifted me up, and imparted wisdom. I hope that these verses also speak to you.

Each cancer journey, like each of our lives, is different. However, many of our fears are universal. If you've walked that walk, you will be able to identify with some of the emotions I share. If you're walking it now, I hope that you find comfort in knowing that what you feel is not uncommon.

Whether you currently have cancer, had cancer, know someone with cancer, or just want to know what it's like to experience cancer, I'd like you to take away the same message: Put your faith in the Lord and He will lift you up. Listen for His voice. You can find Him in other people, in the twitter of a robin, in the rustle of autumn leaves. He can speak to you through a song, a Bible verse, or a sunset. Delight in little everyday things. Find joy in the beauty of nature. Appreciate each day.

But most of all, seek Him.

Preface

"Yes or no?" I looked into my husband's pale blue eyes, but I knew that he didn't have the answer. Dishtowel in hand, I stood in the bedroom with Tad while the guests gathered in the living room. I was about to serve lunch, but I needed to speak to Tad before we sat at the table and I lost my chance to confer with him privately.

"Am I or am I not supposed to write the book?" I continued. "Maybe I misread the signs. Maybe they weren't from God. Maybe I got carried away with the idea of becoming an author. Maybe I'm wasting my time trying to write something no one will read. I would like to know once and for all, am I supposed to write this book or not? I wish God would give me a sign through Pastor Michael."

I had skipped the morning's church service that late April Sunday in order to cook lunch for the visiting pastor, deacon, and others from the Cortland and Ithaca churches and our home church in Rochester, New York. I was sorry not that I had missed the sermons, but that after preaching, I had missed being present while the visiting Pastor Michael walked around the sanctuary and prophesied over various individuals. I so wanted to hear from God about this book that I thought I was to write. You see, the book is about my year battling cancer—not a topic I had ever considered writing about. Yet the day I got diagnosed, a friend told me, "You should journal through your cancer." Two days later, another friend said, "You have to journal through your experience. It will help others." Since two people with whom I can't remember ever discussing journaling told me to journal through my cancer experience, I recognized it was God speaking through them. I hadn't planned on journaling about my cancer, but I journaled. And journaled and journaled, sometimes writing for hours in the hush of the night. At the end of the year, I sent out a Christmas newsletter based on my journal, and a different friend asked me, "Have you considered writing a book?"

I hear you Lord, I thought. So I started to transcribe and edit my hundreds of handwritten pages. I wrote faithfully and fervently— until a couple of months into the project I got sick with a bad cold. I had been working full-time, homeschooling my youngest, and balancing a myriad of household tasks along with the writing when the three-week-long cold sent me to bed and disrupted my routine. The illness completely derailed my book project. And with the coming of spring, the gardens beckoned. Doubts crept in.

"After lunch, I'll ask Pastor Michael to pray for you," Tad assured me.

We went back to our guests, and I served the meal I'd prepared. Conversation bounced from church affairs to mission trips to people we knew in both the U.S. and in Ukraine, where my husband and the visitors were all born. I served sautéed chicken and scalloped potatoes and salad. My younger daughter helped me bring out dessert and tea. At no time did Tad mention my dilemma.

As the guests prepared to leave, Tad spoke up. "Kathryn would like you to pray for her," he said to Pastor Michael.

We knelt on the hardwood floor of the living room. All eleven of us raised our voices together in communal prayer. Then after a moment, Pastor Michael's voice rose above the others:

"Yes or no? Yes, I want you to speak. I want you to share. I will heap blessings upon blessings on you..."

A shock went through me. The Creator of the Universe, the King of kings and Lord of lords, the God of Abraham, Isaac, and Jacob—

He repeated my question to me before He answered it! The one and only God Almighty, the God who had spoken to Moses—He actually responded to this trivial question of one tiny speck of humanity on this earth and answered it so directly. I was amazed. Dazzled. Stunned. For weeks, I was as awed as if I myself had seen the burning bush.

Perhaps it's silly that we don't believe that the God of the Bible is the same God today that He was back when Moses walked the earth and David fought Goliath. Christianity today has been so watered down that many people think that miracles and actual encounters with God don't exist anymore. They do! But you need to slow down, and in the stillness, ask with all your heart and be willing to listen with all your soul.

And you will seek Me and find Me, when you search for Me with all your heart.
– Jeremiah 29:13 (NKJV)

This is my story…

Foreshadowing

When the doorbell rang, I was at my computer in my home office writing e-mails. Why would my husband or kids ring the doorbell when I purposely left the front door unlocked?

I went to the front entry hall expecting to see my three teenage children coming home from the evening youth group meeting, but instead I saw three other teens, friends of my children, on the front porch.

"We came to pray for you," said eighteen-year-old Tatiana in her ever-calm voice.

I was confused. How could she know? I had gotten the diagnosis earlier that evening right before my husband Tad left for the youth group meeting.

I opened the door wider.

"Come into the living room," I invited Tatiana and her two younger brothers, Myron and Michael. "So you heard?"

"Yes, we heard. We were in youth group tonight and Brother Tad asked for prayer for you."

My visitors did not take off their winter coats as they came into the living room. We knelt on the Turkish carpet in the circle of warmth cast by the wood-burning stove. As we bowed our heads, Tatiana began:

"Thank you, Lord, for Sister Kathryn. Thank you for loving her enough to trust her with this illness. Thank you for giving her the strength to deal with it…"

She made it sound like God allowing this illness in my life was a privilege, a disguised blessing.

Next, fifteen-year-old Myron prayed. Referring to Matthew 25:35-40, he thanked God for my hands and feet, for using me to feed Jesus, clothe Jesus, visit Jesus in jail. He thanked God for my example of serving the poor in Africa and Mexico and other places.

I was weeping by then. I had no idea that I had touched the lives of these teenagers. I was surprised that they would drive to my house to pray for me, arriving even before my own family came home. Most teenagers just don't think that way.

Michael, the youngest, remained quiet. I prayed next, thanking God for their uplifting visit. When we got up, Tatiana wrapped me in a big hug. Myron, who towered above me, reached over and hugged me.

"Mom…" he said, and I smiled through my tears. Calling me "Mom" has been our joke since the mission trip to Mexico two-and-a-half years before. My husband and I had taken our three teenagers and four others from the church youth group to Mexico to distribute used clothing and school supplies to the Chinanteco tribe deep in the verdant hills of Oaxaca. We lived in the thatch-covered huts with black scorpions, spiders the size of small rodents, and people who were more hospitable than my grandmother. One day, the missionary we were serving with, Paul Gonzalez, told Myron, "Go call your mom. Tell her to come out here."

"But my mom isn't here," Myron, puzzled, explained to Paul.

"Yes, she is. Go get her."

"But she's not here!"

"Yes, she is. She's in the house," insisted Paul. "Tell her to come out here."

Then Myron realized that Paul had mistaken him for my son Jacob. So Myron went into the house and called me—and has jokingly called me "Mom" ever since.

After their prayer, Tatiana, Myron, and Michael refused my invitation to stay. They left, walking into the brisk darkness of the winter night. Their gesture was so unexpected, so touching.

But it was Tatiana's prayer that echoed in my heart and set the stage for what was to come.

December

Wednesday, 29 December 2010

"For I know the plans I have for you," declares the LORD, "plans to prosper you and not to harm you, plans to give you hope and a future."

– Jeremiah 29:11 (NIV)

Cancer. I have cancer. It sounds so surreal when I say it. So serious. So deadly. Cancer and me in the same sentence? How could this be?

Just three short weeks ago during my lunch break at work, I read the news that Elizabeth Edwards, wife of presidential candidate John Edwards, had died of breast cancer. A lengthy article described her life, her schooling, her marriage, her character, her death. She was sixty-one and had battled the disease for six years. In other words, she was my age, fifty-five, when she discovered the golf ball-sized lump in her breast while taking a shower.

How can anyone have a golf ball-sized lump in her breast and not know it? I wondered.

I filed this article in the back of my mind and went back to my job of writing user manuals. Eleven days later, while soaking in the bathtub on a Saturday evening, I thought, *I never do those breast self-exams that the doctor always tells me to do. I probably should.* So I used the tips of my fingers to feel—a lump? No, could it really be? I felt the other side. Nothing. Then the left side again. A lump.

Definitely a lump, bigger than a marble, smaller than a ping-pong ball. It hadn't hurt. I hadn't known it was there. Like Elizabeth Edwards.

Probably a cyst, I thought. *My younger sister has had cysts before.* So I didn't panic, didn't think it was anything serious. But all that touching, squeezing, pushing did cause the lump to be somewhat sore.

It's all in my head, I convinced myself. *It's just a cyst, and moving that lump all around caused the pain. Just because it's a lump doesn't mean it's cancer.*

But I didn't sleep well that night. The next day I called my sister.

"I had one cyst that was aspirated. The other lump was a fibro-adenoma, and it was removed," she explained.

I didn't know what a fibroadenoma was, but I knew it wasn't cancer.

By now I was fairly convinced that I had a cyst, but I called the OB-GYN office first thing on Monday morning and went in the same day. A physician's assistant felt the lump.

"It's…" She searched for the right word.

"Mushy?" I filled in.

"Yes, mushy," she explained. "I know that 'mushy' isn't a medical term. But the lump isn't hard. I'm not worried about it, but I'll still send you for a mammogram."

Although I thought I'd had a mammogram the year before, the records showed that it had been two years since the last one.

I remembered the debate I'd heard on the radio a year ago and the new recommendation for getting mammograms every two years instead of annually for women my age. Additional cost of false positives? Emotional trauma for those women who think they might have cancer, but don't? Extra exposure to x-rays? I didn't need much convincing to skip a year. My parents are both alive and well at eighty and ninety-one, and besides, I'm so small that I didn't think that breast cancer would have much tissue in which to grow.

The mammogram was scheduled eight days later. I wasn't in a hurry.

The appointment was for 11:45 AM. I hadn't eaten lunch. I didn't realize that I would be at the clinic until 4 PM. After all, I was just having a mammogram: go in, register at the desk, strip from the waist up, put on a gown, wait your turn, get your breasts squashed between two plates, turn this way, turn that way, zap, zap, zap, then wait to have the x-rays read. If an anomaly is found, get zapped again. Get dressed, go home. Should take an hour.

But not this time.

The OB-GYN office had made my mammogram appointment at a place I hadn't been to before, the Elizabeth Wende Breast Care Center. It has a reputation for pampering its patients: free tea, free snacks, crackling fireplace, a tranquil aquarium, and chairs arranged to give you privacy as you wait while wrapped in the blue smock worn with the opening in the front. The piano-and-violin music was peaceful and relaxing. The mammogram experience at this center is meant to be soothing.

I left my clothing in a locker and carried the key on an elastic band around my wrist like at the YMCA. Dressed in my blue gown, I chose a seat near the fireplace and began to read the book I'd brought with me. I remember two younger women sitting in a corner just within earshot, sharing their experiences with breast cancer. *How odd,* I thought. *They're so young. How could they have had cancer? I'm glad I just have a cyst.*

A technician did my digital mammogram quickly, then led me back to the waiting room. I received a yellow sheet offering massages—for a price, of course: one dollar per minute.

Between one and two billion people on this planet make one dollar per *day*—one dollar for a day's worth of hard physical labor, such as hauling cinder blocks up ramps on wooden scaffolding at a construction site. I'd seen women doing that in Ethiopia for one dollar per day. But here they were charging one dollar in one minute! I struggled with this. I craved a professional massage, but had a hard time justifying the cost. Pay someone ten days' wages? Would it really be better than the massages with which my husband has spoiled me? I'm not one to indulge myself—I'm too thrifty—so I don't really know how I justified it that day. If this lump is—I couldn't say the word—is not a cyst, this would be a little treat before the cusp of something that I couldn't even imagine.

So for ten dollars, the minimum, I indulged myself with a ten-minute chair massage. Given in a specially designed chair while clothed, the massage was delightful. The subdued lighting and soft piano music were almost enough to distract me from the real reason I was there.

I was then led into the ultrasound room. Apparently this was standard procedure when one has a lump.

I lay down on a table in the dimmed room. Dr. Khokhar, a man of Arabic descent but without a foreign accent, did the ultrasound. At first I was disappointed that I was being examined by a male in this predominantly female-run clinic, but I quickly got over my disappointment. This twenty-something man, who was balding prematurely, was polite, treated me with respect, and explained everything as he did it.

Instead of looking at the lump first, he held the ultrasound probe under my arm.

"The lymph nodes look normal," he stated.

I looked at the monitor on my left.

"You know how to read this, but I don't know what a lymph node looks like," I told him.

Dr. Khokhar pointed out little C-shaped sausage-like dark objects on a lighter background of what looked like static. "Those are your lymph nodes."

He went on to the lump in my left breast.

"I don't like the way this looks," he said, looking at the lump on the monitor. "There are calcium deposits."

I could see white spots—the calcium.

"Perhaps I take too many calcium supplements?" I suggested.

"No, it's not that. If water collects somewhere, eventually the minerals will crystallize. It's like that."

Dr. Khokhar assured me that the majority of tumors are benign and this one was not necessarily malignant.

"I'll confer and see whether we should do a biopsy," he said, and walked out of the room.

Meanwhile, a nurse came in and asked whether I was willing to participate in research being done on a CAT scan for cancer. They were asking for volunteers who had lumps, so I qualified for their study. I agreed to the CAT scan, though I later regretted it because the scan took additional time, required getting an IV (ouch!), and the injected dye caused some strange side effects: my blood vessels felt warm, almost hot. The flush moved through my body and across my bladder. I panicked and began to pant, which frightened the medical staff. They rushed around like alarmed ants and hooked me up to IV fluid to flush out the dye. I was glad when it was over.

"The doctors decided it's best to do a biopsy," a nurse informed me and led me back into the ultrasound room.

"The needle will hurt like a bee sting," Dr. Khokhar explained, "then the pain killer, which is like Novocain, will take over. You shouldn't feel the second shot or anything during the biopsy. If you do, tell me."

I could see the needle entering my flesh on the ultrasound monitor. I closed my eyes.

"I don't know who designed these, but the biopsy machine sounds like a stapler," said the doctor. He held the machine behind his back so I couldn't see it, then pressed a button so I could hear the loud click. "I'll take four or five samples," he added.

I watched the needle on the monitor, digging through my flesh. I felt the tugging, but no pain. I never felt the initial incision. I don't know when he inserted the titanium marker that would tell the surgeon where to operate, if needed, or inform future mammographers where I'd been biopsied.

I wasn't done yet. I was sent back for yet another mammogram to check the position of the marker in my left breast.

When I came home, I went to the bedroom with my husband Tad so I could tell him my news without the children hearing.

"They'll call with results between five and seven o'clock tomorrow. There's a good chance that it's benign. But we should tell the children," I suggested.

At eighteen, seventeen, and fifteen, our three children are old enough to understand the ramifications of positive results. At the supper table, Tad told them I have a lump that could be cancerous, but the children did not seem at all concerned. Jacob, the oldest, who is in his first year at the local community college, admitted that he'd heard my conversation with my sister Marta the day I told her about the lump.

The answer tomorrow will determine the trajectory of my life. If it's negative, life goes on as usual; if positive, I face a rather frightening unknown.

Before going to bed, I wanted to hear from God about this. What would He tell me? I prayed and asked God to show me what the results would be. Then I picked up my Bible and, avoiding pages with bookmarks, I opened it. The pages fell to Nehemiah, a name that means "comforted by Jehovah." On the left was a heading, and that's where my eyes rested.

Dedication of the Wall of Jerusalem

At the dedication of the wall of Jerusalem, the Levites were sought out from where they lived and were brought to Jerusalem to celebrate joyfully the dedication with songs of thanksgiving and with the music of cymbals, harps, and lyres.

– Nehemiah 12:27 (NIV)

Would I be joyfully celebrating the news that the lump is benign? Or would I celebrate at a much later time that I had beaten cancer? Isn't it much more of a celebration to overcome an adversity than never to have faced it at all? A tiny part of me, oddly and illogically, wanted to have that experience, to know what it feels like to get that frightening diagnosis, to fight that battle, and to feel the victory. For an infinitesimal sliver of time, I wanted the challenge of cancer. A result of "benign" would be too easy, too boring, and life would simply continue as usual. But I pushed that bizarre thought aside. In all honesty, "benign" was what I was hoping for—and expecting.

This year's autumn rains had drawn on for days upon soggy days, but during the night when the calendar turned to December, the rain turned to snow. We awoke on December first to a world of white. The days and days of rain became days and days of snow, which piled up higher and higher. During all of December, the temperature did not rise above freezing. I spent many evenings chipping away the ice buildup on the back patio, ice that was dangerous to my two daughters as they carried buckets of water from the bathroom tub through the backyard to the shed near the end of the property where our two Nubian goats were housed.

Earlier today, as I stood under the patio light in the premature darkness of the winter evening chipping away at the ice with a shovel, my husband called me to the phone. It was 5:22 PM. That would be Dr. Khokhar.

I took the cordless phone in hand and stepped into the house. I heard a faint click as Tad picked up the bedroom phone to listen. I was thankful that he did; later I had a hard time remembering what the doctor had said.

I don't recall the beginning of the conversation, the introduction or the niceties. I was expecting the word "benign," but instead, I heard, "Unfortunately..."

That word said it all; I didn't need to hear the rest. Unfortunately, I was to take the path less traveled, the path less desired, the one full of brambles, fallen logs, and muddy slopes, the path where fearsome beasts hid behind shrubs. It would be a difficult path, but walking it would make me stronger.

Other words stand out from this conversation: Semi-aggressive. MRI. Lumpectomy. He mentioned the word *surgeon* as if everyone has a surgeon the way you have a dentist. I don't know any surgeon; I haven't needed one! Dr. Khokhar said that he couldn't recommend a surgeon, but he could give me some names off the record. I was too stunned to ask for them. My thoughts were dashing about like bumper cars trying to figure out how I would schedule an MRI, find a surgeon, get an appointment with this surgeon, and make sure my operation was scheduled—all before I left for Haiti on a mission trip with the family in ten days.

How does one go about finding a surgeon? I puzzled.

All this was going on in my head while we talked. Dr. Khokhar asked, "Do you want the names of the surgeons?" Of course I did; I just hadn't caught the hint before. So he named some surgeons, and I jotted them down.

The conversation lasted maybe ten minutes, but the ramifications will remain for life. I had just come to a large fork in the road, and I took the one less traveled—the one labeled "cancer."

"Do you want someone to stay home with you?" asked my husband as he prepared to go to the Wednesday night youth group meeting. I usually looked forward to a quiet house for a few hours on Wednesday evenings.

"No, I'll be fine. I'll make some phone calls," I said.

Tad asked again. He knew that women sometimes say "no" when they mean "yes," and "yes" when they mean "no."

"What if I ask *you* to stay?" I asked. He never missed leading the Wednesday youth group, even when he was sick. The "someone" he volunteered to stay home with me was my youngest child, fifteen-year-old Larissa.

"I'll stay if you want me to," he said.

That was comforting, even though I wasn't completely convinced.

"Really, you don't need to stay," I assured him. "I'll just be on the phone. I want to call and tell some people." I had decided that my cancer would not be a secret.

As Tad and the kids bustled around the house in their typical last-minute frenzy of grabbing binders, books, and Bibles, I sat down by the fire in the living room and started a list of people to call. With the news, I'd lost my appetite and didn't want any supper.

I phoned my younger sister Marta first. She already knew I had a lump; now I told her it was cancer.

"Just don't tell Mama yet," I requested. "I'll go over to the house tomorrow and tell her in person."

Next, I called my boss, Betty. My illness would have a large impact on her because she'd have to shuffle around writers in our group to cover my projects while I was out on medical leave.

I started by telling Betty about the Elizabeth Edwards story, the lump, the mammogram, the biopsy, and ended with today's results.

"I'm so sorry," said Betty, sounding truly distressed. Her mother had died of cancer during the summer.

"It's okay to tell people about my cancer," I informed Betty. "I'm not going to keep it a secret. Many people at work go out on medical leaves without sharing the reason, and that just leaves co-workers to speculate and make up reasons. You can tell them."

"I'm so sorry," Betty repeated. "But it's not my place to tell others."

"Just so you know, I will be telling others in the group that I have breast cancer. I don't want it to be a mysterious absence."

Throughout our conversation, Betty repeated over and over, "I'm so sorry." I felt that I had to cheer her up.

"I'm sure things will be okay. It'll probably be a lumpectomy, the doctor said. I may need radiation afterward, or I may not. I'm okay. Don't be sorry! I'm sorry for you because I'm going to be out on medical leave and you'll have to find someone to do my job while I'm out. That's why I called you as soon as I found out, right after I called my sister."

Next, I talked with my brother George, who is seven years younger than I am. Then I reached Tamara, the wife of my youngest brother Peter. By the time I called my friend Tina, I had told the long version of my story, from reading Elizabeth Edwards' obituary through getting biopsy results, so many times that I shortened my news to three simple words: "I have cancer."

Tina, the only believer I had reached, prayed with me on the phone. It was soothing to feel loved enough to be lifted in prayer to the Lord, the one who has my fate and this illness in His hands.

"You should journal through your cancer," Tina suggested. And so that evening, I took a spiral notebook from the shelf of folders, binders, and notebooks that I keep for my children, whom I home-school, and started to write.

Thursday, 30 December 2010

God is for you. God loves you.
God will guide you. God will not fail you.
God will be with you. God will provide for you.
God will bless you. God will give you rest.
God will strengthen you. God will answer you.
God will uphold you. God will keep you.

These comforting words came in an e-mail this morning from Mema, an Indian friend who did not yet know that I had been diagnosed with cancer. But God knew. Mema was raised in Amy Carmichael's orphanage in India. She and her husband Gulshan are devout Christians now living in Rochester. We met them when Gulshan was the mission pastor in a church we previously attended.

How uplifting to read Mema's note, sent at a time when I needed it. God always knows our needs.

I did not go to work. Because of the upcoming New Year's holiday, doctors' offices will be closed tomorrow. I had to make calls today to schedule my medical appointments for next week.

I had a lot to arrange for the following week: schedule an MRI, select a surgeon and schedule an appointment, pick up the MRI films 24 hours after the procedure, then meet with the surgeon and determine the surgery date. On Saturday, January 8, our family will be leaving on a one-week mission trip to Haiti with two others from our church. Because I had traveled to Haiti with this mission organization soon after the 2010 earthquake, I am coordinating the Rochester team. I do not want to miss this trip. I hope to arrange all my medical appointments, including a date for the surgery, before we leave.

I made my first call just after 8 AM to schedule my MRI. I was delighted to get an appointment for Monday.

Next, I tackled that daunting and confusing task of choosing a surgeon. This was a critical decision, yet I had no experience in this area, no guidebook to follow. Not only did I have to select a surgeon, I had to schedule an appointment with this doctor for next week, which meant that I had to complete this task before 4:30 PM.

I had the names that Dr. Khokhar had mentioned, but I didn't want to select a surgeon at random. So I decided on this tactic: I'd call my general practitioner, my gynecologist, and my friends who are nurses and ask for their recommendations. I would make a list, and whoever came up most often would be the one I would choose.

Through the course of my calls, two names came up almost each time. I selected the one who came up most often. However, when I called his office, he was booked for the next two weeks. So I called the office of Dr. Lori Medeiros, who had the impressive title of Director of the Rochester General Hospital Breast Center. She specializes in breast cancer surgery. Dr. Medeiros has fourteen years of experience but since she is in her thirties, she is young enough to still have good vision without needing reading glasses. I like the thought of someone with good vision operating on me. And she had time to see me next Thursday. I succeeded making all my appointments.

After the shock of losing my brother Alex in a bizarre accident two years ago, I knew that the news of my cancer was not a conversation I should have on the phone with my parents. In the afternoon, Tad and I drove the one mile to my parents' suburban home.

We do not typically visit my parents in the middle of a workday, so I was afraid my mother would be suspicious. Tad and I went to the kitchen making small talk with my mother while my ninety-one-year-old dad, who can barely walk due to neuropathy, sat in his usual easy chair. Dad is hard of hearing, so telling him would require a lot of repetition in a loud voice.

When I went into the living room to greet my father, Tad told my mother the news. We hadn't planned it that way, but I was relieved because I didn't know what to say to her, how to phrase it so that she wouldn't be alarmed. The thought of losing another child would surely cross her mind. Tad told Mama simply that I have breast cancer, but we didn't expect it to be serious. The doctor had suggested that I might have a lumpectomy and be back at work as soon as six weeks later. We left it up to Mama to tell Dad.

Mama called me later in the afternoon to share that Dad took the news well. Thankfully, his attitude buoyed up my mother.

"I had prostate cancer, and I survived. My sister Pavlina had breast cancer, and she survived. Kathryn will survive, too," Dad had told her.

It was a relief that I would not have to support my mother as well as deal with the cancer myself.

Cancer is a presence that is always with me, like a new pet, but not as much fun. Granted, it's only been two days since I found out, but it's a new reality, a new mindset, a new path to tread. Cancer. Me. My new identity.

In the evening, my husband, three children, and I gathered for our evening devotions.

Cancer does peculiar things to one's thinking. Was the cancer an answer to a strange prayer that I've prayed ever since the children were young?

"Lord, if it's my time, then take me. Please take me before any of my children. Make it so I don't outlive them. If it's my time, help them not to miss me if I go."

Tad seemed shaken. When we were alone he asked, "Why did you pray that?"

"For a long time I've prayed for God to take me before taking any of the children. I just haven't prayed it out loud in front of you. I don't want to cheat death if it's my time to go. Maybe this is God's answer to my prayer. I don't want to get cured only to have Jacob, Alexandra, or Larissa die before me. I couldn't bear to lose them. I don't think I would handle the pain of that loss very well. I've seen what happens to other mothers when their children die. So I pray for God to take me before any of them."

Friday, 31 December 2010

Consider it pure joy, my brothers, whenever you face trials of many kinds, because you know that the testing of your faith develops perseverance.
– James 1:2-3 (NIV)

Today is a work holiday. There is nothing I can do today about my cancer, so it's a cancer holiday, too, and I focused on our trip to Haiti.

When I volunteered to lead a group from our Ukrainian Pentecostal church on a mission trip, I took on all the stateside logistics of the trip—buying the plane tickets, making sure the deposits and final payments were delivered on time, obtaining the supplies that our team was assigned to bring to the field, delivering the training to my team, even packing and weighing our suitcases before departure. However, the trip itself is organized by a Christian ministry, Mission E4, based in Massachusetts. (The E4 stands for Ephesians chapter 4, which stresses unity in the church.)

I had traveled with Mission E4 to Haiti in March 2010, two months after the earthquake. I felt privileged that I was allowed to go because I heard of many volunteers being turned away by various organizations. What skills could I possibly contribute to the daunting task of rebuilding that devastated country? I wasn't a builder or a medical worker. I had my two hands, a willingness to work, and a driving passion to go. Tad gave me his blessing to volunteer, and as has happened over and over on mission trips, God arranged the ideal job for my skills. While others dug ditches, painted walls, or poured concrete, I was assigned to be the photographer to document the different building projects and ministries of Mission E4.

Although I work as a technical writer day to day, I have a degree in photography. I hadn't expected my skill as a photographer to be useful on the mission field. Doctors and nurses, builders and teachers—they're valuable and practical in the field. But a photographer? Yet God showed me otherwise. Time and again, for different organizations and in different countries, I have been assigned the job of mission-trip photographer. I documented doctors at work in the African bush, village life in Senegal, Mexicans digging through trash on a dump, homes being built for the destitute, feeding programs, teaching programs, orphanages, slums. Several mission organizations have used my photos for websites, brochures, and banners, and I've given many presentations about missions and their work with the needy. A powerful photo can be more effective than words.

On the March 2010 trip to Haiti, I was assigned to work with Caleb, a gifted twenty-one-year-old videographer whom Scott Long, the head of Mission E4, had brought with him from Massachusetts. Caleb was to document the devastation in Haiti and the mission's relief projects—raising the walls of the girls' orphanage, feeding hundreds of schoolchildren, building temporary housing, setting up a new tent camp, and distributing food and water. Since Caleb, who worked for Scott, was timid and a bit intimidated by his animated boss, he was delighted to have a partner. The two of us scurried after Scott like chicks after their mother hen.

Caleb and I made an odd pair—a somewhat shy young man and an older woman egging him on. After I climbed a ladder onto the old orphanage roof for a better vantage point, I urged Caleb to follow me. I encouraged him to explore the neighborhood behind the orphanage with me and photograph the children and crumbled buildings. I discovered when the schoolchildren were served their daily meal and ran to fetch Caleb so he could document the huge, steaming cauldrons of rice and beans and the row upon row of uniformed children eating their simple meal under the tarp-covered frame that served as a temporary school. Caleb was delighted not to be alone with Scott; I was thrilled that I was assigned to spend so much time with Scott and learn about his ministry.

Traveling in a local tap-tap (a wildly painted pickup that serves as public transportation), we dropped by to see—and document—destroyed homes, construction sites, the demolished city of Léogâne, and muddy tent camps where people lived under tarps, cardboard, and sheets. We visited the three schools where Mission E4 feeds eight hundred pupils each school day. Caleb and I followed Scott up a barren hill from which we could see the ocean; we accompanied Scott back to Port-au-Prince for building supplies. All during that time, when he wasn't arranging the delivery of more building materials or answering his cell phone, Scott shared about his life and ministry with hand gestures and such enthusiasm that it was contagious. The more I got to know this man with a trim salt-and-pepper beard and thick, silvery hair, the more awed I was by his dedication to serve the Lord and help the destitute.

This prematurely gray man in his forties grew up in a Christian home. He was homeschooled—a rarity when Scott was growing up. Scott's father was a pastor. When Scott was sixteen, he went to Haiti on a six-week mission trip. He fondly remembered the missionary family that hosted him during this trip.

A few years later, Scott's father had an affair, divorced his mother, and remarried. Of course, that meant he had to step down from his position as pastor.

"If that's what Christians do, I wanted none of it," Scott recalled during one of our bumpy rides, "and I stopped going to church."

But Scott married an ardent new believer, Tanya, who continued going to church. When they had children, Tanya took the children to church. Scott still refused to go.

"I went only once in seven years, and that was to see my children in a play," he admitted.

Tanya and the children fervently prayed for Scott; he fervently pursued his new passion: making as much money as he could. He was a successful businessman and eventually he had his own business. The family didn't see much of Scott.

"When I was about thirty, the missionary family that I'd stayed with in Haiti was in the States," Scott told me. "They were visiting churches. My mother and Tanya urged me to go see them. I didn't want to go to a church, but I did want to see them."

When Scott heard the missionaries speak, the Lord broke his heart.

"I cried and cried," Scott recalled. "I couldn't talk for about twenty-four hours. 'Honey, I'm done,' I told Tanya. 'My whole life is God's.'"

Scott decided to serve Jesus as fervently as he'd pursued mammon.

"The American dream flies in the face of Christianity," Scott explained. "I sold my business. I sold our home. Then Tanya, the three children, and I went to live with my mother-in-law while I prayed and sought God's will for my life."

That's not something most Christians are willing to do.

"Then I read Galatians 2:10. When Paul and Barnabas were leaving to preach the good news to the gentiles, the apostles James, Peter, and John gave them only one piece of advice that was nearest and dearest to their heart: *They desired only that we should remember the poor, the very thing which I also was eager to do.*

"When I read that passage," said Scott, "I felt that God called me to work with the poor."

Specifically, God called Scott and his family to Haiti. They lived in Haiti for four years, then returned to the States.

"Was it too hard to live in Haiti with your family?" I asked Scott during the tap-tap ride.

"No, it wasn't that. Do you know what the second greatest cause of death among teens in the U.S. is? Suicide! Young people in America have what they need materially, but spiritually they're empty inside. They have no purpose. You won't find Haitians committing suicide; they're too busy trying to scrounge for their next meal. But American youth have too much of everything materially—yet inside they have a big void. I went back to the States and started a program for youth so they would find a purpose in serving God. I take them down to Haiti a week after they join the program."

During that post-earthquake trip, I thought over and over, *Tad just has to meet Scott.* I was excited that in a little over a week, we would be in Haiti and they would finally meet one another.

Today, the last day of the year and a day off from work in most companies, was the final training day for the Rochester Haiti team. Sadly, three original members of the team, all eighteen years old, dropped out because of the cholera outbreak in Haiti. The news reports frightened their parents, who forbade their children to, as they perceived, "risk their lives." No amount of persuasion would convince the parents to change their minds: not the fact that cholera had not reached our destination of Léogâne, nor assurances that we would drink only filtered water; not the statistics that show only two percent of those who become infected with cholera die of the disease, nor even knowing that my medical kit contained Cipro, an antibiotic used to treat the illness. They were blinded by media-induced fear. So the team of ten was reduced to seven: my husband and me, our three children, and two others—Ruth, an enthusiastic sixteen-year-old member of the youth group, and Lyuba, the twenty-something wife of Tad's youth group co-leader. The team was our family plus two others.

We went over the rules, practiced skits, and arranged when to meet at the airport. But as we talked, I sensed a weight in the air and an unspoken tension. I realized that Ruth and Lyuba were avoiding mentioning cancer or disease of any kind. I think it's in the back of everyone's mind: Is this a death sentence? Will she die of this disease?

"So, have you heard about my illness?" I asked.

The question relieved some of the strain in the air, and this "taboo" topic was now fair game. I assured them that I still plan to go to Haiti.

The diagnosis is still so fresh and so shocking that it's in the back of my mind during everything I do. It twists my thoughts and leads them down paths I'd rather not take. Will this be my last New Year's celebration? Will this be my last trip abroad?

The cancer must color the thoughts of my family, too. They don't say anything about cancer, but tiptoe around it as Ruth and Luyba had. However, I get extra hugs from the children. Tad or the girls offer to wash the dishes for me. Although I'm no sicker today than I was a week ago, those around me treat me as if I were weaker or somehow impaired. I feel fine, really I do, with only a little soreness and bruising where the biopsy sample was taken. Actually, the pain—and bruise— have spread to my left armpit, but I'm sure—well, almost sure—that it's just from the invasive procedure of the biopsy. Nothing has changed, except that now we know. We know that this thing is lurking in my body, and if left untreated, it would kill me. But this thing—it is part of me, my own cells gone haywire. Again, just like when I had lupus, my body has turned against me and could potentially kill me. There are no bacteria or viruses involved; the body just self-destructs.

I don't want to sound like a hypochondriac, but I've also had an odd, dull pain in the right side of my abdomen for the second day. I'm doing my best to ignore it. It's easy to imagine that the cancer has spread its tentacles to my ovaries. But I can't allow myself to think that or get absorbed by negative thoughts and worries.

People who hide their cancer from others miss many blessings. After supper, the doorbell rang. It was Rony—Mema and Gulshan's son—with his Russian wife Olga and their four-year-old son Ben. They were going ice-skating, and since our house is on the way, they stopped by. Both Rony and Olga hugged me as they came in. The news is spreading.

Tina, who had told me to keep a journal, called and asked me to go on a walk with her. I had to decline because of guests. People are suddenly taking extra time to see me, call me, talk to me, all because of the cancer that isn't even making me feel ill.

January

My son, do not make light of the LORD's discipline, and do not lose heart when He rebukes you, because the LORD disciplines those He loves, and He punishes everyone He accepts as a son... No discipline seems pleasant at the time, but painful. Later on, however, it produces a harvest of righteousness and peace for those who have been trained by it.

– Hebrews 12:5–6, 11 (NIV)

Most people won't understand how my eighteen-year-old son could possibly consider a car accident in which he totaled his beloved sports car to be the best thing that happened to him in 2010. But with his head bowed, Jacob admitted that he realized God had disciplined him with that accident, even answered his prayer.

Our family tradition is to celebrate New Year's Eve at home around the dining room table with a small late-night meal, such as the sushi and artichoke salad we had last night. As we eat, each of us shares the best and the worst event from the previous year. Some highlights or disappointments are obvious. But other times what one shares can be an eye-opener for the rest of us.

Last spring, Jacob bought the sporty Scion tC in an online auction as an investment. The car had been totaled, but Jacob, who is working toward a degree in auto mechanics, painstakingly fixed it to look and run almost like new. He had invested every dollar he'd earned ever since he was thirteen. Then he'd borrowed some more money from Tad with the promise to pay it back after he sold the car.

But there were no buyers. Week after week, month after month, the car sat in the garage. From time to time, Jacob took it out, drove it, and then parked it in the garage again where he lovingly washed and buffed it.

I don't believe that God took away the car because of Jacob's emotional investment in it, although it was high; it was how he drove the car that displeased God. But Tad and I were oblivious. We had no idea that our son, an A student, changed from a responsible young man into a threat to society when he got into that vehicle. Only when he got up in front of our congregation after the accident and publicly repented, thanking God for His protection, His mercy, and His discipline, did I learn that Jacob used to exceed the speed limit by twenty, thirty, up to sixty miles per hour.

Jacob first started speeding virtually during his childhood in what seemed like innocent computer games. At that time, we didn't realize how detrimental the games were. Midtown Madness doesn't take its players looping around a racetrack, but careening through city streets at ridiculous speeds. Need for Speed promotes "the thrill of the chase and the rush of the escape." High-speed chases, hair-raising getaways, exhilarating action—they become part of the player's psyche.

But Tad and I were unaware of this. We limited Jacob's time on the computer, but we didn't realize how the games were affecting our son's thinking. Jacob was a young teen by the time Tad saw how addictive and foolish the games were and took them away. By then, the damage had been done.

Even though we parents didn't know it, Jacob was aware of his struggle with speeding and spent many hours on his knees. He begged God to get rid of this sports car. And God answered his prayer—but not in the way that Jacob had meant it. Instead of finding a buyer for the car, one rainy October afternoon God had allowed Jacob to lose control of the vehicle on an expressway and spin into a guardrail. A one-car accident. Jacob didn't have a scratch.

Since the Scion had no collision insurance, Jacob lost every penny he put into that car, and he still owed Tad money. But that's how it should be: punishment isn't punishment if it doesn't hurt.

We continued going around the table sharing our highlights. For fifteen-year-old Larissa, it was the mission trip to South Dallas last winter and the conversations that she had there with other youth on that trip. For seventeen-year-old Alexandra, it was growing closer to God through prayer and devotions. For my husband, it was his fall trip to Ukraine and the ministering he did there. For me, the highlights were the youth mission trip to Dallas with my two daughters, where I worked with the homeless and spent time with Pastor Chris Simmons of Cornerstone Baptist Church, and the trip to Haiti where I met Scott Long. Both individuals were inspirational examples of godly men. I felt privileged to have met them.

I shared an additional highlight: a donation that I had received for Mission E4. I had given a presentation about my Haiti trip to our small church, which consists almost wholly of Ukrainian immigrants who arrived from the ex-Soviet Union within the last twenty-five years and work blue-collar jobs. About a week after hearing of the utter destitution in Haiti, seeing images of the barefooted individuals in tent camps who slept on cinder blocks, and learning how Mission E4 helps these poorest of the poor, a man sent his daughter to me with an envelope. "For Haiti," she said and quickly returned to her dad.

The envelope was labeled "For orphans, crippled, and homeless." I opened it when I got home and counted the small bills.

"Tad," I said when I found him in the bedroom, my eyes welling up with tears. "There's $2350 in this envelope." For a janitor with five children, this was a small fortune.

Although today, January first, was a "normal" day at home—we cooked, Jacob and Tad spent time working on a car, I talked with a few people on the phone—all day I focused on my aches and pains. This is definitely not normal for me, but since I don't know how extensive my cancer is, my imagination has been working overtime.

My heart hurt—was it from stress, or was lupus coming back?

The localized abdominal pain that I recently noticed twinged once or twice. A woman in her thirties in our church had ovarian cancer; could mine have spread already?

My right hand felt numb. Why do I wake up with this numbness every day for the last few months? Surely that has nothing to do with cancer—but what is it?

And why was I so tired after working outside adding water to the water garden? It was a pleasant day in the forties. The snow was melting, and compared to all of December, it was not that cold. I wasn't outside that long, but I was worn out.

Thankfully, Alexandra and Larissa cooked supper, steaming up the windows and filling the house with savory smells. They worked together to prepare a Russian meal of borscht and baked cheese tarts that they learned to make from Olga, the woman who stopped by yesterday. I'm grateful that my teenage daughters are such good cooks and, like me, they enjoy the art of cooking and trying new recipes.

While they cooked, I lay down on a couch in the living room. For much too long, this had been my customary spot, the place where years ago I had spent days and weeks and months with lupus, an autoimmune disorder that left me fatigued and suffering from chest pains if I so much as sat up. From this spot, I can see the entire living room, dining room, and even into the family room. It's warm because the couch is near the cast-iron wood-burning stove with which we heat the house. The flickering of the fire, visible through the glass window on the stove, gives the room coziness, not just in temperature, but in ambiance, like sitting around a campfire.

As I lay on the couch, I began to read all those booklets on cancer that New York State mandates the clinic send me. I never knew that there were so many types of cancer! I thought cancer came in one flavor, just attacked different parts of the body. But in my brief exposure to cancer, I've learned that there are different types of cancer than can affect one organ. I suspect that reading too much about cancer will just frighten me. Sometimes ignorance is bliss.

Sunday, 2 January 2011

When times are good, be happy; but when times are bad, consider: God has made the one as well as the other.
— Ecclesiastes 7:14 (NIV)

This morning, Tad and the kids left for church without waking me. I heard the front door close and was surprised that Tad hadn't even asked whether I wanted to go. This would not have happened a week ago. But now I have cancer. The only difference between now and one week ago is that I know. I don't feel any different, but knowing colors my thoughts. Although it's highly unlikely that cancer would kill me quickly (it would have to metastasize to a vital organ), I do wonder, for example, whether this coming spring will be my last one, or whether I'll ever see my relatives in Ukraine again.

I believe that the most likely scenario is that I'll be cured of the cancer in a few months. They'll take out the lump and then… well, I'm not really sure what. Chemotherapy? Radiation? Both?

But has it spread? That is the question that is in the back of my mind nearly all the time.

When I went to the kitchen, it was still before 9:00 AM. A freshly made pot of coffee greeted me. Because Tad and I both make our coffee in the same espresso maker—he makes decaf and I make regular French Roast—I immediately wondered whether the coffee was decaf. But, no, a note on the counter stated REGULAR—YOUR COFFEE and had an arrow pointing at the espresso maker. I found out later Alexandra had made it. She certainly wouldn't have done so a week ago; she usually chides me for drinking too much coffee.

I got ready for church slowly, relishing my time alone, my coffee, reading my devotions in the tan recliner by the bow window, enjoying the morning light and sight of green grass for the first time since November 30 when the rains had turned to snow.

I got to church late, but I did not feel guilty about it.

The MRI is tomorrow. Tad offered to go with me. So did my sister. Then my mother. I turned them all down. There is no point in wasting their time. I suppose I'm not letting them feel useful, though. In accompanying me, they would feel that they're helping or at least giving me moral support. But I've always been a bit of a loner. Sometimes it's easier to deal with things on my own than feel that I have to "entertain" people should they accompany me. I won't get any results tomorrow at the clinic; if there's bad news, it will come later.

I spent the late evening checking homeschool assignments and making a daily study schedule for the coming week for the two I'm still homeschooling: Alexandra, who is in twelfth grade, and Larissa, in tenth grade. I write the schedules—subjects, assignments, and due dates—in table form on the computer. It felt good to go back to that usual Sunday evening routine. A kind of reassuring normalcy.

Monday, 3 January 2011

The L*ord himself goes before you and will be with you; He will never leave you nor forsake you. Do not be afraid; do not be discouraged.*

– Deuteronomy 31:8 (NIV)

This was my first day at work since I found out that I have cancer. I won't be able to get in a full week of work because of the scheduled MRI and other medical appointments, but I have a deadline, and I need to hand off my project—a user manual for a printer—to my co-worker. She didn't know yet that she would have to take over my project, and not just for the week that I'm going to be in Haiti. And, of course, I wanted to inform my co-workers that I'm going to be taking medical leave soon after I return from my mission trip.

The drive to Kodak Office in downtown Rochester is just seven miles, mostly by expressways. But the last mile is on city streets—past a large art supply store, by an old brick church building turned into a music school, and past the Open Door Mission, Rochester's best-known rescue mission that works with the homeless. In Rochester, Open Door Mission is synonymous with soup kitchen.

I parked on the street in front of the Open Door Mission, which is just a block from the Kodak headquarters. With much urging from my husband, I had decided to donate my spiny Crown of Thorns cactus to the mission, and I had it with me today. The potted plant, which I had received from my friend Joy when it was maybe twelve inches tall, was now higher than my waist with a mess of thorny branches twisting and reaching in many directions like a modern sculpture. During summer months, the Crown of Thorns basked outside on the front porch, sprouted many lush leaves, and bloomed a stunning profusion of small vermilion flowers; during winters, it retreated indoors where it shed its leaves and looked rather forlorn in its spot behind the metal loop full of firewood where it stayed until the warmer days arrived. Our house is too small with too few windows to accommodate this sizeable plant, though it had managed to survive for years sitting in that corner by the fireplace as if penalized for its less-than-spectacular winter appearance. Instead of continuing to appeal to my husband year after year to spare this plant, I decided to give it a new home in a bright room with skylights where it would get the light it needed and would look good year round. The Open Door Mission's prayer room was such a place.

A year ago, my daughters and I had started to volunteer at the Open Door Mission soup kitchen after we returned from a youth mission trip. Over the Christmas holiday, we had flown to Dallas and met up with about fifty youth and eight leaders from all over the U.S. and Canada.

The trip was organized by Global Expeditions, a Christian ministry based an hour's drive from Dallas. Global Expeditions partnered with Cornerstone Baptist Church, which is located in an area of South Dallas that the media had dubbed "The War Zone." Home to a predominantly African-American community, this spot is just a few blocks from where President Kennedy was shot. This rough neighborhood used to be one of the most notorious crime areas in the United States, known for its drug dealers, violent gangs, drive-by shootings, and prostitution. But over the last twenty years, through the vision of Pastor Chris Simmons and the work of his church, the area has been transformed.

I was privileged to meet Pastor Simmons and spend time with this godly middle-aged man who grew up in Washington, D.C., in a Christian African-American home that took in many foster children.

"When I first arrived here in Dallas in 1988, I was a young pastor just out of seminary," the now bald Pastor Simmons explained. "The older women in the church said, 'That pastor's a nice guy, but he won't stay.' Back in those days, you often had to walk around a dead body to get to church.

"I believe that if we own it, we can control it," the pastor continued passionately. "One of the first things we did when I came to Cornerstone was to buy the liquor store in this area, shut it down, and make it into a soup kitchen."

Cornerstone took over a crack house and turned it into a home for ex-convicts reintegrating into society through the church's jail ministry. Some of the ex-cons work in the soup kitchen.

The "White House," the mansion in which our team stayed the week we were in Texas, used to be a gutted residence; it now houses boys between eighteen and twenty-one years of age who are out of foster care and need a place to live while they continue their education. A live-in mentor oversees the place and the boys.

An abandoned grocery store where drug dealers hung out and started fires is now the new church building. Cornerstone also owns a clothing pantry where donated clothes are sorted and distributed, a shower building where the homeless can bathe, and several homes that the church rents to families whom they screen and select. Many of the buildings, suffering from disuse, were simply donated to the church.

I spent the week interacting with homeless and low-income elderly as well as people who used to be prostitutes, drug dealers, convicts, addicts, and gang members. The experience definitely stretched me.

"Homeless can get a meal many places, but most places don't offer the personal touch we provide here—someone to talk to and look you in the eye and accept you," said Pastor Simmons.

Serving in the soup kitchen was the highlight of my week in South Dallas. But I was as apprehensive as the youth when I started my soup kitchen experience. I'd never talked to a homeless person before. What do I say? How do I start a conversation? What do I talk about that doesn't seem phony or forced?

I arrived at the soup kitchen with a team of volunteers that included my older daughter Alexandra. Some uncharacteristic snowflakes swirled in the Texas air that dark evening. Although I expected a large turnout due to the freezing temperature, attendance was sparse.

"We don't offer a bed for the night here, so a lot are probably at the other soup kitchens that do," explained Uncle Joe, a large African-American cook with a smile as wide as he was. He was one of the ex-convicts now working in the soup kitchen. "Those who eat here may be too late to find a bed elsewhere and will have to sleep outside."

So the men who showed up were the ones who either really wanted that one-on-one attention that Pastor Simmons described or were just hardier and willing to sleep outdoors.

I forced myself to take a seat opposite a black man sitting alone and reading a book. Curtis turned out to be about my age. To my great surprise, our conversation wasn't at all strained. He ended up telling me details about his life—time in prison, death of his wife Tiffany, and why he was living on the streets—he claimed he never shared with anyone before. "I felt something drawing me here tonight," Curtis said to me. "I now know why. It was to talk with you."

I was dumbfounded.

We not only talked about his life; I also shared about mine, especially about the time I was bedridden with a disease that was undiagnosed for months. Eventually a doctor determined that the disease was lupus, but that just put a name on my condition; it didn't make me better. Lupus is an autoimmune disorder for which there is no cure. In lupus, the immune system, which normally protects your body from bacteria and viruses, attacks your own body's healthy tissues, often damaging kidneys, joints, or in my case, my heart. Lupus can also cause crippling fatigue. I spent most of my time in bed, too exhausted to even sit up. My children were then six, eight, and nine years old, but I couldn't take care of them. My husband cooked the meals and got the kids off to school. But a few days after I got sick, Tad broke his leg in three places. After that, he had to lie in bed with his leg elevated. So we had to rely on the help of family, friends, and neighbors, and the kids did a lot more chores than usual.

I told Curtis that God makes promises to us in the Bible, promises that He keeps. I took a Bible off the shelf, flipped the pages to my favorite book of the Bible and showed Curtis the following verses:

> *Is any one of you sick? He should call the elders of the church to pray over him and anoint him with oil in the name of the Lord. And the prayer offered in faith will make the sick person well; the Lord will raise him up* (James 5:14–15, NIV).

"I read this, Curtis, but when I was lying in bed with chest pains, this sounded too good to be true. I didn't want to risk being disappointed. I hung my hopes on this verse, yet dared not call the elders. I didn't want to trouble them. At first when I was bedridden, I was just immensely tired, but is that a reason to call the elders? I didn't know what was wrong with me.

"And what if it didn't work? What if the elders prayed for me and I was still sick? I was afraid that I'd lose faith in what the Bible says. I both wanted to call them and didn't want to. I battled this for months.

"At times I lay in bed negotiating with God. 'Lord, if this really works—if the elders pray over me and I *am* healed—I'll tell everyone about it!

"Yet I was still afraid to test what it says in the Bible.

"After a few months, I wasn't completely bedridden anymore, but I wasn't well either. My health and strength went up and down like a roller coaster. At this time, my husband Tad was planning a summer trip to Ukraine to visit his parents. The kids and I had been there before, but this time I decided to stay home. What was the point of traveling all that way just to lie in bed? But as the time grew nearer for them to leave, I didn't want to be left alone at home. By then I wasn't spending all my time in bed and I was even working part-time. So I asked Tad to buy me a ticket to Ukraine as well.

"The weekend before we left, someone from our small group Bible study arranged for the elders to come to a small conference room between church services and pray over me. It hadn't occurred to me that the elders didn't all have to drive to my house in the middle of the week, that they could pray for me at church when we were all there on a Sunday—although I didn't have the strength to go to church when I first got sick.

"The elders gathered in the conference room that Sunday and prayed for me, and the pastor anointed me with oil.

"Of course I had expected—or at least hoped—that I would be instantly healed. So I was more than a little disappointed that nothing happened that day. Or the next.

"We left for Ukraine on a Wednesday. I was still feeling so ill that at the airport I had to lie down on the floor because in some areas there were no chairs. It takes about twenty-eight hours to travel from our house to my in-laws'. We arrived on a Thursday. I was exhausted.

"I went to bed, and slept and slept. The next day I didn't feel my husband get out of bed. I didn't hear the kids get up and walk through the bedroom. I didn't hear the dogs barking or the roosters crowing. I slept eighteen hours straight and woke up the next afternoon. When I sat up in bed, I knew I was healed!

"All that time when I was sick, my husband used to ask me, 'How do you feel?' and I'd answer, 'Like I'm living in someone else's body.' It didn't feel right. It didn't feel like me. It felt kind of heavy. But that afternoon when I sat up in bed, I had my old body back! That entire time in Ukraine I was on the go. You'd never have known I'd been sick!"

I looked into Curtis' eyes. He'd been listening attentively.

"What the Bible says is true! You just have to put your faith in it. God promises to answer prayer. Look at this:

"Philippians 4:6 says, *Do not be anxious about anything, but in everything, by prayer and petition, with thanksgiving, present your requests to God.*

"You said that pride is keeping you on the streets. Let's pray that you overcome that pride, that you get off the streets and move in with your daughter like she's asking you to."

And I reached over the table, held hands with Curtis, and prayed.

In the midst of our animated conversation, two teens had quietly sat down next to me, listening. At the end of the evening, they asked in amazement, "How did you get him to open up to you like that?"

I smiled. "When I sat down opposite him, I just asked him, 'Are you originally from Dallas?' He wasn't, so he started telling me his life story. And, of course, I shared mine, too."

Most people like to talk about themselves if you can just get them started. That opening question was one that I used again and again during the week in Dallas—with the church security guard who, at twenty-seven, had spent a third of his life in prison; with the widows for whom we cleaned up yards; with the gang member turned church member; and with the ex-prostitute who is now the church receptionist. But while I was listening to life stories, the teens were raking or cleaning yards, sorting clothes or scrubbing showers, teaching or playing with kids, ninety-two percent of whom come from single-parent homes.

"A lot of people who were part of the problem in this neighborhood are now part of the solution," Pastor Simmons shared as he drove another youth leader and me around the neighborhood.

"How do you do it?" I asked, incredulous at the enormous change in this neighborhood where I was not afraid to walk alone.

"Acts of kindness," explained the pastor with a smile. "Painting, raking, and cleaning like the youth are doing; distributing food; teaching children during school vacations to keep them off the streets and away from drug dealers; and helping neighbors in need, whether it's clothes for the children or groceries for a few meals. These acts of kindness draw people to Cornerstone Baptist Church. Once they accept Jesus as their Savior, they are transformed; their lives are completely turned around."

Pastor Simmons told me about Judy. "She owns Judy's Lounge, a bar that was notorious as the congregating point of prostitutes, pimps, and drug dealers. You could drive by in the middle of the night and find up to a hundred people hanging around outside the bar. It was a den of evil.

"Judy has a soft heart, so she started to volunteer at our soup kitchen, which is kitty-corner from her bar. Every time she volunteered, she heard the gospel message. God worked in her heart, convicting her to shut down her lounge. Now, because of other things going on in her life, Judy is going to live in the building that was once Judy's Lounge and hold Bible studies there. So you see, one woman's transformation can change a whole block."

To help her, Cornerstone sent part of our youth team, including my daughters, to paint the outside of Judy's Lounge an intense blue color, covering over the writing on the walls that used to advertise her bar.

Pastor Chris Simmons' charismatic personality is another reason that Cornerstone Baptist Church is such a strong influence on the community.

"Riding around the neighborhood with him was like riding with the pope!" exclaimed a volunteer from Arkansas. "Everybody knows him."

And he knows them all, too—by name. This caring man exudes God's love to all he meets, making everyone he interacts with feel special. I saw him greet elderly and young alike with a few kind words, a smile, and a big hug.

"With all the work this church does, I thought it was a mega-church," shared the same Arkansan. "I was shocked to see a sign above the sanctuary entrance that read, 'Seating capacity: 317.'"

My daughters and I left Dallas changed by our experience. I was buoyed up to see God's work being done through Pastor Simmons; the girls were uplifted to have met many other teens from around the country who are on fire for the Lord, willing to sacrifice holiday time and comfort, ready to rake leaves in the cold and spend nights in sleeping bags on the hardwood floors to be part of God's great commission. One youth member summed it up aptly: A room full of strangers became a family overnight.

The Dallas trip also changed my relationship with my daughters. Like most teens, they find some things that I do embarrassing, other things annoying. Alexandra had been critical of me for some time, and although I knew she'd outgrow it eventually, her cutting remarks still stung and sometimes brought me to tears.

But something happened on this trip.

On the last day, my daughters' team gathered in a circle and everyone shared their "Kodak moment"—their highlight from this experience. Larissa's was the deep conversations she had with her small group. Alexandra's was packing up food that would be shipped around the world to help stop hunger. But one girl said that the highlight of her trip was washing dishes in the kitchen with me and the conversations we had. Another said that she wished I were her mom. I was surprised and humbled.

After we returned home, Alexandra, then sixteen, approached me one evening and apologized for her harsh words and snide comments. We hugged. I choked up. Then we started a new phase in our relationship.

I reminisced as I crunched up the snowy steps to the Open Door Mission hugging the large pot that contained my disorderly Crown of Thorns. It had been Alexandra's idea to volunteer at this soup kitchen after we returned from Dallas. She kept urging me to sign up until I picked up the phone and made the monthly commitment a year ago.

A man inside saw me with the plant and held the glass door open for me. "Captain's gonna be real happy with that plant," he said.

Any plant brought to the mission was automatically Captain's plant. He cares for all the plants in the glass-enclosed prayer room—watering, repotting, nurturing cast-off houseplants back to health. The prayer room, which looks like a luxuriant greenhouse furnished with couches and armchairs, is a warm and inviting place that envelopes you with a sense of peace. Daily Bible studies are held here for men who were once homeless, but now reside in the Open Door Mission and take part in their Christian Life Recovery Program.

I had seen the room last year during a tour of this building, a tour that Captain personally gave my children and me. (I am still sad that Tad had been too busy to join us.)

I don't recall how my friendship with Captain came about. Perhaps this tall, sturdy man with a slight paunch is friendly to all volunteers, and, like Pastor Simmons, makes everyone feel special. I do know that whenever I volunteer, I look forward to talking with Captain.

Captain was the cook the first night my daughters and I volunteered. Something about his appearance hinted of homelessness. Was it the bad teeth? The untrimmed moustache and slightly too long gray hair that was parted in the middle? The mannerisms?

After introductions, Captain immediately teased us as he told us how to make the sixty or seventy salads, poked fun at us as we set the tables, and joked that we dished out too much or too little as we served the meal he had prepared. Captain constantly ribbed, kidded, and teased. Sometimes jokers like him are the ones hardest to get to know. But between the wisecracks and humor, I was able to have a serious conversation with Captain and urged him to tell me his testimony.

He described his slide from a successful construction business owner to a drug-addicted homeless man.

"I made too much money for my own good," Captain admitted. "I didn't know what to do with it all, so I got into drugs."

"Why didn't he buy a boat like most people?" my son later asked. Perhaps he didn't think of it. Perhaps God had other plans. Sometimes it's only when one sinks to an unimaginable depth that he turns to God for help.

Because of the drug addiction, Captain lost his family, his home, his business, his dignity.

"I was like those men out there," Captain waved his arm from the kitchen area where we stood toward the front of the hall, where around sixty men and a few women were listening to the evening's preaching. "When it got cold, I'd come here for a meal and a bed. I'd hear the preaching. Little by little, it began to soak in, even though I didn't know it at the time."

As the service continued, Captain led my daughters and me upstairs to the area where the men sleep and showed us the bunk bed in which he'd been lying one night.

"I was in this bed," he said, pointing to an upper bunk, "when it all came together and I chose to turn my life around and follow Jesus. It was about 2 AM, but I couldn't sleep. I felt I had to tell someone, so I got out of bed. There was a security guard there by the door. When he saw me, he said, 'You don't have to tell me what happened. One look at you and I can see that you're practically lighting up this whole room.'"

Since that first evening, every time I come to the Open Door Mission, Captain greets me with a crushing hug. Although he still jokes and teases, we have genuine conversations, and he shares what's going on in his life. Today, after presenting him with the Crown of Thorns, I shared what's going on in mine.

"I just got diagnosed with cancer. Breast cancer. I'm going to Haiti with the whole family next week, but when I get back, I'm going to have surgery. I don't know just when yet."

I could tell that Captain was a bit taken aback. "I'm sure you'll be alright," he said.

We chatted a bit longer, but I had to get to work.

"I'd like to pray for you before you leave," said Captain. And standing there in the entryway of the building, we bowed our heads and Captain prayed for my healing, for my family, for our mission trip.

"You call me every once in a while and let me know how you're doing," he insisted as I left.

Most people associate the C word with death. So it's not a surprise that many co-workers reacted with shock, even tears, when I told them of my cancer. The tears took me aback, though, because I hadn't expected that sort of reaction. I hadn't thought that any co-workers cared that much. I'm on friendly terms with everyone, but I consider my co-workers acquaintances rather than close friends. And I wasn't planning on dying... yet.

While Jim and Anais, who work closest to my office, stood in my cubicle absorbing the news, our boss walked in. It was the first time Betty had seen me since I called her; she asked whether she could give me a hug.

"You have to ask that these days?" Jim questioned.

Betty nodded. In today's working world, there are so many rules to follow, especially when you're a supervisor.

Betty hugged me, and all four of us stood in my cubicle a bit longer than we were comfortable with. In illness and death, people often don't know what to say.

I heard Jeanette, a short African-American woman who dyes her hair a reddish blond. She was outside my office getting a drink from the water cooler, so I invited her in. Then I shared my news.

"Before you hear from someone else, I wanted to tell you that I have cancer," I told her.

She looked at me and her eyes filled with tears.

"This shouldn't happen to you! Of all people…"

I knew that Jeanette was thinking back on conversations that we'd had about my mission trips and destitution in the developing countries I visited, about her childhood spent in poverty and how she overcame it, and about her work with inner-city schoolchildren. She is one of just a handful of Christians in my work group, so we had discussions about faith, Sunday school, and churches as well. Because of blog posts I'd written for the Kodak corporate blog about my mission trips, most people in my work group know about my heart for the poor and for God, even if I hadn't personally told them.

I took on my role of cheering up Jeanette, telling her I expected to be back at work six weeks after the surgery. Admittedly, I was touched because I hadn't realized that my presence at work had made much of an impact on my co-workers.

I spent only half a day at Kodak. Then I walked out into the frigid air and to my Volkswagen Golf on the sea of asphalt.

The day, like all too many Rochester winter days, was cloudy, but not with picturesque cotton-ball clouds. Instead, our winter cloud cover, caused by masses of air picking up moisture from the Great Lakes, tends to be a solid milky-gray curtain that shuts out the sun for days, even weeks at a time. The cloud cover drapes the city with a dreary gloom that seeps into my inner being no matter how much I try to keep out the bleakness.

I drove to the same Elizabeth Wende Breast Center as last week, but this time I entered through a side door, as if hiding from the public. This was the door to the MRI area, the place where the less fortunate—and perhaps the more frightened—enter.

I am familiar with magnetic resonance imaging (MRI), which uses a very strong magnet, pulses of radio waves, and a computer to produce pictures of the inside of the body. I had an MRI taken of my brain about ten years ago, and still recall the claustrophobic alarm that swept over me when I opened my eyes inside that tomblike machine. I vowed never to open my eyes inside one of those cryptlike chambers again. That first MRI, which was prescribed by my ophthalmologist to determine why the vision in my right eye blacked out on occasion, found an optic glioma, a type of brain tumor that affects the optic nerve. Today's breast MRI, which provides more information than a mammogram, will show whether the cancer has spread beyond the known lump in my left breast and whether there is any cancer in the right breast.

Mothers, daughters, sisters, friends,
The circle of caring never ends.

I found this written on a sign on the door in the waiting room. I'm now part of this sisterhood, the one that flaunts the pink ribbon. I had not previously understood that symbol of breast cancer. Cancer and pink ribbons were not part of my world. Now, less than a week after my diagnosis, I already identify with that pink ribbon. I want to display it so that other women know that I'm a member of this growing community. I want to reach out to them and have them reach out to me.

The small waiting room in the MRI area was empty. As I waited to be admitted, I asked the receptionist some questions.

"How many biopsies do they do at this facility each day?"

"Well, of course it varies," answered the receptionist, thinking. "I'd say about seven to ten biopsies per day. Of those, eighty to eighty-five percent are benign."

"How common is breast cancer?" I continued. "How many women get breast cancer?"

"One out of eight women will get breast cancer at some point in her life. Those who get breast cancer at a younger age are in more danger from the disease; it tends to be more aggressive." I figured that at fifty-five, I fell in the middle of that range—not so young, but not yet elderly.

After I was admitted into the MRI area and changed into that ubiquitous blue gown, I got to talking with Nurse Teresa. It started with the typical, "Hi, how are you?" I didn't give a typical one-word answer; I told her that I was going to Haiti in just a few days. The conversation took off. I described Haitian orphanages, schools, and churches, the tent camps I'd seen, and the history of the country. The conversation touched on materialism, my kids, her kids, slums, Honduras, other mission trips. I think I almost talked Teresa into taking her children on a mission trip to Haiti. Perhaps God meant me to be an ambassador to all these medical people whom I normally would not have met.

This MRI was not as traumatic as the brain MRI because the machine was open at both ends. Some clever individual had rigged up a mirror at an angle inside the cylindrical scanner. When I was placed on the patient table and slid into the MRI, the mirror allowed me to see out one end and watch Nurse Teresa. This dispelled any feelings of claustrophobia.

The MRI was loud and thumping, like a bad rock concert. Fortunately, I was given earplugs, and then earmuffs. To take my mind off the noise and my constrained position, I daydreamed about walks along the seashore, birdsongs, and mountain scenes.

Dr. Khokhar called me at 4:30 PM with good news: the MRI showed only that single mass in the left breast and none in the right. It appears that the cancer has not spread.

"Most likely you'll need a lumpectomy, then probably some radiation, not chemotherapy," he assured me. "The mass is 2.3 cm in diameter. If it had reached 3 cm in size, then we would probably need to do other things."

I was a little calmer during this phone call than I'd been during the previous call, and I was able to ask some questions I had thought of since his initial call.

"You said the cancer is a 'nuclear grade 3.' What does that mean?"

"It's a more rapidly growing type," explained Dr. Khokhar. "It can pop up in a few months."

"So how long do you think this lump has been growing?" I asked.

"Probably six or seven months."

I calculated that it had started in May or June.

To keep family and close friends abreast of developments, I sent them an e-mail.[*]

My days are so full lately, full of medical appointments and phone calls, writing lists and packing suitcases for Haiti, exchanging e-mails and entertaining guests.

Later in the evening, Cheri came over to drop off presents and letters for the three children she sponsors in Haiti. I had offered to deliver these gifts to the schoolchildren next week while distributing gifts to my own sponsored children.

It's a rare treat to visit with Cheri because she lives almost an hour's drive from Rochester in Geneseo, an upstate New York college town. Spending time with Cheri is like basking in the sunshine. Her warmth and exuberance are uplifting and contagious. No wonder she was Alexandra's favorite teacher.

Cheri and I became friends in an odd way: We met during a rocket launch of her sixth grade science class when Alexandra was one of her students. All the parents were invited to this event, so as a supportive parent, I came to the school grounds during lunch to watch my sixth grader launch her mantis-green Estes rocket. I ate my sandwich on a blanket spread on the expansive lawn as I observed one set of students after another shoot their colorfully painted rockets into the blue sky. When an hour later Alexandra still hadn't launched her rocket, I introduced myself to her clipboard-wielding teacher with the chin-

---

[*] See Appendix, Date: Mon, Jan 3

length brunette hair and asked how much longer I had to wait.

"I'm on my lunch break from work," I explained.

She assured me that Alexandra would be next up in line.

"By the way, Alexandra told me that you're retiring at the end of this school year—and that you plan to go to Africa in the fall. I was in Africa twice on mission trips. If you give me your e-mail address, I'll send you a link to the photos from that trip," I offered. I couldn't help thinking that she looked much too young to retire.

Although Cheri taught science, she was an artist. She loved the photos of African village scenes that I sent her. We met for coffee. We discovered that we both loved gardening—and Africa. So a friendship was born.

During summers, I've stopped at her home many times, often with the children as we drove home from Camp Cherith, a Christian summer camp. Geneseo was right along the way. Cheri always welcomed us warmly with lunch, a walk through her town, ice cream cones, a tour of her garden or art studio.

Years later, when we met on a Saturday morning for breakfast, I described my relief trip to Haiti—orphans, abject poverty, tent camps, collapsed buildings, illiteracy rate of fifty percent, the Mission E4 school program that feeds eight hundred children one meal per day, child sponsorship.

"I sponsor a girl through Mission E4. It pays for her schooling, uniform, and schoolbooks—and one meal per day, quite possibly her only meal. Three times a year, I can send her a letter or gifts," I told Cheri. "I met the girl when I was in Haiti; she chose me as her *blan mama*—her white mother."

Cheri leaned across the table a little closer toward me.

"I've been thinking about doing something like that, but I just didn't know whether my money would go where they say it goes. If you trust this organization, then I'd like to sponsor a child," said Cheri. "Actually, I'd like to sponsor three. I'll put part of my Social Security check to good use."

So Cheri began to sponsor three Haitian children. Tonight she dropped off presents for me to take to them.

When she arrived, the whole family gathered, as we often do around a special guest, talking, listening, laughing, singing. We sang hymns a cappella in four-part harmony as we do every night for our devotions. We included her in our prayers, singing, and Bible reading. I know that Cheri is not a church-going believer, but she does believe in God. Like many individuals, she feels there's something more outside her grasp—something that we have found, but she hasn't yet.

Before I went to bed, I received this note from her, which reminded me how important it is to invite people into our home:

Date: Mon, Jan 3, 2011 9:41 pm

Hi Kathryn!

First, let me say that I thoroughly enjoyed your family. You are wonderful. Your family was quite gracious to take the time to sing for me. Thank you. I enjoyed Tad's remarks, and tell him I do sing (in the car, in the shower...Ha!).

I will continue to pray that your health is restored to perfect and you may continue to do God's work. We need Kathryns in this world!

It is always a spiritual refreshment to spend time with any member of your family. You have lovely children who are learning the many opportunities afforded to become good citizens of both the church and state. As parents, you and Tad must be proud!

I find myself with a foot in two worlds at times. Many of the people that I have come to know in this village are well meaning and church going, but do not lead the life they preach. This is not to say that they are bad, but are often mislead with the ideas our society crams down our throats. They do not feel spritually happy to me. But I continue to be independent and pray that God will lead me to the water. Use me. Help me to fulfill my purpose. I always feel refreshed and back on track after a visit or chat with you. We were meant to be friends!

I am currently involved with a decision to open an art school for kids. Charging those who can afford it so that I can offer scholarships to those who are very needy. Art is a therapy in itself and can help children who need some time, attention, and love to nurture their talents. But at the same time, I want to go to Africa again or maybe South America and Haiti. I am trying to sort all of this out in my head. My husband always says, "Look around, Livingston county has some of the neediest children in the world. Their bodies may not be starving as in Africa but their spirits are in very bad shape!" They, too, are poor and neglected in ways that are profound. He thinks that I do not have to go to another continent to help poor people. So I struggle. But I will figure it out. Perhaps do both. Meanwhile, I wish you safe travels, and interesting adventures. If you get nervous about anything, imagine that you're sitting right smack in the middle of God's palm. Ha! What a grand place to be!

God Speed.
Cheri

Wednesday, 5 January 2011

A friend loves at all times…

– Proverbs 17:17 (NIV)

I ran into co-worker Roseanne while walking through the cubicle maze at work. She hugged me. No words were needed. She had heard.

"Lisa was looking for you when you were away from your office," said Jim, whose cubicle faces mine. Lisa is our boss's boss.

I went to her office.

"I just want you to know that I know…"—of course she didn't say what she knew because no one liked to say that word—"and that we'll do everything here to support you as you go out on medical leave. Anything you need, you be sure to tell me," said Lisa.

Annemarie, another co-worker, came to my office. More hugs.

There was one more person I wanted to tell before she heard about my cancer from others. Marilyn, a vivacious and expressive woman my age, works for another department at Kodak. I've known her a long time because I did a project for her as a freelance writer before I was hired by Kodak. We've had lunches together and exchanged e-mails. When she learned of my upcoming trip to Haiti, she single-handedly rounded up boxes and boxes of donations— food, toys, children's clothing, personal hygiene items.

When I sat down across from Marilyn at her desk and told her that I had breast cancer, her jaw fell, eyes glistened with tears, and she reached for a tissue. "No! Not you!"

I was bewildered by her emotional reaction.

At work, we tend not to show our emotions or voice our feelings toward one another. But my news has jolted some people onto emotional turf, and I heard thoughts that can be difficult to voice.

"I really admire what you do," Marilyn said with a voice that lacked her usual joviality.

I blushed. I didn't know how to respond. The mission trips that expose me to slums and tent camps, garbage pickers and homeless, street children and lepers—I don't take them to impress people or seek points for doing good works. I go because it's my passion, because it makes me feel more alive than anything else I do. When I'm sitting in a smoke-filled hut sharing a bowl of deer stew with an old Kuna Indian woman or handing out lemonade to Mexicans who dig through the trash for a living, I feel so much more jubilant than at my climate-controlled, fluorescent-lit office at the world headquarters of Kodak. How can I explain that joining a relief team in Haiti after the earthquake is not a sacrifice, but a privilege? How can I convey that the people I meet and the experiences I have on the mission field are such blessings that they far outweigh any sacrifices I make? That going on a mission trip is so much more meaningful and fulfilling than taking a beach vacation or cruise?

'It is more blessed to give than to receive' (Acts 20:35) are not

empty words or a cute saying; they are the truth. God's truth.

"Come with me to Haiti next time I go," I invited.

"I can't... Not yet. Maybe someday..."

Thursday, 6 January 2011

Be strong and courageous. Do not be terrified; do not be discouraged, for the LORD your God will be with you wherever you go.
— Joshua 1:9 (NIV)

Lying in bed this morning, I suddenly remembered. Overcome with both fear and awe, I recalled a strange event that took place—was it six or seven months ago?

I had sent out an e-mail to a friend at the time, so I searched in my sent folder for that e-mail.

Date: Monday, April 12, 2010, 3:54 PM
Subject: shaken

I may have mentioned that when I was ill with lupus my second time, a prophet in Ukraine had told our pastor, "She has to be ill for a while, but she will eventually be healed." And I was—one year after getting ill. I was healed while in Mexico a year ago through the impassioned prayers of the missionary's wife, a woman who had the gift of healing.

But now this same prophet, who lives in Ukraine, had a vision about me. (I met him briefly when I was in Ukraine in 2009, but find it odd that he would ever think of me—or that I'd appear in visions.) He even called our pastor today to tell him—warn him—that a deadly illness is hovering over my head. My husband just called me to relay this message.

Our church often prays for my health because that's where I get attacked. Even last week it was my eyesight. But a deadly illness? Could you please pray for my health?

I just wanted to share because I am a bit shaken and you seem to be a prayer warrior. Please pray for me.

God bless you.
Kathryn

In April—eight months ago—when I heard the prophecy, I thought it had to do with my heart. Chest pains and heart palpitations had been all too common when I'd struggled with lupus, then menopause.

Why had Brother Shtyher, who lives in Ukraine, gone out of his way to notify our pastor of his disquieting vision? What good was it for me to know? Was there anything I could do?

I knew this man's reputation. Brother Shtyher was a man of God who had the gift of prophecy, one of the spiritual gifts described in 1 Corinthians 12:

There are different kinds of gifts, but the same Spirit... To one there is given through the Spirit the message of wisdom, to another the message of knowledge by means of the same Spirit, to another faith by the same Spirit, to another gifts of healing by that one Spirit, to another miraculous powers, to another prophecy, to another distinguishing between spirits, to another speaking in different kinds of tongues, and to still another the interpretation of tongues (1 Corinthians 12:4, 8–10, NIV).

When we had met Brother Shtyher and prayed with him, I was astounded at his acute perception of my children's characters. He revealed things he could not have possibly known; only God knew. For example, when he prayed over Larissa, he said, "On her heart is written, 'good.'" Indeed, of all of us in the entire family, Larissa is the most kind-hearted and helpful individual, often going out of her way to help others with their chores or fetch things someone needs. She is calm and humble, avoids conflict of any kind and—well, is just plain good. Brother Shtyher could not have known this.

During that summer meeting, Brother Shtyher had prophesied that I would face fear and would call to God in psalms.

That April night after I heard the prophecy about illness, I lay in bed, thoughts fluttering like bats in a cave. I had heart palpitations and shortness of breath. I could not sleep. I was terrified of this deadly illness hovering over me. What was it? Would I die prematurely?

I eventually convinced myself that the prophecy had to do with that one fear-filled heart-pounding night of palpitations, and it was behind me.

But this January morning, I realized that the cancer had either started or was about to start growing in my body about the time of the phone call. I was facing this deadly disease now.

I sat on the patient's table in the doctor's office dressed in a blue gown, the surgeon in front of me, my husband Tad and sister Marta to my right sitting on chairs. My eyes welled up with tears, then overflowed. My throat was closing and I could barely speak.

"I... didn't think I'd need a mastectomy. I thought you would just take the lump out and reconstruct my breast, maybe put in a little implant..."

I realized that the size of the lump was large compared to the overall size of my breast. But the thought of losing the entire breast, cutting it off, being not only flat but with a zipper scar like the doctor explained—I couldn't picture it. I couldn't grasp it. I couldn't believe it. This was not part of the script.

Marta stood up and hugged me. My tears continued. The nurse's aide handed me a tissue.

"If you keep it, you'll have to come in for a mammogram every six months," Dr. Lori Medeiros explained gently.

Well, there would be that peace of mind of knowing that nothing could ever grow there again. If there was no breast, there could be no breast cancer.

"You're so small and the lump is so big that there won't be much left of your breast if we take the lump and the tissue around it," Dr. Medeiros continued. "Really, I think you'll be much happier with a mastectomy. I also seriously recommend you consider reconstruction, either with an implant or using your own tissue—though considering your size, I'm not sure there's much of your own tissue to do reconstruction with. Insurance will cover the cost in either case."

I liked Dr. Medeiros immediately. She was professional, friendly, and approachable—and explained things in a way that I could understand. She also didn't try to downplay the difficulties: it would be emotionally traumatic to lose a breast.

"What's your stress level?" Dr. Medeiros asked me.

Before I could answer, Tad chimed in, "High."

Working full-time while homeschooling our three children through the high school years had definitely taken its toll on my emotions and health. I was surprised by Tad's answer, though, because I didn't think that he was aware just what kind of strain I was under.

"Studies suggest cancer is tied to stress," the doctor noted.

The doctor made sure that Tad and Marta understood what she said, and answered their questions. Tad was there for moral support; Marta was taking notes. Because there was so much to absorb during that first visit, the surgeon's office had recommended bringing a note taker. Even before the office suggested it, Marta had volunteered. Here was something concrete she could do to help. Like my mother, Marta has a servant's heart.

Dr. Medeiros looked at the films and pathology report, did a breast exam starting with the healthy breast, and examined both breasts with ultrasound right there in the office.

"The tumor is very mobile, and that is a good thing," she commented. This meant it had not grown into the surrounding tissue like a seedling spreading its roots. "The MRI did not show any cancer in the lymph nodes, but there may be microscopic cells present, so I will take out the sentinel nodes during surgery and send them to pathology for a biopsy just to make sure."

"Sentinel nodes?" I asked.

"Those are the first set of lymph nodes where cancer cells would travel if they spread from the tumor," the doctor explained. "The day before surgery, you'll go in and have some radioactive dye injected into your breast near the tumor. That radioactive blue dye will travel to some lymph nodes—the sentinel nodes. Using a device, I'll be able to detect the radioactive dye in the sentinel nodes, and I'll remove these lymph nodes. I do that first and send them down to pathology. We used to take out all the lymph nodes, but that's not done anymore. We just take out two or three. Then while I'm doing the breast surgery, I'll get the pathology report back. If cancer cells are found, I would then take out the next set of lymph nodes, and send those for analysis. If no cancer is found in the sentinel nodes, I won't take out any more lymph nodes."

The appointment was long, filled with new information and many questions, which Dr. Medeiros patiently answered. My cancer is an invasive ductal carcinoma, probably a stage two based simply on the size of the tumor, and a nuclear grade three, which means pretty fast-growing.

My head was swimming with terminology I never thought I'd need to learn.

"It's a common 'garden variety' cancer," Dr. Medeiros went on, "so there are known treatments and protocols that are very effective." She expects the outcome to be good; there is an excellent survival rate. Dr. Medeiros doesn't think that I'll need chemotherapy. However, nothing is certain until lab results are back, about a week after surgery is complete. If I do require chemotherapy, the side effects would be nausea and hair loss. Dr. Medeiros described how her brother went through chemo in his thirties when he had been an athlete—"the epitome of health." He bought himself some gym equipment and intended to work out through the chemo treatment. But he didn't use it once. Chemotherapy is rough.

I opted for the mastectomy and no reconstruction. Surgery frightens me, and the idea of undergoing additional surgery for vanity's sake does not appeal to me. My husband supported this decision.

"Don't make your decision quite so quickly," urged the doctor and introduced me to the nurse navigator, Andrea, who would help me through the cancer process. The doctor left the room, and then it was Andrea's turn to talk, listen, and answer questions. It was already four o'clock. The appointment went on for another hour. During that time, Tad had to leave for a business appointment. Marta stayed with me to the end taking notes.

Andrea, an expressive Italian with curly dark hair, described her own breast cancer journey. She included a lot of details from her personal life—marriage, divorce, raising children on her own, nursing school, career, and how she ended up as the breast cancer nurse navigator.

Andrea was a godsend. She talked about faith, and how those with faith and with a positive outlook have better survival statistics. "Your attitude is the single most important factor in determining the outcome of your disease," she shared. "Those with a strong belief system and with a good support system do well. I can see you have a good support system. I don't know what your belief is, but I used to be a Catholic; now I'm a Christian," Andrea continued.

"I'm also a Christian," I interrupted, delighted to have a sister in Christ helping me through this bramble-filled journey.

We talked about Haiti, Scott Long, suicide, materialism, and, of course, breast reconstruction.

"I was diagnosed with breast cancer when I was thirty-nine. I didn't love my breast enough to put my life at risk. I chose a mastectomy. I know that it's easier said than done. You have to be at peace with your decision. What's right for me may not be right for you. I chose to have reconstruction using my own muscles and fat. But I have a friend who chose not to have reconstruction. She doesn't even wear a prosthesis. She's quite comfortable to wear a bikini on a beach just like that—completely flat on one side.

"If you do choose to have reconstruction, there are two ways of doing it: using your own tissue, like I did, or having an implant. If you decide on the implant, which might be the way for you to go because of your size, the plastic surgeon would coordinate surgery with Dr. Medeiros. This surgery would be a two-step process. The day of the mastectomy, you would get a small implant between your muscles and chest wall. This implant would be gradually expanded over a period of weeks, sort of like filling a water balloon. It would stretch out your muscles. Then you'd have a second surgery to remove that implant and put in a permanent implant, either silicone or saline-filled.

"I had the reconstruction, and I'm very happy with my decision. But it must be your decision whether to have reconstruction or not. I suggest that you don't make your decision today. Think about it. Talk to a plastic surgeon. Then you can decide and call us. And even if you decide not to have the reconstruction now, you can always change your mind and do it later. By law, insurance has to cover the cost of this surgery."

"And if I don't have reconstruction?" I asked.

Andrea told me about Thelma's Boutique, a store on Park Avenue in a chic part of town, and gave me a flyer. Thelma's is in a structure that used to be a large house; there are no storefront windows. A discreet sign facing the road simply states the store name. There is no hint of its contents. I have driven by Thelma's hundreds of times, but never noticed the place.

"They have prostheses there. Also wigs and headscarves, should you go through chemotherapy."

She let me handle a prosthesis and introduced me to a world I hadn't known existed.

The appointment had started at 2:45 PM; my sister and I walked out of the medical building after 5 PM. I was hungry, tired, and overwhelmed—and I still had to buy fifty-six packages of flatbread, plus dried fruit, raisins, and other food items for our Haiti trip. This food was for our on-site lunches while doing construction projects.

"Would you like to go out for coffee and talk?" my sister offered as we neared the parking garage.

I felt information and emotional overload, and just wanted to go home. But I couldn't. "I can't tonight. I still have to buy groceries for the Haiti trip, and I haven't finished packing!"

Flatbread was a little difficult to find. I had looked in my regular grocery store earlier in the week and not found any. So I headed to a higher-end grocery store, Wegmans. There was one not far from the medical building where I'd had my appointment.

As I drove and parked and walked, I was in a daze, in a surreal state where I barely noticed the fruit, bread, or people around me. On the outside, I looked like anyone else who had stopped for groceries on the way home from work. But inside, everything had changed.

Cancer. Surgery. Mastectomy. Zipper scar. Prosthesis.

I was traumatized. I had thought they would take the lump out and life would go back to normal after some radiation or even chemotherapy. I was prepared to have my hair fall out; I was not ready to lose a breast. Life never, ever goes back to normal after that. There is a permanent physical reminder of what you went through, which had never occurred to me. No wonder there is such a sisterhood of survivors.

Oddly, I ran into Andrea, the nurse navigator, at the grocery store. I made small talk, telling her I was doing my shopping for the Haiti trip. Somehow her presence there cheered me, reassured me. Her cancer, which had been about a decade ago, was so far behind her, she probably didn't think about it anymore.

But my cancer journey was still ahead.

Wegmans had a variety of flatbreads, but even after I purchased all they had, it was still not enough. I so wanted to go home, but I drove instead to Price Rite, a discount grocery store. They usually carry tortillas at a reduced price. Tortillas were flat, would not crush in my suitcase, and we could make sandwich wraps out of them. I bought a dozen packages. Plus dried fruit. And granola bars. Another hundred dollars.

At the checkout, a young Hispanic woman with hair pulled back tightly into a bun asked casually, "How are you?"

"You don't want to know," I grumbled.

All day long at work, I had answered "Good"—but that was before the doctor's appointment.

"You don't want to say…?" asked the cashier.

"I just got diagnosed with cancer," I blurted out. I wasn't sure why I had phrased it that way; the issue was not the cancer, which I already knew about, but the mastectomy—losing my breast. I suppose this was easier to say, and I didn't have to get into the details.

The cashier's eyes brimmed with tears. Was it compassion?

"Are you okay?" I asked, not at all expecting this reaction.

She wiped a tear. "My mother died from cancer," she shared.

"When? What kind of cancer?"

"Colon cancer. Last year."

I could see that the wounds were raw. I paid for the groceries and walked over to hug her. We both stood there, crying and locked in an embrace. Not the usual checkout counter experience.

Friday, 7 January 2011

Be joyful always; pray continually; give thanks in all circumstances, for this is God's will for you in Christ Jesus.
                                        – 1 Thessalonians 5:16-18 (NIV)

The ringing of the phone awoke me. I glanced at the glowing red numbers on my radio alarm clock as I jumped out of bed. It was just after seven.

"Hello?"

"Kathryn?"

"Yes."

"I'm sorry to be calling you so early, but I just got notification that your Delta flight from Rochester to New York City was canceled for tomorrow morning. You're going to have to fly out today in order to make your morning flight to Haiti tomorrow."

It was the travel agent. I was immediately wide awake.

"Can you get us a flight today?" I asked with a sinking feeling.

"I'll call you back," said Lori and hung up.

The original reservation was for Saturday morning at 6 AM. That early flight would get us to JFK Airport early enough for us to catch the New York – Haiti flight. We were supposed to be at the airport tomorrow at 4 AM, which meant getting out of bed before 3 AM. We had planned on a long day with tight connections.

With one phone call, those plans were shattered like a broken glass.

"If I can do anything for you, do me the honor of asking me," said Jim as I walked into my office later that morning.

It was an interesting way to word his offer, and I thought immediately of an account I'd read about a pastor who had been in a tragic car accident and was bedridden for an entire year afterward. Whenever anyone stopped by to visit and asked the pastor whether he could help him, bring him a cup of tea or anything, his pat answer was always, "No, thanks." An elderly pastor observed this and suggested to the bedridden man, "When people want to help you, to bring you something or serve you somehow, don't immediately turn them down. You are robbing them of the opportunity to serve. Do them—and yourself—a favor by allowing them to serve you. You will both benefit, and it will bring you closer together. Don't automatically say 'no.'"

I remembered this well.

"Could you water the plants in my office while I'm gone?" I asked Jim.

I could stay at the office only a couple of hours; we had to be at the airport at 4 PM. Lori had gotten us tickets for an evening flight with a different airline. I had e-mailed my boss and two of my co-workers to tell them of my sudden change of plans and that I had to leave work by 11 AM to finish packing. I asked for a 9 AM meeting with Shelley, my project lead, and Gina, the co-worker who was going to finish writing the manual I'd been working on.

"I'm sorry," I said to Gina when I arrived at the small conference room. "I didn't finish writing the manual. There's a whole chapter on remote printing that still needs to be written. With all the medical appointments, I just didn't get to it."

"Oh, Kathryn, that's all right! I completely understand. Your health is more important. How was your meeting at the doctor's yesterday?" asked Gina.

Suddenly I couldn't talk again. My eyes pooled with tears. I looked down, and the tears spilled. Gina, who is so kind that she probably thinks twice before swatting a mosquito, must have regretted asking. I felt so unprofessional at that moment and was glad that there were only two women in the room with me.

"I have to have a mastectomy," I said in a shaky voice. "I wasn't expecting that. The doctor who diagnosed the cancer thought that I'd just need a lumpectomy. Maybe some radiation. I didn't think I'd lose my... that I'd have to have a mastectomy."

Saturday, 8 January 2011
JFK airport, New York City

Because of the LORD's great love we are not consumed, for His compassions never fail. They are new every morning...

– Lamentations 3:22–23 (NIV)

From seat 36A on Delta flight 0699, I could see a luminous flush of pink gleaming like a beacon of hope on the metallic body of a nearby airplane. The rest of the scene was the monochrome gray of planes and tarmac and airport buildings. But the dazzling reflection of the predawn eastern sky on that one plane signaled an imminent sunrise, a new beginning.

It had been a short night in New York City. We rose at 4 AM, had group devotions in the girls' hotel room, and boarded the airport shuttle from the Marriott Courtyard Hotel at 5 AM. Then, in the expectant dimness that precedes dawn, we shuffled our twelve suitcases through the crowds and chaos that spilled outside the Delta terminal at JFK Airport. We pushed our baggage through long, snaking lines, exchanged stories with other anxious passengers, and finally made it on board the flight to Haiti. I smiled to myself as I recalled yesterday's flight on JetBlue from Rochester.

At the Rochester airport yesterday afternoon, we weren't able to check our luggage all the way through from Rochester to Haiti because our travel was on two different days. Since we were not traveling internationally the first day of the trip, we would have to pay luggage fees for the domestic flight. I was the treasurer for our group, but with the unplanned cost of two hotel rooms in New York, I didn't have enough funds for the baggage and would have to cover the cost out of my own pocket. Fortunately, I had a credit card with me, but I voiced my concern to Tad.

"You go and check in," said my husband soon after we arrived at the Rochester airport. "I'll go to Ruth's dad and we'll pray."

Good idea, I thought, but without a lot of conviction. Mentally, I was getting ready to make a case for not charging us the luggage fees, getting ready to argue our cause.

I went up to the JetBlue counter to check in. Ruth, Lyuba, and my three children clustered around me.

"Where are you going?" asked the agent brightly.

"Haiti," I responded. "Well, not today. Today we're flying to New York and we have to stay overnight in a hotel. Early tomorrow we're going to Haiti. We're going to be building a boys' orphanage there. The suitcases have lots of relief supplies and food that we collected."

"Haiti!" declared the agent. "You're all going to Haiti?"

"Yes, I was there two months after the earthquake. Now we're all going there. These are my children and"—I motioned to Ruth and Lyuba—"two women from our church. My husband is coming, too. You know," I shifted topics, "they really need our help there in Haiti..."

As she printed our boarding passes, I told the agent about the tent camps and poverty I'd seen on my previous trip. Suddenly she announced, "I'm not going to charge you for these bags." She turned to a co-worker. "They're going to Haiti! Let these bags go."

In fact, she didn't even weigh the suitcases. I was reminded to never underestimate the power of prayer.

The Rochester – New York flight was sixteen-year-old Ruth's first airplane flight. Ruth, the third of six children born to immigrant parents, has a bold and mischievous spirit. Solidly built like her peasant grandmother, brown-eyed Ruth loves to challenge young men to arm wrestling. It's rare that she loses. She's spirited and expressive on a regular day; during the flight she could hardly contain her excitement.

I had been assigned seat 1A right in the front, but noticed that Ruth did not have a window seat. I still remember my own exhilaration as I looked out the window during my first flight, which I took at seventeen. "Here, Ruth, switch seats with me so you can sit by a window," I offered.

Our male flight attendant enlivened the trip with his wit. At the beginning of the flight, he pointed to the other attendant and announced, "Keisha has been nominated for flight attendant of the week. To vote for Keisha, press this button up here"—he pointed to the flight attendant call button—"as many times as possible."

Ruth "voted" for Keisha, of course.

At the end of the flight as we were gathering our carry-on luggage, I asked Ruth, "So how did you like the flight? You got the special seat, 1A in the front, because it's your first flight."

"Really?" she beamed.

I smiled broadly. "Just kidding. Don't you remember I swapped seats with you?"

"Oh yeah…"

As everyone disembarked the plane, Ruth stood at the front with the flight attendants, and taking her cue from Keisha, she smiled at each passenger. "Thank you for flying JetBlue!" Ruth said over and over again.

Afterward, the pilot let her sit in his cockpit and I took a photo of her there. Then we caught the shuttle to our hotel.

We settled into our seats on the Saturday morning New York – Port-au-Prince flight and waited for all the passengers to board.

The mood of this flight was much more subdued than on my previous flight to Haiti. Today there was a mix of black Haitians and white Americans calmly taking their seats. But last March, two months after the earthquake, the air had been charged with excitement and apprehension, and the plane had been filled to capacity with nervously chattering teams of American volunteers sporting matching green or red or yellow tee shirts with names of organizations, churches, and Bible verses. At that time, my tee shirt had been lime green.

Haiti. The word has so many connotations. To most, it's now associated with the tragic 7.0 magnitude earthquake that killed a staggering 316,000 people a year ago. But I had been interested in Haiti before that catastrophic event, before Haiti became a household word.

The seed was planted during a company-sponsored bike ride for racers and bicycling enthusiasts that I was covering for a Kodak blog article in the summer of 2007. As I panted near the back of the pack of riders, I fell into a conversation with a kind software engineer who decided to keep me company as I fell further and further behind, and eventually brought up the rear.

Instead of rushing to the finish (and to the promised pizzas), we enjoyed the rural scenery and chatted as we pedaled. Work, children, outside interests—we covered a large range of topics. He told me about his daughter's obsession with soccer; I told him that my husband and I try to get our kids involved with activities in which they'll learn skills that they'll use the rest of their lives.

"Most high school kids who participate in sports no longer play the sport in college," I noted, "or afterward. But if you learn to play a piano, you'll have a life skill and will be able to play piano the rest of your life. That's my husband's opinion—and I think he has a good point," I added.

Then I shared about mission trips, which I consider character-building experiences that shape a person's outlook on life.

"My son, who's fifteen, is crazy about sports cars," I related. "My husband and I don't approve of his obsession with something that is vain and could prove to be dangerous. I consider a car to be a form of transportation that gets you from point A to point B, not something that you show off to others. So to introduce our son to something on the other end of the spectrum from the sports cars that he's so enamored with, I went with him to Mexico last summer to build homes for the destitute on a landfill next to a garbage dump. When I say 'home,' I mean a twelve by twenty-foot plywood structure with a door and two windows—no electricity, no running water. And the stench of the garbage was so strong that I can still smell it in my mind.

"Our children—and most Americans—don't know what real need is. They've never seen it. Each day 25,000 children die of hunger and preventable causes, such as illnesses treatable with antibiotics that they can't afford, while our kids think about iPods and sports cars. There's such a disconnect between the rich Western world and the rest of the world. I hope that through mission trips, like the one to Mexico, my kids will broaden their horizons and be a little less self-centered."

"Have you read *Mountains Beyond Mountains*?" asked the engineer as he pedaled next to me. "It's a book about a doctor's work in Haiti. My wife read it. Sounds like something you'd be interested in."

I borrowed the book from the library the following week. It sowed a burning desire to go to Haiti.

How do you describe Haiti, a land so poor that people resort to eating mud cookies to fill their bellies and fend off hunger pangs?

Perhaps it's best to start more than two centuries ago when Haiti, a lush, mountainous land with tropical climate, was the single richest colony in the world, "the jewel of the Caribbean." The mahogany, coffee, sugar cane, and other goods it exported brought more wealth to France than all thirteen American colonies brought to England.

The French exploited the land using slave labor. Although we associate the African slave trade with American plantations, in reality, the United States (or the colonies) imported only five or six percent of the ten to twelve million slaves taken from Africa. A far greater number went to the Caribbean and Brazil, where a large number of them worked on sugar plantations. In Haiti, life expectancy was short and slave masters were cruel. They felt that they had to be to assert control over slaves: the slaves outnumbered them fifty or a hundred to one.

The slaves rebelled nonetheless. On August 14, 1791, a slave named Boukman met with voodoo priests under a large tree, and in a religious ceremony, they slaughtered a black pig, drank its blood, and made a pact with Satan: if he would help them win independence from France, they would dedicate the country to him and to the spirits of the island for the next two hundred years.

In 1804, Haiti became the first country created by a black slave revolt and the first—and only—country in the world dedicated to Satan and his dark forces.

The main religion in Haiti is voodoo. A common saying is that Haitians are 70% Catholic, 30% Protestant, and 100% voodoo, which means that most Haitians both go to church and practice voodoo. Voodoo combines beliefs in ancient African gods and ancestral spirits with demon worship. Casting spells and creating potions, trances and animal sacrifices, and demon possession—voodoo spirits entering bodies and making the people act like animals—are some typical voodoo rituals. Voodoo is epitomized by ceremonial bathing not in water, but in mud. Death curses, drunkenness, wild orgies, and even child rape and sacrifices are also part of this dark religion. Intoxication, lying, stealing, and violence are extolled in voodoo.

No wonder Haiti is considered a dangerous place.

Dedicating their country to the dark forces seems to have cursed the land. Haiti's history has been marred by instability and violence. Bloody coups and dictatorships, violent confrontations between rival gangs and political groups, drug trafficking and a corrupted judicial system have made this potential tropical tourist destination a place to avoid rather than visit. The infrastructure has all but collapsed. The human rights situation, according to the UN, is "catastrophic."

Haiti is not only the poorest country in the western hemisphere, but close to the poorest in the entire world. Half of the population is illiterate. Of the ten million Haitians, eighty percent live in poverty. In fact, fifty percent—that's five million people—live in abject poverty, defined as eating only one small meal or less per day. One article I read states, "…most Haitian children receive less nutrition than the average American house pet."

The media mocked the suggestion that the earthquake was God's vengeance. Not so the Haitians. Léogâne, the center of voodoo, was the epicenter of the earthquake. The Haitians did not see this as a coincidence; they saw it as God's judgment. They know their history. They know that every year in August, Boukman's sacrifice is reenacted under the great tree where he is said to have made his pact. They know that year after year, the country is dedicated and rededicated to Satan.

They also go to church. They know that God is a jealous God.

The unseen is more real than the seen. But we close our spiritual eyes in the Western world, distracting ourselves with material pleasures. This spiritual battle seems to be more apparent in Haiti—if you choose to see it.

For our struggle is not against flesh and blood, but... against the powers of this dark world and against the spiritual forces of evil in the heavenly realms (Ephesians 6:12, NIV).

In 2001, a Haitian pastor bought the land next to the tree where the annual sacrifices took place and began to pray against the evil powers that this tree symbolized. The voodoo priests were enraged. But in 2003, word spread that the tree had died. No sacrifices were held that year. The two hundred years were up. The powers of darkness seemed to be loosening their grip on Haiti.

Scott was in Haiti at the time of the earthquake and told me during my first trip, "The night after the earthquake and the entire week afterward, people gathered in churches and sang through the night. It was as if in that moment when the earthquake happened, the power shifted from Satan to God," Scott explained. "These are not my words; this is what the Haitians themselves are saying."

The Haitians noticed that the earthquake devastated manmade structures, but nature was virtually unaffected.

Since the earthquake, a revival has been spreading across this island nation. But you only learn of it if you spend time in Haiti or talk to someone who has. The news doesn't talk about it. The three days of fasting and prayer that Haitian President Preval declared one month after the earthquake were not widely reported, even though the country came to a standstill as churches overflowed and voices pleaded for God's mercy.

When people deny that the spiritual history of a country has an effect on the land, they are denying God's supremacy and power. Who controls nature anyway?

Being in tune to the spiritual world is not something that just happens. In North America, it's difficult to do when you're cushioned with material possessions and distracted with entertainment. Blaring radio and television, text messages and Internet, social media and cell phones, sports events and movies, shopping sprees and dinner parties—they fill our worlds. When we are listening to other voices, surrounding ourselves with perpetual commotion to purposely keep out the quiet; when we are busy, busy, busy, driving from here to there, keeping appointments, filling our time with hectic activities, how can we expect to be in harmony with the spiritual world? How can we hear God's voice whispering? It's only when you slow down and allow God to speak into your life that a world outside your five senses can open up to you. Or you can travel to a place like Haiti, and for a brief time, disconnect yourself from the din of your daily life and open the ears of your soul.

Saturday evening
Villa Ormiso, Carfou, Haiti

Every experience God gives us, every person He puts into our lives, is the perfect preparation for a future only He can see.
— Corrie ten Boom

During the one-hour ride from the Port-au-Prince airport to the guesthouse in Carfou, I sat in the front seat of the bus so I could photograph out the window: gaudily painted tap-taps overflowing with people, vendors squatting by the roadside with their bunches of plantains and a few cabbages, pigs rummaging in piles of garbage. A whiff of diesel exhaust and burning trash affirmed that I was in a developing country. That smell raises my pulse with excitement and anticipation.

Paul, our team leader, sat behind me in a fold-out seat. Admittedly, I was a little disappointed that Scott wasn't our team leader. I had wanted Tad to get to know Scott during the week. Because there are over seventy people on this mission trip, we were divided into three teams, one team per bus. Scott is leading team A; his twenty-year-old son Taran is leading team B; and Paul is leading our team, team C.

I had just met Paul, who looks like he's in his forties. He is unusually thin with no padding to soften the sharp angles on his chiseled face. His dark eyes match his dark hair, but the hair is thinning, receding.

When he wasn't making announcements to the team or pointing out landmarks, I tried to find out a little about him.

"How many times have you been to Haiti?" I asked Paul.

"This is my fourth."

"So do you work for Scott?" I continued. I hoped it didn't sound like an interview.

"I've been on staff for a year. I went to Haiti with Mission E4 for the first time two years ago. Then I took some courses at Mission E4. I caught Scott's vision. I was unemployed, so when Scott asked me to join Mission E4, I did."

"Are you married?" I asked. I figured that it would be hard to do this kind of work if he had a family.

"My wife died in 2004 from cancer."

This was getting close to home.

"Was it breast cancer?" I ventured.

"Started there."

I paused a little, wondering how to put my whirlwind of thoughts into words. Surely Paul was one of many people that God purposely put in my path this week. It was no coincidence that he was our team leader.

"I was just diagnosed with breast cancer ten days before this trip. About a week after I get home, I'm going to have a mastectomy."

We were both silent for a while. I realized that Paul could identify with my struggle more than most.

Sunday, 9 January 2011
Carfou, Haiti

Do not conform any longer to the pattern of this world, but be transformed by the renewing of your mind. Then you will be able to test and approve what God's will is—his good, pleasing and perfect will.

– Romans 12:2 (NIV)

Yesterday evening, after we'd settled into our rooms, sorted our donations of toys, clothes, and food, and taken showers, our small group of seven from Rochester sat in the guesthouse courtyard with our hymnbooks and sang a cappella in four-part harmony. Our voices carried through the lower courtyard and up to the pool area. As people strolled up the stairs toward the pool and dining area, they passed by us. Some smiled, some walked by quietly as if not knowing what to do. I got the impression that my children were a touch embarrassed to be singing in this public spot.

Our family has been singing hymns a cappella for about five years, inspired by a request to sing for a Christmas Eve service at a community church. Tad, a gifted musician, has trained the family, and later the church youth group, to sing without musical accompaniment. Hymns sung in four-part harmony are so lovely that we've often observed moist eyes and dabbing tissues. We are far from professional, but all three children have inherited Tad's musical gift and are much better at staying on pitch than I am.

I've often found it interesting how differently Tad and I take in the world. As a musician, he learns by hearing, and so he easily picks up languages. He's also good at puns. He appreciates songs and melodies, sings perpetually, and can perceive discord in music that I can't hear. It's no surprise that a few years ago, he changed his career and become a piano tuner.

I take in the world through my eyes. I see light as it wraps around a person's face or skims across a field. Every scene is a photo opportunity composed in an imaginary frame in my mind. I see things that others miss. I don't say that to brag; I only recently discovered it when traveling through the Ukrainian countryside at dawn with my husband, his sister Ira, and her husband Andriy. I would ask Andriy to stop the car, then I'd run out and photograph a shepherd with a cow. Or mist rising from a pond. Or men with scythes cutting hay, backlit by the rising sun. Later that evening, I showed Ira, Andriy, and Tad my early morning photos on a laptop computer, and all admitted that they hadn't seen any of what I'd captured in my viewfinder.

"Why, that's really beautiful," my sister-in-law admitted with some surprise. How could they not have seen it?

After most of the guests had wandered up to the dining area, we stopped singing and joined them. Following supper, Scott gave the group a rundown of a typical day, introduced the rules, and encouraged us to turn in early. Many had been up even earlier than we had been.

I told Scott that I had been diagnosed with breast cancer just before this trip and asked him whether there was anyone in Haiti who could pray for my healing—other than the group, which I also wanted to pray for me.

He paused for a moment, then said, "Tomorrow your group is going to Fauché for the church service." (Ah, yes, the place where the 'twenty-four hour bug' almost got me.) "Be sure to tell Paul to ask Madame Wooldolf to pray for you. She's one who will remember to keep praying for you even after you're back home."

Madame Wooldolf, a mother of five, is the wife of a pastor in Fauché. She's also a fervent worship leader who raises her voice in song and leads the congregation in worship. I remembered her—and her passionate singing—from my previous trip.

And the twenty-four hour bug?

During my March 2010 trip, Caleb and I had accompanied Scott to Fauché, where a medical team was setting up a clinic under a tree—the same tree where we'd had a church service the day before, a tree blooming yellow blossoms and abuzz with bees and insects. After taking some photos of the medical team, I stood under the tree waiting for Scott. I felt something plunk down on my wide-brimmed sunhat, but I dismissed it as a leaf. Suddenly, Scott's daughter Morgan shouted, "Get it off her! Get it off her!!"

Morgan's face registered fear. Had a tarantula dropped down on me?

I bowed my head slowly, very slowly toward Caleb, who was standing next to me, video camera in hand.

"What is it?" I asked quietly, as if afraid to frighten whatever was on my hat.

Caleb took a step toward me and gradually reached for the brim of my hat. He gave it a sharp little tug.

"What is it?" I asked again.

"It's gone," said Caleb.

"What was it?" I turned to Morgan.

"A twenty-four hour bug."

"A twenty-four hour bug? The only twenty-four hour bug I know is the stomach flu."

"It's a hornet that if it stings you, you die in twenty-four hours," Morgan explained.

"It was about that big," explained Caleb, marking off a distance of about three inches on the microphone of his video camera.

It was my turn to be in shock. I felt at that moment that someone must have been praying for me.

"Caleb, you saved my life!" I grinned. "But you didn't get a video of that bug?"

During the bus ride to Fauché this Sunday morning, we picked up our translator, Emanuel, at the girls' orphanage, which is the "base camp" for Mission E4. In fact, because there are so many volunteers on this trip, Team B, led by Scott's son Taran, is staying in tents on the orphanage grounds; there aren't enough rooms at the guesthouse for us all.

When Emanuel saw me on the bus, our eyes connected. "I remember you," he smiled. I was surprised. He must have met many people between last March and this January. I remembered him, too; he had ridden in a tap-tap with a small group of us to the church service in another location in Fauché—that memorable tree. But today's church service was held in a school building, which is really just a wooden frame with a corrugated metal roof and an earthen floor. Blue plastic tarps were hung for walls. The red and green and blue school benches served as pews.

A drum and a tambourine accompanied the singing. The service ran two hours, maybe longer. Some of the locals fanned the sultry air with papers, trying to chase away the perspiration from their faces. There was a lot of singing, some preaching, more singing. When Paul preached, Emanuel translated into Creole for the congregation. When the pastor preached, Emanuel translated into English for our team.

We took part in the service, too. Our Rochester group sang one of the hymns that we'd practiced last night. Then, when the service was over and the Haitian children from the congregation were playing with our team members, some of whom were blowing up long balloons and twisting them into animal shapes for the children, I reminded Paul of my request.

We gathered at the front of the church: Madame Wooldolf and her pastor husband, Tad and my children, Paul and Emanuel. Someone pulled up a chair, placed it on the dirt floor in front of me, and motioned for me to sit. Madame Wooldolf began to sing. Others joined in. Sitting on that chair in the tropical heat, I bowed my head. After the song, Madame Wooldolf raised her voice to God, fervently beseeching Him on my behalf. Her husband joined the prayer. The voices of other team members intermingled, weaving a tapestry of prayer on my behalf.

I know that God can heal miraculously. He's done that in my life before. Twice. Here I was again, humbled before Him and begging Him to extend my life and restore me to health once more.

I thanked Madame Wooldolf, and we hugged. Soon afterward, our team boarded the bus.

All three teams had lunch—a large spread of Haitian foods— together at the girls' orphanage. Madame Bazile (the wife of the pastor who runs the orphanage and church in Léogâne) and the orphans had been preparing the meal since before sunrise, chopping everything by hand and cooking over charcoal fires. How they managed to cook enough to feed our army of seventy is a mystery.

I'd have trouble cooking for that many in my kitchen with its four-burner gas stove and my host of modern appliances.

Today was a day of rest; tomorrow we begin work in earnest. We spent much of the day hanging out and getting to know one another. Scott encouraged us to sit with different people during meals, to mingle and mix and not dine with the people with whom we arrived. That's how I met some of the individuals who had been in Haiti a year ago during the earthquake. About ten of them returned this January. All described the event as a faith-building experience.

Back at the guesthouse in the evening, Scott led worship in the dining room after supper. Tables were quickly cleared and chairs moved into a semi-circle around the piano.

Like Tad, Scott is a talented musician who plays both the piano and guitar. Scott played the worship songs on the piano and sang with enthusiasm. About fifty of us sang with him. We prayed. And we listened to one of Scott's thought-provoking sermons. In modern Christianity, he said, many people accept Jesus and want Him to be their Lord, who follows them wherever they lead Him. But that's not what Jesus said. He never asked anyone to accept Him; He asked people to follow Him. Were we ready to go where He calls?

After the sermon, we were free to spend time as we wished. Larissa played hymns on the piano. Tad joined her. Then Scott joined the two of them in song. The rest of the family congregated around the piano and sang inspirational hymns in harmony.

As we were breaking up to go to our rooms, I heard Scott say, "Tad and I have a lot in common." My dream of them meeting had come true, and they even saw similarities in one another.

Back in the room that I share with Ruth, Lyuba, and my two daughters, I quickly checked for the lump. Perhaps after that heart-felt prayer it was gone? For a second, I couldn't feel it and I was both hopeful and nervous. Then I found it. The lump was still there. Maybe a miraculous healing would be too easy a way out for me, and God would not have the opportunity to show me all He has in store.

Or maybe I didn't have enough faith for such a miracle.

Someone pointed out that just because my lump didn't disappear miraculously, it didn't mean that God didn't answer our prayers. God heals through doctors and medicine, too. God is sovereign; He has all in His control.

As I lay in bed, I thought about the pain in my right abdomen, sometimes a sharp twinge, sometimes a dull ache, sometimes not there at all. Is it in my head? Am I imagining it? Is it related to the breast cancer? I keep pushing thoughts about this odd pain to the back of my head. Should I have it investigated after I get back home? Or is it psychosomatic?

Yes, I know, God has all in His control.

Monday, 10 January 2011
Carfou, Haiti

...give me neither poverty nor riches, but give me only my daily bread. Otherwise, I may have too much and disown you and say, 'Who is the LORD?' Or I may become poor and steal, and so dishonor the name of my God.
– Proverbs 30:8–9 (NIV)

You look at the Bible differently after spending time in a place like Africa or Haiti. Dirt roads. Wells. Fishermen casting nets.

During a medical mission trip into the sub-Saharan bush in West Africa eight years ago, I rose before dawn hoping to see the colorfully dressed women drawing water from the village well. Instead, I found the nomadic shepherds pulling, pulling on a long rope and hauling out pail after pail of water for their bleating flocks of sheep and goats. I suddenly realized that there was no other source of water for the animals in this vast beige expanse of sand—no sparkling river or lake, and certainly no convenient water faucet. Drawing water from a well that's one hundred and fifty feet deep is grueling. Watching those men, and later in the day the women, gave me a new appreciation for the passage in Genesis chapter 24 about Rebekah drawing water for Abraham's servant and his camels. She had to do a lot of physical work.

Scott described that a few years ago, his team was walking along a beach in Haiti and saw two men who were too poor to own a boat spreading a net in the water. "Let's help them," Scott suggested to the team. He expected it would take them ten minutes, but after two hours and a lot of physical exertion, they had hauled in only five small fish, which the men gave to a widow to eat; the two men had nothing. In John chapter 21, it was an act of faith that Simon Peter threw his net back into the water at Jesus' command after a night of catching nothing. It's not as simple as just tossing a net and pulling it in a few minutes later, Scott's team discovered. It's hours of labor.

The streets of Carfou come to life before sunrise. Vendors set up their baskets of vegetables, or spread a sheet and display items for sale—a pyramid of oranges, a few heads of garlic, a dozen melons, a stack of charcoal. Cars, buses, trucks, tap-taps all drive within inches of their wares, swerving, honking, belching diesel exhaust.

The scenes out the bus window during the ride to the orphanage display a sad state of disrepair and disorder: Crushed cement, piles of rubble, and burning heaps of garbage line the streets. Wretched creek beds filled with trash provide an area for goats and pigs to rummage for scraps. Horns blare as trucks and cars swerve around each other. Crashed and crumpled vehicles sit abandoned by the roadside, covered with thick dust. Trucks bump along, brimming with so many passengers perched on mounds of produce that you wonder how they hang on. And people walking, walking everywhere—some with children in tow, some straining to pull a wooden cart fit for an ox, some balancing a sack or a chair on their heads, some weaving through the traffic and around vendors on their solitary journeys.

Tent camps still clutter the landscape with their distinctive blue tarps crisscrossed with silver duct tape and coated with impressive deposits of dust. One year after the earthquake, 1.3 million Haitians still live in these clusters of structures that are shabbier than the tent I use when camping.

During the bus ride, Paul mentioned that the president of World Vision said that an estimated $400 billion was spent on Christmas presents this past holiday season, but it would take only $8 billion to solve the world's water problem—that is, for everyone on earth to have access to clean drinking water. This lack of access to clean water is the main reason that cholera is spreading in Haiti. It's the reason many children all over the world die from dysentery. And typhoid. Hepatitis A. Diarrhea. The World Health Organization states that waterborne diseases are the world's leading killer. Lack of safe drinking water takes a greater human toll than war and AIDS combined. The majority of the more than three million annual victims are children.

Words cannot describe the ache in my heart when I heard how much had been spent on presents in the last few weeks. Why, we could make huge progress toward solving the water crisis in one Christmas season! But it will never happen. People aren't willing to not buy what they perceive to be obligatory presents. So much of holiday buying is senseless extravagance or giving to fulfill obligations—feeling compelled to buy something even though the recipient doesn't need the item. If everyone would donate not half, but just *one-fifth* of what they'd normally spend during only one holiday season to a charity that digs wells and provides clean water, what a better place this world would be. But most people in the West are not even aware of this need. If they were, would they donate? Would they really be willing to not buy stuff? Unaware of the problem, they buy more electronics, sweaters, toys, and goods that will end up in our landfills.

Fortunately, we're spending our family's Christmas money on this trip, not on stuff. Even in the years when we don't go on a family mission trip, we have a different approach to Christmas.

Many years ago, we put an end to the senseless present exchanges with our extended family—though not without some resistance. A few years later, we changed from buying presents for our children to giving them each a check made out to a charity and a catalog from that charity. Jacob, Alexandra, and Larissa could then choose a variety of items in the catalog that add up to the dollar amount on the check— a goat for a poor family in Africa, a pair of chickens or rabbits for a family in India, an education for a year for a Senegalese child. It's interesting to see the selections that the children make.

Each of our children also receives some chocolates and a practical item or two, depending on need: wool socks, a blanket, a cookbook. This journey took years, but we've gone from a family who lavished presents on our children to one who has taught our children that they have everything that they need. The children themselves recently told me, "I have everything, Mom. I don't need anything for Christmas." They really don't, and they've come to see it themselves. Not only have we taught them this, but they have also seen need with their own eyes. There's no better present for children than mission trips that take them to a destitute country so they can see how blessed they truly are. Our children have stopped comparing themselves to their local peers who "need" designer clothes or the latest smartphone and can see where they fit on the global scale.

Tuesday, 11 January 2011
Haiti

Be still, and know that I am God...

– Psalm 46:10 (NIV)

A knock on our door awoke me at 6 AM.

"Thank you!" I shouted to the mysterious door knocker whose duty it was to go door to door and wake everyone.

It was time to shower, get dressed, load the charged batteries into my cameras, organize my camera bag, put on sunscreen, then choose a place outside where I could read my Bible and record my thoughts and impressions in my journal. Every morning when Scott starts playing the piano in the dining room by the pool, it's time for the group to assemble for morning devotions.

Early morning at the guesthouse is a tranquil and enchanting time—birdsongs, golden sunlight on the lush tropical plants in the courtyards, and a hush that precedes the day's activities. This verdant spot, isolated from the chaos and filth of the Haitian streets, is a little slice of tropical paradise, a haven from the hard life that is the daily reality of most Haitians.

Daybreak is a time to spend with God, a time to thank Him for bringing me here to Haiti and extending my life yet another day. It's a time to meditate on the messages Scott has been sharing and to bask in the rich Christian fellowship I have here.

The mission trips I've taken have been times of spiritual revival. I return home invigorated. Renewed. Glowing inside. On a mission trip, I live each moment of the day solely for God and spend it with fellow Christians. I make new friends, am inspired by the work of missionaries, and feel much closer to God. I thank the Lord for every moment I have on a trip like this. I wish I could stay in Haiti weeks or months, not just seven days.

Word is getting around that I have breast cancer. I share it with most people I talk to—on the bus, during meals, on the work sites, or hanging around the guesthouse. I'm thankful for the words of encouragement and support, and the promises of prayer.

Today I met Rose, a thin woman with hair cut in a short bob and dyed a platinum blond. At sixty-three, Rose has been a breast cancer survivor for seventeen years. She had a mastectomy when she was forty-six. I'd been hoping I would meet a survivor with whom I could talk.

"I know it sounds odd," said Rose, "but the cancer was an answer to prayer. I'd been praying that my husband and I would grow closer. Through that cancer, our marriage strengthened and we grew much closer to one another."

Her story actually didn't sound so odd. Years ago, when I was an assistant in my daughter Larissa's Sunday school class, the teacher, who was younger than I, told me that she had prayed to get closer to

God. Then she got breast cancer. Through that cancer—and a double mastectomy—that she had in her thirties, she indeed drew very close to God.

"Did you have reconstruction surgery?" I ventured to Rose.

"Not at first," she replied. "I went for four years with a prosthesis. The prosthesis was sticky and uncomfortable in hot weather like this. Four years after the mastectomy, my husband was going to get off the health insurance we were on. 'It's your last chance to get reconstruction,' he said, so I went ahead and did it. I'm glad I did. I'd feel awkward changing in a room full of women like we have here. I know one woman in her seventies who is in a new relationship with a man, and she now regrets not having the reconstruction."

"Did you have an insert put in?" I asked.

"No, I had reconstruction from my own body fat. It became infected, though, and they had to cut away half of it."

Despite Rose's testimony, I am still inclined to stick with my original decision. When rooming with women I don't know, I can get dressed discreetly. Today's prostheses are much improved over the older ones, I've heard, and not as likely to be uncomfortable in hot weather. And I certainly wouldn't want the pain of additional surgery only to lose half the work. Still, it was good to get the opinion of someone who has had both the prosthesis and the reconstruction.

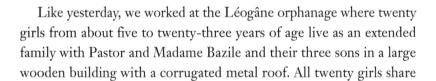

Like yesterday, we worked at the Léogâne orphanage where twenty girls from about five to twenty-three years of age live as an extended family with Pastor and Madame Bazile and their three sons in a large wooden building with a corrugated metal roof. All twenty girls share one room, sleeping on the cement floor without any mattresses.

Tad's task is to build triple-decker bunk beds for the orphans. Several women sanded the two-by-fours so the boards for the frames would be smooth and the orphans wouldn't get splinters. Alexandra and Lyuba spent most of their time sanding by hand, back and forth, back and forth, smoothing the wood with sandpaper. Later in the day, one of the men brought an electric sander and plugged it into a generator. Lyuba, with sky-blue eyes and hair the color of sunshine, beamed with delight at her new skill with this power tool. The sanding and Tad's bed-building are considered "light construction."

Ruth and my son Jacob are part of the "heavy construction" team, which is working in full sun on the flat cement roof of the building that contains the medical clinic and gift shop. This team is putting up the wooden frame and walls of a second-story apartment where a young missionary family is going to live. Several of the men on this team are experienced builders. I noticed one of the men, whom Ruth dubbed "Grandpa" Rich, teaching Ruth how to handle a hammer properly, how to pound in nails when you need to hammer at an angle, and how to make a frame square. With dark eyes sparkling and brown hair speckled with sawdust, Ruth worked with enthusiasm, glowing with delight even as she sweated while carrying lumber, hammering nails, or holding boards while others measured, cut, or nailed. She loved doing construction work, she announced, and it showed.

Larissa and I are in charge of preparing lunches for our team and making sure each team member is drinking enough water. Larissa and I hound everyone to drink, drink, drink, then refill their water bottles from the blue plastic five-gallon jug of filtered water. We climb to the top of the medical building, search inside the orphanage, and scour the grounds for the workers and their water bottles, making pests of ourselves. Despite drinking a minimum of half a gallon of water, few of us need to use the toilet. We just sweat, sweat, sweat.

Lunches are simple: your choice of a wrap made with peanut butter and jelly or canned chicken breast with mayonnaise, plus crackers, dried fruits, and a granola bar. Lunchtime is the busiest time for Larissa and me. The rest of the day, I monitor water bottles in between taking photos of our team or the Haitian children; Larissa helps with the sanding.

Although the days are muggy and sweat perpetually trickles down my back, work time passes quickly. All too soon we have to return to the guesthouse. There's always a rush for the front seat next to the bus driver because it has the best view, and it's the best spot for photo opportunities.

At the guesthouse, there's another rush for the showers. We have only one hour to clean up and rest before dinnertime. Ruth, Lyuba, and Alexandra, who are covered with sawdust from their work, have first dibs on the shower.

"AAAaaaah! Ooooh!"

Those of us in the room giggled. Lyuba hadn't caught on that we could hear her exclamations through the bathroom door as the shock of cold water hits her in the shower. That cold water is bracing, but after the initial jolt, it feels good on a hot, sweat-covered body.

I prefer to shower last, after dinner and Bible study, and just before I go to bed. That way I wash off the day's grime and perspiration, and feel refreshed before slipping into bed. If the city electricity does not shut off, the ceiling fan provides a gentle breeze.

When I shower, I still feel for that lump. With so many people praying, maybe it will disappear?

Wednesday, 12 January 2011
One-year anniversary of the earthquake in Haiti

All nations whom You have made shall come and worship before You, O Lord, and shall glorify Your name. For You are great, and do wondrous things; You alone are *God.*
– Psalm 86:9–10 (NKJV)

Nights are not peaceful in a place like Haiti. Dogs bark during the night. Roosters crow at odd hours. Loud, thumping music blares through distant loudspeakers. I try to keep out these sounds with silicone earplugs that I push deep into my ears every night, but even these wax-like plugs don't keep out all the noise. They mute it, and usually that's enough for me to sleep through the night.

But this night was different. I had fallen asleep at the usual time, but awoke in the predawn grayness. I took out my earplugs. Faintly,

I could hear the singing of hymns coming from unseen churches, voices in the distance singing to God.

It was the one-year anniversary of the earthquake. What it was like a year ago is hard for me to imagine.

For my devotion this morning, I read Psalm 86. Penciled into the margin of my Bible is a note: I had read this psalm as a devotional in Ethiopia while on a mission trip. This psalm is dear to the hearts of the Ethiopians: it is the cry of the needy.

> *Hear my prayer, O LORD; listen to my cry for mercy. In the day of my trouble I will call to You, for You will answer me* (Psalm 86:6–7, NIV).

How the Haitians cried to the Lord that fateful day one year ago! I was inspired by their individual stories of those who had been in Haiti a year ago. None on the Mission E4 team were hurt even though the destruction around them was catastrophic. Through a series of "coincidences," God protected them. For example, one bus was tied up in traffic, so it didn't get to the guesthouse at the usual time. When it finally arrived, the driver parked on the left side (the wrong side) of the road—something he had never done before. Just as the driver was about to open the bus door, the ground began to shake. The ten-foot high guesthouse wall, which was made of cement, toppled. Had the bus been in its usual spot, it would have been crushed by the wall. Had the driver arrived even thirty seconds sooner and opened the door, the passengers would have been under the wall as it collapsed.

The second bus was further down the narrow, vendor-lined street. During the earthquake, the bus rocked as if on ocean waves. "That was some pothole!" thought the passengers. Soon they realized that the earth was moving under the vehicle, but they were safe, away from any collapsing structures.

Scott's story was even more remarkable. He was in the Port-au-Prince Hospital visiting a student when the earthquake occurred.

"I thought it was tanks exploding or bombs dropping—you know Haiti is not a very stable country," Scott explained. "It took me a few seconds to realize that it was an earthquake. And then I wanted to run down this corridor with glass windows. I threw my arms up and prayed to Jesus for protection, and two Haitian women grabbed my hands. They held on to me, one holding each hand, and prayed and prayed. I was getting impatient. I wanted to run, but they were keeping me from doing that. Then the whole corridor exploded with glass! Had I run down that corridor as I'd intended, I would have been severely injured, if not killed. When I turned to look at the Haitian women, they were gone. I still don't know whether those were real women or angels."

God had indeed guarded each one of them. A part of me wished that I had been there, too.

Businesses and schools are closed today. It's a national holiday. During the bus ride to Léogâne, I saw church after church crammed full of people. Many of the church buildings were wood, tarp, and tin structures much like the church we attended on Sunday. But these simple churches, unlike many magnificent structures in America, were alive and full—full of people, full of songs, full of God's spirit.

We arrived in Léogâne at nine o'clock to continue our construction projects. As we hammered and cut, sanded and painted, climbed stairs and filled water bottles, we could hear music and preaching coming from the school building next door, a building—actually, another wooden-framed structure with those ubiquitous blue tarps for walls—that functions as a church on Sundays.

Tad and I, along with a few others, had the opportunity to walk over to see the church service, which had started before 7 AM. The school benches had been moved off the cement floor of the building, the tarp walls had been tied up to make one large, open area, and on the hard floor were dozens and dozens of blankets on which sat women and children. Some of the children were lying down; others were fidgeting; still others dozed. The men sat on the school benches outside the building under the open sky. It was mid-afternoon, but the singing and preaching continued and would do so until evening.

The sermons the last few evenings have challenged me. When Scott preaches, I listen with my pen.

"Today there are 33,000 Christian denominations," Scott told us. "That's *denominations*," he reiterated, "not churches. Now that's staggering! There are doctrinal differences between all these denominations, but even so, we can all serve together. For this week, the differences aren't so important. The seventy people on this mission trip are from twenty-three churches, but all want to help the poor. We are all working here together.

"In many American churches, the pastor is paid, and we're the cheerleaders—or the critics—sitting in the sidelines. But we are all supposed to work."

People want to find a purpose, Scott explained. And that purpose should be serving the Lord in some capacity, just as we are doing this week. What a feeling of satisfaction to be here with my brothers and sisters in Christ sweating under the sun. What a blessing to be removed from my day-to-day work life, which I feel is too closely aligned with the secular world. It's wonderful to be here where the world's pull is not so strong.

Thursday, 13 January 2011
Haiti

As the body without the spirit is dead, so faith without deeds is dead.
– James 2:26 (NIV)

Today we carried rocks. Our team carried white rocks, some the size of baseballs, some the size of basketballs, and some the size of buckets. All day long under the searing tropical sun, we carried the rocks from a pile by the school where we had church on Sunday, across a plank laid over a muddy area, and to the place in the lush, green field where three Haitian masons were constructing the foundation of a boys' orphanage. These rocks were their building materials. When we were almost done carrying the rocks, a dump truck arrived and deposited another mountain of large, white rocks.

God's people are all supposed to do works of service. After all, faith without works is dead. So we worked, sweated, drank quarts of water, rested in the shade for a while, then worked some more.

While team members were carrying rocks, I peeked into the school building. On Sunday, we had attended church here; now, school was in session. Such a minimal structure: a wooden frame, blue tarp walls, corrugated metal roof, earthen floor. And so few tools: chalkboards, notebooks, a few textbooks, and some boards nailed together to create simple desks, which were painted in primary colors. No PA system for announcements, no science labs, no gymnasium, no computers—not even any electricity. Yet the level of education for those in school (though only fifty percent of children go to school) is fairly high. In our entertainment-saturated culture, we are led to believe by our school districts that we need to increase taxes to provide more modern structures equipped with interactive whiteboards, bigger auditoriums and better sports fields, and more advanced computer equipment. But do they really lead to a better education?

There's a huge disconnect between our lives and the lives of typical Haitians. We, for example, own so much stuff. A Haitian hut couldn't accommodate a fraction of my family's belongings—furniture, appliances, clothing, books, tools, music instruments, electronics, papers… I overheard a group back at the guesthouse discussing this concept. "Makes me feel like a rich jerk," said a teenage girl who is in Haiti with her dad.

"We tend to think that being blessed means having a lot of stuff. But you can have a lot of stuff and be miserable. On the other hand, you can have very little stuff and be joyful." These words, which I heard a year ago on my Dallas mission trip, ring true here, too.

Life is a battle for survival, not a playground. For some, like the

Haitians, it's a physical battle—getting enough food, providing shelter, overcoming disease. For the rich—and most Americans are rich compared to the majority of the world population—life is the pursuit of a bucket list of pleasures. However, for both rich and poor, it's a battle for spiritual survival. Sadly, many are completely unaware that there is a spiritual battle being waged for their souls, and spend their lives pursuing pleasures—seeking fun rather than seeking the Lord's will for their lives.

> *What good is it for a man to gain the whole world, yet forfeit his soul?* (Mark 8:36, NIV)

Most of what the world teaches us is against Scripture. For example, the "American dream" emphasizes material wealth, power, status, individualism. Yet the Bible says that the greatest of all is the servant. Jesus was the ultimate example of servitude.

> *For even the Son of Man did not come to be served, but to serve...* (Mark 10:45, NIV)

We tend to surround ourselves with material comforts that insulate us from a closeness to God. We don't need God's help the way the world's destitute do. We rely on health insurance and doctors; the poor rely on God. We pray calmly, "Lord, give the doctors wisdom"; they plead, "Almighty God, heal my child!"

In some ways, my cancer seems trivial compared to the day-to-day struggles of the Haitians where poverty and hunger are the norm. Yes, I have a deadly disease—a time bomb—in my body, a bomb with a short fuse. But I'll go for surgery soon and be under top-quality medical care. If I were born Haitian, I'd probably be illiterate (one out of two Haitians are), constantly hungry and struggling to feed my family its one meal per day, and ignoring the lump in my breast. That lump would grow and the cancer would spread and eventually kill me because I would not have access to medical care. In Haiti, there's only one doctor for every four thousand people. Haitians ignore small problems and bring their loved ones to a doctor only when they are so sick and weak that a doctor is their last hope. Typically Haitians go to a voodoo priest before they come to a medical doctor. By the time they see a doctor, it's often too late. On my previous trip, the nurses in my group had a feverish baby die on the examining table in front of them. The high fever and respiratory infection that could have been treated with ibuprofen and antibiotics turned out to be fatal for this child.

At a time when I could be feeling sorry for myself or simply worrying about my upcoming operation, coming to a place like Haiti is a refreshing change in perspective.

Meals at the guesthouse are served buffet-style, so we each take a plate, help ourselves to the food, and walk around searching for an empty spot at a table, sometimes by someone we know, sometimes not. Most evenings we don't sit together as a family because Scott had urged us to mingle. I know that it's more difficult for teens to circulate among the mostly adult team, but our children have spent a lot of time visiting the elderly with Tad, and they usually sit with us when adult company comes to visit. The company of grown-ups is not new to them. Even so, I could tell it was stressful for them to choose seats.

I was delighted to see that tonight Alexandra and Larissa sat at a table with Scott and his wife Tanya and were talking with them during the meal. It seems like a privilege when the head of the organization and his wife grace your table, sort of like sitting with the President and First Lady.

After dinner, Scott and Tanya retired early. Scott had delegated Tad to lead worship and Paul, our team leader, to lead the devotions. Tad selected some hymns in advance from the hymnbook he brought, and I wrote the words on the large whiteboard near the piano. We as a family led the singing with Tad on the piano.

One hymn stands out: "Holy, Holy, Holy." It's a hymn our family sang in Spanish in a Mexican church one muggy evening during a mission trip to Oaxaca. We sang it in Ukrainian in Tad's hometown in Ukraine. Alexandra and I sang it just a few months before in a kerosene-lit church on the tiny island of Ailitupu in the San Blas Archipelago off the coast of Panama. And now, here in Haiti, we sang it again. We sang out from our hearts. We sang out from our souls. We sang out from our entire beings, lifting our faces, and radiating joy and reverence. Soon the entire team stood to their feet. We sang the last verse without piano accompaniment, forty to fifty earnest voices ascending to the Lord in harmony. I closed my eyes and felt I was among a choir of angels. I wanted the song to never end. I wanted this feeling to buoy me up forever. Is this what it's going to be like in heaven worshipping the Lord? No, it will be even better!

If only I could hang on to this joy in my everyday life.

Solemnly, we sat down after that hymn. Paul gave a short testimony from his life, and we split up into discussion groups, each sharing something from our lives. When devotions were over, one woman from Wisconsin hung back.

"You don't know what you did for me," she said to Tad, blinking back tears. "Your singing is so special." And she told of a time long ago when her aunts and uncles and parents used to get together and sing as we did here.

But people are too busy now. Too involved with their big-screen TVs and computers and text messages. Too busy socializing through social media to actually socialize in person, to sit together and talk and sing. They don't even know that they're robbing themselves of some of the most precious memories they could make.

I sat with my new friends from Wisconsin and Massachusetts and Minnesota. I realized in a moment of bittersweet comprehension that after this week, this group of people from so many different cities will never again be gathered in the same place on this earth.

When the group broke up, Alexandra said quietly, "I wish Scott would come out. I'd like to talk with him."

I was delighted that his company and his words built her up, and that she wanted, as I understood, his advice with something. I'm also glad that Alexandra enjoys talking with adults. She seems to prefer the wisdom of grown-ups to the foolishness of teens. I'm pleased that she, too, is connecting with people.

Friday, 14 January 2011
Haiti

Speak up for those who cannot speak for themselves, for the rights of all who are destitute. Speak up and judge fairly; defend the rights of the poor and needy.
– Proverbs 31:8–9 (NIV)

While sitting on the faux-patchwork-quilt bedspread in my guest-house room, I could hear Scott's piano-playing drifting across the courtyard. It was 6:45 AM.

The music lured me into the dining room, and I chose a seat on a couch near the piano. Whenever I hear Scott playing worship songs, joy radiates in my heart. I sipped some black coffee from a white mug and waited for the others to gather. Slowly, the couches and chairs filled up.

As Scott led the singing, I could see Lyuba's face shining and eyes smiling. This time of morning worship is so delightful and inspiring.

There's a camaraderie here, a unity in spirit that I don't feel in my church back home. Here is faith in action: about seventy people crazy enough to use their money and vacation time to labor and sweat and share rooms with strangers just to spend all day serving the Lord. Individuals, husbands and wives, mothers with sons, fathers with daughters, friends, and our entire family—all came to give of ourselves. But instead, we found that we were the ones gaining, learning, being blessed by our fellowship with each other and by our relations with the Haitians.

For me, each mission trip is a spiritual retreat. Nothing that I can do in the comfort of my home compares to traveling to a difficult place, meeting like-minded Christians and sacrificial leaders, and spending all day working for the Lord.

It's hard to believe that it's our last day.

This morning we lifted our voices in unison, beseeching God to let us see what human eyes cannot.

Open the eyes of my heart, Lord.
Open the eyes of my heart.
I want to see You.
I want to see You...

The bus took our team to Lacquil, the village with Mission E4's largest school. To get to the school, we hiked about half a mile from the asphalt road along a dusty dirt road, down a small rise and back up, under banana leaves and past some huts. Through the school gate came our pale parade of daypacks and ladders and pails trailed by a local dog. The Lacquil school, unlike the other two, is made of cinder blocks and cement with a corrugated metal roof.

With our arrival, classes were dismissed and a couple hundred rambunctious pupils were shepherded into the largest room, which serves as an auditorium or church meeting place, depending on the occasion. The children were closely packed on the benches in rows from youngest to oldest. They were not dressed in their red gingham uniforms today. As I stood at the front of that tightly crammed room, I had the impression of looking over an animated field of dark-faced flowers. Their excitement was contagious. Inside, I felt like one large smile. I tried to capture the passion of the moment with my camera.

The children responded in unison to Scott's questions and enthusiastically accompanied him in praise songs. Tad later confided that the eager singing touched him. Once again, he was impressed by the musical and I by the visual.

My family, Ruth, and Lyuba presented the skit that we'd practiced in our Rochester living room. Other groups also acted out the life of Jesus. We sang the Creole worship songs as best we could, played games, and listened to Scott present the gospel message. When the formal presentation was over, the children flocked around the team and clung to us like iron filings to a magnet. We picked them up and held their hands; they smiled at us and we smiled back; they spoke to us in Creole and we replied in English, and neither knew what the other said. It was impossible to find our translators in that crush of humanity.

After the program, some of the men set up ladders and did construction work among the swarming children. My daughters and I found a bench in a corner of a classroom and made lunch for the team. Those who sponsor children had the opportunity to meet with them in a corner room. How Scott and Lynn (the child sponsor coordinator) managed to find the correct children in the pandemonium of the schoolyard and match them up with the American visitors who sponsor them is probably a trade secret.

I got to sit and, through an interpreter, talk with twelve-year-old Roudnesa, the girl who had grabbed my hand on my previous trip and selected me to be her blan mama. How could I refuse to sponsor her? The $30 per month ensures that she eats one meal per day and has an education.

I gave Roudnesa a bright yellow dress and other gifts I had bought for her, then distributed the presents that I had brought from Cheri for her sponsored children. I also presented nine-year-old Pierre, my mother's sponsored boy, the gifts that we had bought for him: a soccer ball, a shirt, a Matchbox car, and some practical items—soap, washcloths, toothpaste, toothbrush, a few granola bars.

After my meeting with the children, I wandered around the schoolyard trying to avoid the children's hands clamping onto mine so I could be free to take pictures. I came upon my daughter Alexandra talking through a translator with the ten-year-old girl she sponsors.

"What would you like me to bring or send you next time?" my daughter asked Yvekar.

Uh-oh, I thought. Here it comes, the request for an iPod or something ridiculously expensive.

"Pencils," answered Yvekar. "I need pencils for school. And a backpack."

I was humbled. It was not the answer I had expected.

The day was packed with activities, even more than the previous days. After lunch, a baptism service filled the classroom where earlier we had held the children's program. The worship music was upbeat, accompanied by drums and tambourines and clapping. Many school-children stayed for the service and joined our march to the green-blue sea. Back to the asphalt road went the surge of humanity, across the blacktop, down another dirt road through fields and past oxen, and all the way to the sandy beach and rippling waves. The Haitian worship team did not stop their animated singing and drumming during the mile-long walk.

Standing waist deep in the ocean waters, Scott and Pastor Bazile baptized about twenty new Haitian believers. Meanwhile, Haitian children stripped down to their underwear and ran splashing into the salty waves, chasing one another, shrieking, and adding a sense of disorder that seems to prevail in Haiti.

After the baptism, while others took a swim, Scott led a group down the garbage-speckled beach to some land where he was considering building a guesthouse. The walk took us past crude dugouts used for fishing, goats tied up on the sandy shore, children playing with a starfish, and primitive fences made of sticks and rope. I had to half jog to keep up with Scott and thought of how much more exercise I get during a mission trip than in a usual day at the office.

Next, we hiked back across the main asphalt road to the local pastor's home. In the courtyard under tall tropical trees, we were offered drinks of coconut water straight out of the coconuts and chunks of peeled sugar cane. I especially enjoyed the sugar cane: the crunchy bite, the juicy rush of sweetness, then the fibrous mass that you spit out.

The day was waning, and sadly, we had to board the buses. Before returning to the guesthouse, we stopped at the girls' orphanage one final time. Some bought souvenirs. Some hugged the orphan girls. Some sat and visited with one another. Just before we left, we gathered around Pastor and Madame Bazile, and with Scott translating for them, they thanked us for sacrificing our time and finances to come and help them. "Don't forget about us," they urged.

After supper at the guesthouse, I was delighted to see Taran, Scott's newlywed son who had stayed with his team at the orphanage all week, leading worship with his father. Scott played piano; Taran played the guitar. Both sang joyously.

"It's not okay to do nothing," Scott reminded us as we sat in a half-circle around him. "Now you are responsible for what you know about the poor. Proverbs 31:8 says, *Speak up for those who cannot speak for themselves.* Find a way to speak up for Haitians. That's our duty."

At the end of the evening, Scott took up a collection for mattresses for the girls' orphanage. Until this week, the girls had been sleeping on the cement floor. Yesterday was like Christmas morning when they returned from school and found bunk beds in their room. Each girl grabbed a pencil and claimed a bed by writing her name on it. Soon these wooden beds will have mattresses, something considered a luxury here.

At my request, before the group dispersed to their rooms to finish packing, Scott announced that I had recently been diagnosed with cancer and would soon be having surgery. He invited anyone who wanted to come pray for me. About seventy people gathered up front, surrounded me, lifted up hands and voices, and prayed for my healing. I feel confident that many of these brothers and sisters in Christ will continue to pray for me long after we've left Haiti; long after we're back home in our snowy, wintry surroundings; long after the tropical heat is but a memory.

Saturday, 15 January 2011

For with much wisdom comes much sorrow; the more knowledge, the more grief.

– Ecclesiastes 1:18 (NIV)

The buses wove through the gray predawn streets of Port-au-Prince on the way to the airport, past a perpetually smoking garbage dump;

by an outdoor market with its hordes of people, herds of goats, and heaps of vegetables; and by the only working traffic light that I had seen—not that traffic obeyed it.

Back in the airport, we re-entered the modern world of air-conditioning and fluorescent lights, coffee shops and public announcements. Already the huts and dust seemed far away.

What is the hardest thing about going to a place like Haiti?

You would think that it's experiencing the destitution: Seeing shacks worse than my backyard shed house entire Haitian families. Or seeing a boy pounce on a crumpled gum wrapper, unwrap the previously chewed gum, and pop it into his mouth.

Those are certainly difficult.

But it's far harder to come home and see the tremendous opulence in our country. To know that you have lived through and seen things that your family and friends at home have never experienced and can't relate to. To grieve for the masses of suffering people you just left—people you personally met—when your friends are having parties, oblivious to or not caring about the misery of so many. Or to watch food being thrown away and ache inside, wishing you could beam it into a hut you visited. You want to belong to the world that you were once a part of, but you can never again truly fit in because you have left your heart behind, because you can't selfishly enjoy things you used to indulge in, because you know that while you spend money on some frivolous thing, others are going without food. And you not buying that thing won't make any difference to the hungry child, but somehow it doesn't seem right to indulge yourself anymore.

A man from India living in the U.S. once wrote, "I sometimes refused to eat the desserts... This made no difference in supplying food to hungry families, but I couldn't bear to take pleasure in eating while workers in Asia were going hungry." [*]

---

[*] K.P. Yohannan, *Revolution in World Missions* (Carrollton TX: Gospel for Asia Books, 2004), p. 42.

I completely understand. I try not to beat myself up because I was born in North America and have so much. But it just doesn't seem right that they have so little.

After our basic needs are met, material possessions do not significantly add to our happiness. In fact, it seems that some of the more unhappy people are those encumbered by their possessions. Those with huge homes and impressive furnishings seem to echo with emptiness inside. Possessions have not filled the void. Only God does.

I wish everyone in America would experience a place like Haiti.

Monday, 17 January 2011

"Meaningless! Meaningless!" says the Teacher. "Utterly meaningless! Everything is meaningless." What does man gain from all his labor at which he toils under the sun?

– Ecclesiastes 1:2–3 (NIV)

Back to work today, back to the "real world"—at least in my daily world. I often question this world that I live in, this fluorescent-lit, climate-controlled monochrome cubicle with five-foot tall partitions delineating 9 by 12 feet of industrial carpet with a beige desk, beige drawers, beige bookcases, and a beige computer. Only my chairs and plants add color: the blue chair I sit in, the red chair for guests, and the green leaves of my philodendrons, which wrap half the office walls with their long, leafy vines. It's such a peculiar and unnatural spot in light of the rest of the world. It's so out of touch with the Haitians I just visited, so disconnected from the day-to-day reality of the majority of the world's population, so detached from the land and nature and family. Is this cubicle really what I want as my world? Yet this spot, where I can't even see whether it's sunny or snowing outside, is where I spend a large portion of my days, my life. At meetings, we talk in code words and acronyms. If my husband or children happened to listen in, they wouldn't understand the discussions. OOBE and OPMT,

BUGs and RUGs*. So meaningless. So pointless. When people around the world are perishing from hunger and children are dying from preventable diseases, how can I put my heart into gates and go topics, firmware upgrades and FAQs, domains and downloads? Perhaps I never should have been a company employee. I didn't plan to be. But I am.

Don't get me wrong. I'm thankful for the income and grateful that the writing I'm expected to do comes easily to me.

"Not everyone gets to work his dream job," a friend once told me. "In fact, I think that most people don't. You're fortunate you have a job!"

A job I like, to a certain point. It's not my dream job, but it's not a difficult job. The dilemma is that this job is not my life's passion. I just can't get whole-heartedly behind my projects and cheer them on. I do my work, and do it thoroughly and well and within deadlines, but my heart is not in writing user manuals or Frequently Asked Questions. It's in Haiti. And Kenya. And Ethiopia. It's with the poor and suffering of the world. I love the people I work with and the company, and I enjoy my work on a pedantic level, but the greatest satisfaction I've had in my ten years at Kodak is writing a few posts about my mission trips for the corporate blog. There I got to share my heart. I could touch people through my words and photos.

I don't have the same passion for technical writing.

I often question whether I couldn't be doing more with my life. Something meaningful. Something that will make a difference, such as helping to alleviate hunger and suffering by raising awareness and spurring others to action. I've felt that this is my calling. I've spoken at churches and stirred up audiences to help the poor or go on mission trips. But instead of following my passion, here I am at Kodak writing user manuals for printers that scan, copy, and print documents and photos. This does not feel like a contribution to the world, some-

----

* Out-of-box experience, Online Printer Management Tool, Basic User Guides, Regulatory User Guides

thing that I'd want mentioned in my obituary. "She wrote easy-to-understand user documentation." No, I feel a bit of a failure because I have not trusted that God would financially provide for us if I were to follow my passion. In this area, I'm a cop-out, a chicken. I haven't had the courage to take a risk.

Someday I'll be able to follow my passion, I tell myself. Someday I'll be out of here. Someday… Or will I? Will I even make it through the cancer? Am I already too old? Too arthritic? Too weak physically? Have I missed my chance?

Yes, I'm back from Haiti, back to my working world.

I walked right by the new plant in my office without noticing it at first. Then I did a double take: a cedar-like tree in a blue pot sat on my side bookcase. A note by the plant read:

Kathryn—
Welcome back! And look… one more plant to worry about. Hope you like it.
Jim

"Another plant you'll have to take care of when I'm out on medical leave," I told Jim when I walked into his cubicle to thank him. His wife, an avid gardener like me, had picked out the plant.

Co-worker Jeanette stopped by and told me that her congregation had prayed for our group and all the missionaries while we were in Haiti. They also prayed for healing from my cancer.

Marilyn, who works in the Entertainment Imaging department, sent an instant message welcoming me back as soon as she saw the green light by my name indicating that I was online.

My sister Marta e-mailed me, asking me to stop by her house on the way home because she had something for me.

I went through e-mails, talked to co-workers, caught up, and settled back into my cubicle world. After work, I stopped at my sister's house, which is about a mile from my home. When I walked in, she handed me a bag.

"Open it," she insisted. I found an envelope, but because I hadn't brought my reading glasses, I asked her to read it to me.

"It's a certificate for three one-hour massages. For stress relief. I got a deal on them. They're good for one year."

Marta hugged me and her eyes got watery. Once again, I got the feeling that people were treating me as if they expected me to die.

Tuesday, 18 January 2011

The LORD does not look at the things man looks at. Man looks at the outward appearance, but the LORD looks at the heart."
– 1 Samuel 16:7 (NIV)

Though I realize that plastic surgeons repair birth defects, such as cleft palates, and disfigurement caused by accidents, I associate plastic surgery with vanity: facelifts, tummy tucks, breast augmentation, nose jobs. Thus I had not expected to ever visit a plastic surgeon. But to satisfy Dr. Medeiros and my sister as well as my own curiosity, I scheduled a consultation appointment with a plastic surgeon. I could thus make a more educated decision: should I or should I not have breast reconstruction? So that I would not be swayed one way or another, I insisted on going to this appointment alone.

My 11 AM appointment was with Dr. Andrew Smith. When I walked into the waiting room, I couldn't help but wonder about the others in the room. What were they here for? A curious range of patients sat in the chairs: a young Hispanic woman with a toddler, a man who looked like a construction worker, and an elderly couple. The woman was wrinkled as a crumpled paper, but she obviously cared about her outward appearance: Her coiffed hair was dyed a bright pumpkin orange, her nails painted fire-engine red, and her conversation with the man who must be her husband was a long monologue about a lost earring that used to get caught on things. If only people cared as much about their inward beauty as they do about their looks, what a different world it would be.

A tightly clad woman in high-heeled boots showed me into an inner room and handed me literature on breast reconstruction.

"You have about twenty minutes to read this," said the young woman with a strong Russian accent. "Then the doctor will be with you to answer any questions."

Cuts and tucks and implants, though shown as line drawings and not photos, made me queasy. I imagined each line in the diagram as a painful incision on my own body. I read about silicone implants and saline implants and reconstruction using fat from one's own body (which involves additional surgery to remove that tissue). Breast reconstruction is not considered cosmetic surgery and is thus covered by health insurance. But that doesn't make it less painful. The idea of willingly subjecting myself to that much surgery seemed kind of ludicrous. All for looks? Is my self-image all about appearances? I couldn't believe people did all this to themselves voluntarily for vanity's sake, not as a medical necessity!

Then I read about return rates. Infections. Leakage. Ruptures. Scar tissue. Additional surgery. Six in ten women with reconstruction have to return for additional surgery within ten years due to problems. With an implant, you have to monitor your breasts for leaks and problems for the rest of your life. The longer the implants are in, the more chance that you may have to replace them. That means more surgery.

If I had any doubts about my decision to not have reconstruction, those doubts were dispelled after reading the literature. I didn't even need to talk to the doctor, but since I was there for a consultation, I might as well learn all I could from him.

Dr. Smith walked in wearing blue scrubs. He was thin, even bony, with graying crew-cut length hair. After he examined me, he said that I had just enough belly fat for reconstruction using my own flesh. He could do a tummy tuck, which is a large cut, and also take out an artery and vein so this transplanted flesh would have a blood supply. And he'd insert a mesh in my belly to prevent hernias.

I felt faint just listening to this.

Or he could use implants. He explained a little about silicone versus saline.

When he was done explaining medical procedures, I voiced my concerns. "About once a year, I try to go on a mission trip to an out-of-the-way place like Haiti. I carry a heavy camera bag with me everywhere I go. What if I swing this bag from one shoulder to the other and accidentally whack my chest with the bag and—well, could the implant pop?"

"It's possible."

"What then?"

"You'd have to seek medical help immediately."

"In Haiti, I doubt they'd even know what an implant is!"

I found out that Dr. Smith had been to Haiti right after the earthquake, so he understood the conditions in countries I visit. He had also been to Rwanda in Africa. I liked Dr. Smith and enjoyed our conversation about the developing world, but my mind was set after this meeting: no reconstruction. I would go with a prosthesis. Dr. Smith understood why.

Wednesday, 19 January 2011

As for man, his days are like grass, he flourishes like a flower of the field; the wind blows over it and it is gone...
– Psalm 103:15–16 (NIV)

While I was away from my desk during lunch, a single white chrysanthemum in a wineglass full of clear water gel beads appeared by my keyboard. Such an elegant presentation. Such a thoughtful gesture. But who put it there?

I'm deeply touched that people continue to reach out to me and show that they care. I would have robbed myself of this opportunity had I simply disappeared on medical leave and not said why.

I found out later in the afternoon that Jeanette and another co-worker had received the chrysanthemum at the Athena Awards luncheon and brought it back for me.

Our technical writing group of about twenty had its monthly meeting in the afternoon. Betty, my boss, handed me a fancy folder and announced that it was my certificate for ten years of service. After all that griping of meaninglessness, I've spent ten years of my life working at Kodak.

Saturday, 22 January 2011

Who of you by worrying can add a single hour to his life?
— Luke 12:25 (NIV)

I awoke at 9:15 AM and heard footsteps. I had thought that the house would be empty. Tad was to take all three of our kids, plus Igor and David from the youth group, to the Calvary Chapel Prophesy Conference.

"We found out that the conference ended yesterday," Jacob informed me. "Dad took Igor to David's house for two to three hours."

Igor is our part-time child. With a father who's an alcoholic and a mother who is schizophrenic, Igor hasn't known normal family life. When his mother was pregnant with him back in Ukraine, Igor's father had urged his wife to abort him. But family pressure on the wife persuaded her to carry the baby full term. As soon as Igor was born, the father said, "Take him away! Have him made into sausage!"

Igor was raised by his great uncle in the city of Lviv. He did not know his parents—until they won a green card to come to the United States. At age ten, Igor was reunited with his birth parents and came to America with them.

When Igor began to attend the youth group meetings at church, Tad often invited him to our house after Sunday service. We took him bicycling, hiking, and on local excursions; we even took him on a family camping trip to Canada last summer. Once we invited him sledding—we live on the street with one of Rochester's best sledding hills. Igor seemed shocked that I accompanied him and my children, hurtling down the great snowy hill with the others on our ancient

Flexible Flyer, then trudging up, up, up, pulling the sled, panting great frosty clouds, and laughing with the joy of the moment. Why would he think it odd? Was I being too childish? Then I realized that his mother never did anything like that with him.

Igor is fourteen now—about half a year younger than Larissa. David is about the same age. I'm not sure why Tad wanted to take Igor to David's house, which is seventeen miles from ours. Perhaps Tad had wanted to spend time with David's dad, Slavik, who is one of his close friends. Or maybe he wanted to take Igor to the home of his friend David. Igor's dad would never drive him that far.

I was somewhat disappointed that Tad hadn't stayed home. Igor could have hung out at our house, as he so often does. The day was sunny, though cold, but we could have had a cozy time indoors. Our family loves to just hang out together—talk, share, bake, eat together, sit around the cozy fire in the wood-burning stove.

Even though they are teenagers, the kids need attention, and I sat in the living room in my pajamas far too long talking with them rather than working on the homeschooling schedule as I'd planned. Since I'm going for surgery this coming Wednesday, I need to plan out my daughters' assignments for the next two weeks or so.

1:00 PM came and went, but not a sign of Tad. Should we eat lunch without him, or wait until he and Igor return? I experience unease when Tad is gone like this. I feel hollow inside, like something is missing. Like I'm incomplete. I shouldn't feel like this, I chide myself. But I do. I want the family together. I want my other half. Reluctantly, we ate without him.

1:30 PM. I called Tad's cell phone and left a message.

2:00 PM. It's been five hours, not two or three. Why is Tad away from home so long? It's sunny outside, which is rare this time of year, but it doesn't seem as bright with Tad gone. I want Tad's company. I married him because I want to be with him. I like his presence. The whole atmosphere in the house is different when he's home. Why is he away so much? Doesn't he want to be with me? With us?

2:30 PM. Five-and-a-half hours. I left Tad another message. In tears, I begged him to come home. "I know it's not logical. But I need you. I'm having a bad day. Please come home." I was crushed that he didn't pick up the phone.

2:45 PM. The hollow place inside had gotten bigger and bigger, and become a yawning hole about to swallow me up. I was feeling frantic. Why hadn't Tad called back? I called Slavik's cell phone. Slavik answered, then handed the phone to Tad. Tearfully, I begged him to come home. He said he'd come as soon as he ate. They were just sitting down to lunch.

Lunch! It's bound to drag on for another hour. Then there's the drive home. It'll be at least 4 PM before he's home—gone almost as long as during a full workday. Why? Why can't he be with his family? Why did he prefer the company of friends? You show love with your time, and he showed that he did not want to be with me.

I was beyond distraught. I felt myself coming apart. I could not concentrate on schedules or assignments or books. I needed Tad desperately. Two or three hours had turned into seven.

I had to get out. I could no longer remain in the house and just wait for Tad to return. The feeling of abandonment was more than I could bear. I knew that the children were all home. I knew it wasn't logical. But I wanted Tad to hold me. I was beside myself. I felt rejected, unloved. I considered going to a friend's house, but I didn't want anyone to see me in this state. I grabbed my journal and the car keys.

"Are you okay?" asked Larissa as I was heading out the door.

"No, I'm not okay," I said through tears. "I need Dad, and he's not here. He's not here for so long!"

I backed the blue van out of the driveway and headed to the library. I'd have to dry my tears before I went into public.

Unbeknownst to me because the rearview mirror in the van was set for a taller person and I just saw a reflection of the ceiling, Tad was in a car behind me as I drove up the hill. I heard honking, but I was sobbing and the honking didn't register—until I crossed the Blossom Road intersection, and in the side mirror saw Tad standing on the road by the VW Golf. He'd gotten out of the car when I stopped at the stop sign.

He didn't follow. I no longer wanted to go to the library, but was afraid that Igor, whom Tad was to bring home for dinner, would see me crying. I turned the van around and pulled into our driveway. Then I beeped the horn. Tad came out. I got out of the van and buried my head in him.

I am so terrified of the surgery. More afraid of it than anything else I have faced in my life. Not only am I afraid of going under and losing consciousness, but of the pain, of maybe not waking up. Of losing my breast and the emotional repercussions. Of Tad's reaction to my disfigurement. So many unknowns. So scared.

"I took Igor home. I will sit with you and be with you," Tad said. "It's not an effort for me."

And suddenly, I was much better.

Sunday, 23 January 2011

Fear not, for I am with you; be not dismayed, for I am your God; I will strengthen you, yes, I will help you, I will uphold you with my righteous right hand.
                                                    – Isaiah 41:10 (NKJV)

I went into a public restroom. *Kind of dark. Can't see well in here,* I thought. As I walked into a stall, hands grabbed my hips from behind. Someone had been hiding in the next stall. Then the hands lifted me up, up off the floor. I tried to scream, a strangled voice rising in my throat, "Aaaaaa!" I finally choked out—and woke myself.

It was 4 AM.

I lay in the darkness, my heart pounding. In the night, my fears become magnified. Little things that are mere footnotes in life take on exaggerated significance in the still of night. Time slows down and thoughts no longer dart through my mind one after another, but become ensnared like insects trapped in a web. My worries of the surgery flapped futilely, caught in the forefront of my mind. Anesthesia. Scalpels. Stitches. Pain. What if I get the wrong dose of anesthesia? What if I don't wake up from surgery? Why does my underarm hurt? Will they find cancer in my lymph nodes? Has it spread beyond the lymph nodes? Why do I have pain in my abdomen? Will I be able to face cancer with dignity if it spreads? How does it feel to know that you're going to die? How will my children take it if I die? How will Tad manage?

Oh, I know that fear is from the enemy. God promises to be with us, strengthen us, help us. In the daylight, I am able to keep most of my fear at bay. I'm at work or cooking or correcting homeschool assignments. I'm thinking about other things; these thoughts flit through my mind and back out so quickly that I can't entertain them. But at night in the overpowering silence when I can't sleep, fear nibbles at me, and I cannot keep these thoughts out. In my sober daylight moments, I feel strong; but at night, doubts slither in like a venomous snake and I am weak with worry.

How many thousands, tens of thousands, hundreds of thousands—or is it millions?—have surgery every year and live to tell of it? Yet I would rather hike the wilds of Papua New Guinea and risk facing hostile tribes than go under a surgeon's knife. Illogical? Certainly. I'm battling an illogical fear of improbable consequences. And at night, I tend to lose this battle, and fear engulfs me.

Just three more days until surgery. Three more days until they remove my breast. Three more days until they look at my lymph nodes. Three more days until my life changes...

It's in God's hands. I know that. I believe that. And in the daylight, I'm even upbeat about it. But lying alone in the darkness, I'm nervous about what's ahead and pray that God gives me the strength to face whatever happens. I feel so terribly feeble in faith.

All day I was so tired, so very tired. Is the tiredness from not sleeping well during the night? Left over from the Haiti trip? Or, dare I even consider, a symptom of my illness? Am I just oversensitive? Imagining things?

In the evening, Slavik, whom Tad visited yesterday, stopped by with five of his six children to pray for my health and healing. He's a sensitive man in his forties with a gentle voice. Slavik said that when I called his phone yesterday and told Tad that I was having a difficult time, Tad's whole countenance changed. (I thought he'd just be annoyed that I called.) Slavik teared up as he shared, "I realized that it would be very difficult for me without my spouse."

I'm sure Tad has thought about that, too.

Tina called later in the evening to ask how I was doing. I appreciate her checking up on me and encouraging me. I confided that I dreaded not only the surgery, but how hard it will be to look at myself in a mirror after the mastectomy. "Every time I see myself, I'll see this maimed body."

"Look at yourself in the mirror and praise God that you're still alive," Tina suggested. "Think of all the others who are born deformed."

I hadn't thought of that as I focused on fear and self-pity. What words of wisdom. Focus on the positive—on life, not on my disfigurement. What a minor thing it truly is in the grand scheme of things. Something that no one besides my husband will see; something that does not hinder my walking or thinking, seeing or hearing.

"God permitted this for His reasons," Tina continued, "so praise His wisdom in allowing you this challenge. He will help you through this."

Monday, 24 January 2011

The LORD is my helper; I will not be afraid.

– Hebrews 13:6 (NIV)

The temperature plummeted to -8° F during the night. The cold seemed to penetrate my winter coat during the minute that it took to walk over the squeaky snow and start the Dodge Caravan. I didn't have time to let the engine idle; I had a 7 AM appointment at Rochester General Hospital for my pre-op, and considering the long walk from the parking garage to the lab, I was running late.

Even with all the salt that the salt trucks had spread on our road, the snow had not melted. The sun was not yet up to help thaw the slippery coating on the asphalt. I headed downhill on the snow-slicked street toward Browncroft Boulevard, the four-lane thoroughfare through the Ellison Park valley. Although the van had started just fine and I had driven in reverse down the steep driveway, once on the road, the van would not go into drive. The transmission was acting up again. I coasted to the bottom of the road (sometimes it's an advantage to live on a hill) and stopped where Landing Road North meets Browncroft. In reverse, the van worked; in drive, it was like being in neutral. I had fifteen minutes to get to the hospital for my appointment. But the van would not go no matter how much I pressed on the accelerator. I sat in the vehicle at the intersection warming the engine, realizing that I should have given myself more time to do this while in the driveway, not at an intersection blocking any car that might come up behind me. Fortunately, traffic was light and eventually the van clunked into gear.

Even though I wore boots and gloves, my feet and fingers ached with cold. As I chugged up the hill and out of the valley where I live, a little ball of apprehension settled in my stomach: I worried that the transmission would again fail in this bitter weather. Perhaps I should have said yes when Tad offered to come with me.

My trek to the hospital felt more lonesome because of that wintry rawness and fear of breakdown. I puffed through the parking garage, then wove through the corridors and hurried into the waiting room. I was admitted immediately.

A friendly young woman weighed me and questioned me about my medical history and allergies. She took my temperature and blood pressure. She then explained what time I was to stop eating the day before surgery. She instructed me to bring a completed copy of my Health Care Proxy form, then read a list of warnings. They give so many warnings of what can go wrong that it's a little frightening.

I also had my blood drawn to determine my blood type (just in case) and to check for kidney function. I'm sure there's more that they checked, but I didn't write it all down.

Then I had to change into a gown.

I was allowed to leave my socks on, but the temperature in the room was so low that my feet were painfully cold. The heating system seemed to be straining to create that seventy to eighty degree differential between the outside and inside. The longer I waited, the more uncomfortably cold I became. I waited. And waited. Then waited some more. Finally, I wrapped my fleece sweater around myself and put on my boots.

And I waited some more. I guess I had time to heat up the van in the driveway after all.

Back at work, my co-workers said their good-byes to me through-out the day. I stood in the hallways talking far more than usual, getting little work done. My medical leave starts tomorrow.

Rod caught me in the hall. Slight of build and with light brown hair cut short, Rod is mild mannered, even a bit reserved. His cubicle is next to the coffee area, so he gets a lot of walk-by traffic. But he was in the hallway as I walked by.

"You just got back from somewhere, didn't you?" he ventured.

"Haiti."

"That was your vacation?"

"Well, yeah, you can call it that. Probably costs less than a vacation to Disney World, but the kids get so much more out of it. We live in Disney World compared to the rest of the world. It's good for the kids to see how the rest of the world lives," I explained.

We talked of my current medical "adventure" and his family's history of pancreatic cancer, which grows and spreads painlessly so that by the time of diagnosis, it's usually too late. Rod's mother died of pancreatic cancer. So did his grandmother.

We also talked about more pleasant topics, such as our children. When Rod mentioned that one of his daughters likes animals, I asked, "What pets do you have?"

"A couple of dogs, and we just got some guinea pigs."

"Ooo, do they smell! We took care of some guinea pigs for a week. My husband said that the girls' bedroom smelled like his grandmother's farm when the guinea pigs were in their room. Since your daughter likes animals, you should get some chickens," I suggested. "They're more practical, and your girls will learn some useful skills."

"We live in Brighton," Rod explained as if that dismissed the possibility of chickens. Brighton is a suburb of Rochester.

"So do I." I proceeded to explain Brighton's zoning laws and the benefits of keeping chickens—they lay fresh eggs and you learn farming skills. Besides, if you want pets, chickens can be very tame. Ours allow us to pet them.

I also talked about American kids not having a purpose because they have everything they need, and that, following accidents, suicide is the second highest cause of death among teens.

"In general, American kids have everything handed to them. Haitian kids don't, so they have a purpose: to get their next meal!"

I described how Tad and I make our children work around the house and how the girls now enjoy the work—cooking, baking, caring for their animals.

"Having too much robs kids of a purpose," I sighed.

I told Rod about one winter when Jacob, who was in junior high school at the time, decided to earn the money to buy himself a new mountain bike. He did this by shoveling our next-door neighbor's steep driveway. All winter long, he hoped for snow and would get out of bed extra early to shovel the driveway before the school bus came. By springtime, he had earned just enough money for an inexpensive mountain bike.

"If he'd asked for a mountain bike for his birthday, we would have bought him one," I explained. "But he didn't. He wanted to earn it himself. He had a goal—and he achieved it. He took way better care of that bicycle because he had worked for it. Had we bought him a bike, it wouldn't have been quite so special."

"Having a dream—an unfulfilled dream—gives a person a reason to live," Rod agreed.

Later in the afternoon, I walked by Rod's area again and saw him.

"I'm still thinking about what you said. I'm always challenged after talking with you."

While I was at work, my friend Josie, a nurse, stopped by our house and dropped off a bag for me, which my daughters pointed out as soon as I got home. I peeked into the bag: toiletries for the hospital, a CD player, a book and a journal, and a small stuffed teddy bear with a gauze pad and bandage taped across its entire left chest. I smiled. On the bandage written in pen were the words, "The Lord is my helper. – Hebrews 13:6." It's so sweet, so cute.

"One more thing in the house," said Tad. But the girls understood.

When I called Josie to thank her for the presents, she mentioned how I reach people, touch people. I don't see myself that way at all.

"That's what drew me to you," she continued. We had met at church eight years before during a series of training sessions that preceded a mission trip to Africa, the first mission trip that either of us had taken. "You should write about your cancer experience," Josie urged me.

"Tina told me to journal that first day when I was diagnosed," I said. "So I've been doing it. Even down in Haiti."

I wanted to add that she, too, had also told me to write, but somehow I knew that Josie didn't remember it. It's interesting how people can say something that touches you or triggers you to action, as Tina and Josie had, yet not recall what they said. That's how God works: He uses people as His mouthpieces.

I changed the subject. "Remember the youth who didn't go to Haiti because of the cholera scare on the news? The woman who started that whole panic is terrified of places like Haiti and didn't want her son to go there. She has an irrational fear of poor countries and diseases. The whole thing was completely illogical. Tad explained that we'd be drinking clean filtered water and eating properly prepared food. But she wouldn't buy it. She wouldn't let her son go. And others followed her example. She's a doctor, after all, and others figured she knew the dangers of cholera. Well," I took a breath, "I found my own Haiti and cholera. I realized this week that I'm as terrified of surgery and anesthesia as this woman probably is of Haiti and cholera. I guess I shouldn't have judged."

Before I hung up, Josie informed me that she and our friend Phyllis would come to the hospital and pray for me before surgery on Wednesday morning. I was overjoyed.

After supper, the phone rang. Less than a month ago, I rarely received phone calls; now the majority of the calls are for me. This call was from Betsy, my best friend from high school, who now lives in California. We hadn't talked in about a decade, maybe more. Our lives are now as different as the terrain on which we live; it was thoughtful of her to call.

Around nine o'clock in the evening, I was lying on the couch in the living room near Tad when the phone rang again. Larissa picked it up.

"Yes," I heard her say. "She's here."

As she handed me the cordless phone, Larissa mouthed, "I don't know who it is."

"Hello?" I said tentatively.

"This is Dr. Shamaskin," said the voice on the phone. "You may have wondered whether I knew about your medical situation. I just wanted you to know that I am aware of your cancer. I'm so sorry to hear about it."

I was stunned. How many primary care physicians call their patients at home like this?

"Do you have any questions?" Dr. Shamaskin continued.

I thought for a while.

"As a matter of fact, I do." This was my opportunity to ask about that dull localized pain that I'd been having in my abdomen. "I have some odd pains, and I've been trying to ignore them, but I must admit that since being diagnosed with cancer, I'm afraid that any internal pain might be a sign of cancer. The pain seems to come from the area of my female organs, but it also moves around. It's probably nothing, but…"

"Tell your surgeon on the day of surgery, and also make an appointment with your OB-GYN. If you don't get resolution, then make an appointment to see me," Dr. Shamaskin advised.

Tuesday, 25 January 2011

Even though I walk through the valley of the shadow of death, I will fear no evil, for You are with me...
– Psalm 23:4 (NIV)

During this first day of my medical leave, Tad drove me to my 11 AM appointment at Rochester General Hospital for the sentinel node injection. The radioactive blue dye injected near the lump will help Dr. Medeiros find the sentinel lymph nodes, which are somewhere near my underarm, in order to remove them tomorrow. If my cancer has metastasized, the microscopic examination of the sentinel nodes conducted while I'm on the operating table will reveal cancer cells. And, of course, if cancer cells are found in lymph nodes, there is a greater chance that the cancer has spread to other organs.

To my delight, the boisterous nurse navigator, Andrea, was with me through this procedure. I lay on a table and had four bee sting-like injections in the areola of my left breast as Andrea stood beside me. Then I had to massage the breast to get the injected material to move through my lymphatic channels while Mary, the technician, took pictures to see where the radioactive tracers migrated.

This evening was hard. I removed my bra, a bra I will no longer need, and in my mind, I parted with my left breast. The lump, which was originally "mushy," has become hard and now hurts with a dull ache. This lump has grown quite large—most of the width of my small breast. I can see that a lumpectomy would be impossible now. Had the surgeon known that the lump would grow so big in such a short time? It frightens me that it grew so quickly. Seems much more likely that the cancer has spread. Isn't that why my armpit has ached for the last week? Is it because there's cancer in the lymph nodes there? I would be very surprised if there isn't.

From finding a lump five-and-a-half weeks ago to this. It's so unexpected. So out of control.

"You're taking this so calmly," my mother said to me today. "I never once heard you say, 'Why me?'"

"Why not me, Mama? That's what I think. God allowed it for a reason."

I remember lying in bed nine years ago with crushing fatigue before I knew that I had lupus and thinking, *I may never be healthy again. I may always be tired and too sick to travel even as far as Buffalo. But I've had a blessed life so far, much more so than many others. Many people get sick, but I've been healthy all my life until now. So why not me this time?* I did get well after six months. Since then I traveled not only to Buffalo, but also fulfilled dreams of driving cross-country and camping with the family and of going to Africa. Perhaps I will get well again. But that time of illness nine years ago stretched me in faith and developed much compassion for those who are ill and bedridden. I know that I have this cancer for a reason, too.

I felt weepy this evening. As I sat next to Tad on the living room couch, I laid my head on his chest. Tomorrow I will no longer have my female figure. Forever maimed. But other times I just want this time bomb out.

"What are you thinking?" I asked Tad as we sat together.

"*Even though I walk through the valley of the shadow of death, I will fear no evil, for You are with me...*"

Wednesday, 26 January 2011

Day of surgery

When you pass through the waters, I will be with you; and when you pass through the rivers, they will not sweep over you. When you walk through the fire, you will not be burned; the flames will not set you ablaze.

– Isaiah 43:2 (NIV)

I did not sleep well. I awoke near 2 AM and stayed awake trying to tame my fears, which whirled around like leaves in an autumn squall. I was heading into the great unknown later this day. My only operation had been a routine tonsillectomy when I was four years old.

The storm of thoughts was amplified by the stillness of the dark room. I tried to reason with myself. I tried to convince myself that God is in control. But sleep would not come. What will the doctor find? Is this the beginning of the end?

I was not allowed to eat any food after midnight, and could drink only black coffee and water before 7:30 AM. "Nothing after that, not even chewing gum," a nurse had warned me. To make sure I had time to make myself some coffee, I got out of bed at 7:00 AM. I drank the black coffee. Then I waited.

Winter still gripped the area, so when I packed my bag for the hospital, I included a fuzzy fleece blanket and my warm flannel pajama bottoms. I packed the wash kit that Josie gave me, the bandaged bear, my Bible, my reading glasses, my journal, and some pens.

Then I waited some more.

I was to arrive at Rochester General Hospital at 10 AM to be prepped for the surgery, which was scheduled at 11:30 AM. Tad would be there with me all day, but I didn't want my daughters skipping a day of homeschooling just to hang around waiting rooms. There would be no point to it; they could visit in the evening.

As we pulled into the ramp garage, I saw Josie in the car behind us. When we walked into the hospital, Phyllis, who is also a nurse and had also been on that first mission trip to Senegal, was waiting for us in the spacious main lobby. We followed the instructions on the blue paper I'd been given: up the gray elevator, follow the ceiling tags to the green elevators, then to the third floor OB/GYN surgery unit.

When we arrived at the surgery unit, I was escorted to the corner "cubicle" and seated in a large, soft chair—the seat of honor. The hard chair in the small cubicle was for visitors, but I had Tad, Josie, and Phyllis with me, so there was standing room only.

The cubicles had full-length curtains that could be drawn for privacy, and I had to do just that to change into a hospital gown. I had been cold before; in the gown and hospital socks, I was colder still. And nervous. My hands were ice. A nurse brought a heated blanket and put it over my lap.

As Josie and Phyllis stood beside me, I reminisced about how we'd met eight years before. We were part of a medical mission team traveling to the bush in Senegal, West Africa. For each of us, it was the first mission trip. Traveling to Africa was a great adventure. Africa! Just the word gives me a tingly thrill. Both Josie and Phyllis are nurses, and in Senegal they did what nurses do, but without all the paperwork. I went along as the group photographer. I not only documented the work of the doctors and nurses, I also meandered through the thatched-hut villages and photographed daily life: Pounding millet. Drawing water from a well. Herding sheep and goats. Children in school.

My favorite time of day on a mission trip is dawn. I'm not an early riser at home, but on a mission trip, I set my alarm early to see a village coming to life. After I described the scenes I'd observed on my first morning of wandering, on subsequent mornings Phyllis popped out of bed at the sound of my alarm and came along for a pre-sunrise walk in the sub-Saharan sands.

These warm thoughts raced through my mind on this cold morning.

Even if, I thought, I never go on another mission trip again, the Lord has blessed me so very richly. I have met so many precious people and experienced so much in my life. I am far more blessed than those who invest their time and lives in gathering material possessions. I will always have the feel of a sub-Saharan morning with me no matter where I go, how rich or poor I am. And if I want to experience overwhelming joy, I can hum "Holy, Holy, Holy," and return to Haiti.

A few minutes later, Andrea, the nurse navigator, arrived. And then Gulshan (who'd been the missions pastor in our former church) and a Nepali pastor. This morning it was not just Tad and me grimly facing the uncertain future; it was almost a festive gathering. It meant so much to me that they were there—a whole community supporting me, not only my spouse. But it wasn't just their company (I could imagine others coming and feeling burdened by their presence); it was because they weren't there to fret and worry, but to lift me up in prayer. Theirs was a calming presence, like that of sunshine breaking through stormy clouds.

Holding hands in a circle around me, they prayed for me. I felt so buoyed up.

It took two painful tries to start my IV. And then it was on to the operating room.

A metal table.

Big lights overhead.

The anesthesiologist.

My personal Haiti…

When I awoke after the operation, Tad was not far. I was wheeled to a private room near the maternity ward with an IV attached to my right hand, oxygen tubes in my nose, and a large bandage across my chest.

I had survived the operation. What I had feared most was over.

I was grateful for Tad's constant company and moral support. But I also craved to see others, and was thankful when Alexandra and Larissa showed up at 5:30 PM with Igor. They didn't stay long because they had a youth group meeting at 7:00 PM, but this time Tad did not lead it. He stayed with me.

While my daughters and Igor were still in the room, my sister and mother came with chocolates, flowers, and books for me to read during my recuperation. Then Ivan, a gray-haired member of our church who works at the hospital, stopped by to pray for me. When he left, my mother, a devout Catholic, asked whether we ever pray Our Father or Hail Mary. She isn't used to the Protestant way of praying as if speaking directly to God.

"Yes, we pray Our Father," Tad answered. "But we don't always pray formal prayers."

To her, praying means reciting prescribed memorized prayers. The idea of praying as if talking to God is rather strange to her, possibly not reverent enough. But I think of it like this: Would I like my son or daughter to come to me with a prepared speech beseeching me for help, and always the same speech and the same memorized words—every single time? How could I possibly have a relationship with a child who simply recites words learned by heart, perhaps without even thinking about the meaning of the words? And what kind of relationship is it if you just talk, but don't listen for an answer?

Although visiting hours ended at 8 PM, around 10 PM, the pastor from our church appeared in my doorway. I was surprised and honored. Behind him came his grown son (who leads the church youth group with Tad) and his wife Lyuba (who had been to Haiti with us earlier this month). The Wednesday night church service and youth meeting end at 9 PM, so they were on their way home.

But that wasn't all. Following them came the deacon and three of his daughters, including Ruth (who had also gone to Haiti with us). The girls were bubbling about going to Haiti someday. Lyuba said that she dreams of Haiti every night and that she hopes to go back with her husband.

Their visit warmed me like a campfire on a cool night.

Thursday, 27 January 2011

I will say of the LORD, "He is my refuge and my fortress, my God in whom I trust."

– Psalm 91:2 (NIV)

The intermittent psssht of the compression pumps on my calves, the unfamiliar sounds of the hospital ventilation system, nurse's aides measuring vital signs every few hours, and of course, a strange bed and unfamiliar surroundings did not make for a restful night. Tad had offered to stay the night with me. He even lay down on the foldout bed for overnight visitors and turned off the lights.

"Tad," I said into the darkness after a few minutes. "I think you should go home. You're not going to be able to sleep much here." Even on a good night, Tad has trouble sleeping.

Tad protested, but I saw no point in him staying the night with me. He'd get far more rest at home. The hospital staff would take care of all my needs. He finally agreed and left.

It was one of those nights of watching the clock. Midnight, and I still wasn't asleep. *Seven more hours until it's time to wake up.*

One o'clock. *Six hours of sleep left if I fall asleep right away.*

Psssht!—one calf sleeve inflated, promoting circulation in that leg. Pssssssht!—the other sleeve inflated to prevent blood clots in the other leg. And so it went, all evening, all night, the entire time I was in the hospital bed, inflating the compression sleeve around one leg, then the other.

Three o'clock. *My, I'm going to be tired tomorrow…*

At five o'clock, I gave up on sleep and called a nurse, who unhooked me from the compression machine and walked up and down the halls with me and my IV stand.

I was delighted to see Tad shortly after seven o'clock. Breakfast was delivered a little while later, and with it, a cup of coffee. It was decaf.

"Can't I get some real coffee?" I asked. The nurse in the room suggested that Tad buy me a cup of coffee in a coffee shop downstairs. Hospital meals come with decaf only. I needed a caffeine jolt after the last two nights.

My mastectomy warranted only one night's stay in the hospital. I was to go home in the late morning. But before I did so, nurse navigator Andrea stopped by.

"I heard the good news: they didn't find any cancer cells in your lymph nodes!" she stated.

"Yes, I was really surprised," I replied. Even so, I feared that a vagrant cell might have wandered off undetected to some organ.

"You're being discharged this morning," said Andrea. "But before you go, I want you to take a look at yourself in the mirror. Come!" she urged.

I understood immediately that she wanted to be there with me when I saw my new mutilated figure. Andrea had me take off my hospital gown and look at myself in the bathroom mirror. She stood near me.

"I look like I'm ten years old," I bemoaned.

I was completely flat on the left with a big bandage over my left chest, just like the teddy bear Josie had given me. Tubes with drains came out of my body—one from the incision on my chest, the other near my underarm where my sentinel lymph nodes had been removed. I was a rainbow of colors; the disinfectant painted on my body was an odd blue.

Before I was discharged, a nurse came one final time and jabbed a shot of anticoagulant into my thigh as if shooting into a dartboard.

I jumped from the pain. These shots, which I got intermittently during my short stay at the hospital, were particularly painful, and that final jab on my thigh continued to hurt through the day.

At home, I settled in on the living room couch. There I was in the nerve center of the house. Through the bow window, I could see anyone approaching the front door. I could bask in the warmth of the wood-burning stove. I could see the dining room table and hear family conversations. This is where we sing and hold devotions, have discussions and entertain guests. It's also where I spent many, many weeks while sick with lupus.

This first evening at home, guests arrived: Tina, a homeschooling mom, with her three children, and Sandy, my deceased brother's fiancée, with her daughter Alexis. Sandy brought flowers and cookies.

"I had to get cancer for all of you to come!" I said, delighted by their visit.

Friday, 28 January 2011

My grace is sufficient for you, for my power is made perfect in weakness.
– 2 Corinthians 12:9 (NIV)

I slept soundly in my nest, which is how I view the bed in the finished basement bedroom, especially after the room is warmed with a fire in the wood-burning stove. The corner wall of this basement room is curved and lined with stones from our own yard—Tad's handiwork. It's a cozy place away from the activities of the home, a quiet place to rest or sleep in.

I finally had a good night's sleep. I woke just once in the night with a sore throat. I hope I'm not coming down with a cold. Most of the day my throat and ears hurt when I swallowed.

When I awoke, I found it challenging to sit up. With the tubes and bandages and soreness on my left side, I had to wiggle like a worm until I positioned myself on my right side and pushed up to a sitting position.

I'm not to shower or bathe until I get my two drainage tubes removed in a week. It's odd to have them hanging from my body. Last night Tad gave me one of his white tee shirts and safety-pinned the two tubes to it. He tenderly dressed me, drained the discharge in the tubes and measured the red liquid as instructed, then changed the dressing at the site where the tubes are stitched to my body.

Josie had offered to spend all day with me and be my personal nurse today. After a decadent breakfast of raspberries with cream and sugar (thanks, Mama!) and some strong French Roast coffee, I arranged for Josie to come in the afternoon. Meanwhile, Chehreh called from California. Chehreh, who left Iran as a child, and I had worked together back when I was just pregnant with Jacob. Then she and her husband moved to the San Francisco area where they are raising their two young children.

"Kathryn!" Chehreh said in her ever-enthusiastic manner. "That really sucks that you got breast cancer! You of all people!"

Once again, I felt like I had to make excuses for why it was okay that I—of all people—got cancer.[*] Why not me?

"I want to buy your family pizza for supper," Chehreh offered from across the continent. "What's a pizza place near you? And what time do you eat?"

I mentioned Captain Tony's Pizza and told her that we eat around 5:30 PM. Although Chehreh and I e-mail one another occasionally, we had not spoken on the phone for years. This was another blessing of my cancer.

When Josie came, we chatted and looked at photos of Haiti in an album that I'd put together from my first trip. Josie emptied my drains

---

[*] Less than a year later, Chehreh was also diagnosed with breast cancer and had a double mastectomy.

and changed the bandages, and was at the house when a basket of flowers from my cousins was delivered. She left around 4 PM. I lay down.

Chehreh had said that she'd call back and tell us when to expect the pizza. But 5 PM came, then 5:30 PM, and no pizza delivery. And no call. Tad asked the girls to make a salad so he could at least eat that, and then the pizza would come, he said. But although they made the salad, Alexandra would not serve it. "Wait for the pizza!" she insisted.

5:45 PM. We hovered by the front window watching every car that drove up or down our street, hoping for a pizza delivery. I was sorry that I had told Alexandra not to make supper. Maybe there was a mix-up?

Someone suggested that we pray, so we all got up and prayed for a meal to be delivered to us—not that we didn't have food in the house or couldn't fix a meal, but it was getting late and—well, why would Chehreh call and promise a pizza, then not follow through? Although she called from California, her sister and parents live in New York City and she knows that there's a three-hour time difference.

We watched the vehicles that drove up or down our street some more. It was dark. We were hungry.

"Hey, that one is slowing down," Jacob noticed. "It's backing into our driveway!"

All five of us peered out the window.

"Someone is getting out. And someone else—a woman. It's the Stetsiuks, and they're carrying something!"

That something turned out to be poppy seed rolls and a box of chocolates.

"Well, dessert arrived," Tad commented.

In the chaos of the guests coming in with their two grandsons, ages three and seven, and taking off winter coats, the phone rang. It was Chehreh.

"I'm *so* sorry! I forgot about the time difference. I just ordered your pizza. It'll be there in forty-five minutes."

The pizza was a large one with all sorts of toppings—onions, peppers, mushrooms, broccoli, olives, anchovies, pepperoni. It arrived around 7 PM. We shared it with our guests. Then we had dessert.

Slavko Stetsiuk, who's about a decade older than me, told stories from the old country. He had emigrated from Ukraine with his family about the time that the Soviet Union fell apart in the early 1990s. We sat around the dining room table as Slavko recounted how his father had returned from World War II with one leg. His mother had married him that way. He had been very hard-working and managed somehow with that one leg. When Slavko was just three, the head of the town council forged his dad's signature on a list of Banderivtsi— a national partisan movement considered enemies of the state—and his dad was sent to prison. Because he had one leg, he couldn't do hard labor, so he did office work. He returned from prison with a wooden prosthesis with which he learned to run, dance, and ride a bicycle. God had turned a bad situation into good.

Slavko told story after story about his parents, his childhood, his family. Around 9 PM, I started to feel ill: my heart was racing, and I was exhausted and hot. I had been up sitting and socializing way too much today. I lay down on the living room couch while the guests were still here. I didn't want to break up the gathering, nor did I want to miss out by going to the bedroom. So I lay on the couch and listened.

Before they left, they sang and prayed while I continued to lie on the couch.

Saturday, 29 January 2011

He will have no fear of bad news; his heart is steadfast, trusting in the LORD.

– Psalm 112:7 (NIV)

After she finished giving my father his morning bath, Dusia, Dad's part-time caregiver, stopped by our house to visit me. Until today, I knew little about this immigrant from Ukraine. She was simply the smiling gray-haired woman who attended our church, went to my parents' house and bathed my dad three times per week, and took care of other elderly in a nursing home. Until today, we'd only exchanged polite formalities; I'd never really talked with Dusia. After her visit, I realized how each familiar face has some interesting—and possibly poignant—stories behind the facade.

Dusia, about ten years my senior, grew up in Ukraine in a poor village family. Her parents couldn't afford shoes for their children, so her father made boots for them from discarded rubber tires. They were uncomfortable and cold. She didn't have socks, only rags to tie around her feet. "We were so glad when spring came and we could run around barefooted again!" recounted Dusia. "I went to school barefooted, but one day there was a big notice posted at the school that starting the next day, no one was allowed to school without shoes. I cried and cried. I was a good student, and I liked school—but I had no shoes. We were too poor. My father made three hundred Russian rubles per month, and he knew exactly how he would spend every ruble: gas, taxes, food… I knew there was no money for shoes. But when my father saw how much I wanted to go to school, he bought me a pair of sandals. I would walk to school barefooted, then wash my feet at a spring by the school and put on the sandals."

Most of the Western world has no idea that there are not millions, but billions on this earth who still live this way today. We don't appreciate our material blessings a fraction as much as Dusia did back then. She was thankful for a single pair of sandals; in the Western world, we have closets full of shoes for every purpose and occasion, and think nothing of buying yet another pair.

I could listen to Dusia's stories from the old country for hours. She described growing up in the Soviet Union and going to an under-ground church, which met in homes. During home church services, Dusia's mother would ask her to copy a few verses or pages of the Bible by hand because there was only one Bible for the entire community. I've read many accounts of persecuted Christians, but Dusia had lived that life.

Another story she told was about a Christian family with six children whose house was demolished after the KGB found that they were hosting church services in their home. One day as a Christian mechanic was fixing a KGB agent's car, from under the vehicle he began a conversation about this family.

"Where are they living now?" asked the agent.

"In the barn."

"How do they stay warm?" the agent inquired. It was winter.

"The cow's breath warms them."

By the time the car was repaired, the KGB agent had agreed to give the family a permit for a new home. Fellow Christians then built the house for the family.

Before Dusia left, I shared an odd thought that had been bothering me: I told her that I was afraid that by battling cancer, I may be cheating death that could have been an answer to prayer. I revealed to Dusia my prayer that God take me before any of my children, that I couldn't handle the pain of losing a child. "What if God allowed the cancer so that I don't outlive my children, as I've often prayed?"

"Don't say that!" Dusia said. "Of course you should overcome this cancer. Your children are still young!"

But I know that even young people die.

After two hours of conversations, I had to recline, so Dusia left. I'm frustrated that I get exhausted just from sitting. Sitting! Just like when I had lupus. Fortunately, today the muscles on my upper chest aren't as sore. Yesterday I took Tylenol only once in the evening; today I took no painkillers at all. But I am tired, more tired than yesterday. Perhaps I don't appreciate what a trauma my body has been through. I still have a sore throat from being intubated, and my ears hurt when I swallow. And I still cough. I had thought I was coming down with a cold, but it turns out that these are aftereffects of the surgery.

Sunday, 30 January 2011

I call on the LORD in my distress, and He answers me.

– Psalm 120:1 (NIV)

I sit with two drainage tubes hanging from my body and a part of my feminine anatomy missing. Two months ago, while Tad was still battling pneumonia, who would have thought that my life would take this sudden turn? The discovery of cancer is usually unexpected and necessitates quick actions. The diagnosis sweeps you away, and you're thrust down a cancer waterslide, unaware of the next twist or bump, down, down a predetermined course.

And so it was: discovery of lump, doctor's appointment, mammogram, ultrasound, biopsy—all predetermined steps. Then the paths branch: Lumpectomy or mastectomy? Radiation or chemotherapy? Or am I cancer free?

Am I cancer free? I sit and wonder. No cancer cells were found in the lymph nodes that the surgeon removed. So after I recover from the mastectomy, am I done? Was that it? If so, that wasn't so hard. The fear factor was the most difficult part.

These thoughts tumble in my mind, but I have peace with where God is leading me. I can almost feel His hand around mine.

I had a rough night: coughing, throat still sore from being intubated. The ultra-dry winter air heated with the wood-burning stove is irritating my throat. At 1 AM, I got up and fetched a washcloth, moistened it, and slept with this washcloth over my mouth and nose. In the morning, when I swallowed, my ears did not hurt. That was a first since surgery. I'm getting better.

The family went to church this morning, but I slept in. Since surgery, I tend to sleep long, and then spend most of the day reclined on the living room couch by the wood-burning stove, listening, talking, or dozing. I thought I'd have more energy.

Monday, 31 January 2011

...the LORD turn His face toward you and give you peace.
— Numbers 6:26 (NIV)

Beautiful though they are, the vases of daisies and roses, sunflowers and carnations distributed throughout the house hint of illness or loss. I see them on the coffee table, on the mantel, on the dining room table, in the entry hall. Pinks and yellows, the colors of cheer and sunshine and thoughtfulness.

More guests today. And more phone calls. I'm humbled at the outpouring of concern and love, delighted by the distraction and attention, overwhelmed by the meals and flowers and gifts.

Jeanne and Grace, two retired women from the community church we once attended, visited in the late afternoon. They didn't come empty-handed. Grace brought a mix for broccoli cheese soup; Jeanne brought a patchwork pillow in shades of taupe and pink that she had made especially for me, with a heart and a looped pink ribbon symbolizing breast cancer. The pillow matches our recliner perfectly.

Grace, who was widowed only two months ago, is still struggling with solitude. "I wish I'd had more girls," Grace lamented as Larissa brought a tray with cups and tea and sugar, and a plate of cookies that she and Alexandra had baked. Both Jeanne and Grace were impressed with how nicely Larissa served them. I was surprised that they seemed surprised. Perhaps it's because teenagers are better known for rebellious behavior than for good manners.

After supper, more guests came: Lyuba and her whole family. They brought baked chicken and sandwiches and borscht, food that we'll have for tomorrow. With hair the color of corn silk and eyes like the summer sky, her two boys melt my heart. They're delightful and obedient toddlers, springs of energy and playful giggles. Like their mother, they are sunbeams of joy.

Lyuba, still under the spell of her recent Haiti trip, shared a story about her friend Mary, a woman about twenty-eight years old, who had immigrated to Cleveland from Ukraine just four years ago. Like many new immigrants from the ex-Soviet Union, this woman loved to shop. But then she went on a mission trip to a mountain village in Haiti where they slept on the ground and drank rainwater.

"I just talked with Mary," said Lyuba. "Since her return from Haiti, whenever she sees clothes and shoes in the stores, she just can't buy them for herself anymore. She looks at them and sees the needy children of Haiti. She told me, 'How can I buy myself something when children in Haiti have nothing?' Instead, she sends her money to Haiti to help those in need."

Haiti completely changed her life. Testimonies like these are why I lead mission trips to poor countries, why I speak in churches, why I encourage people to go, to see, to experience.

Lyuba sat next to me on the couch and patted my arm. "I love you so much," she beamed.

I smiled politely but didn't know how to answer.

"And I know you love me," she continued, "because when we came to visit you in the hospital, there was a room full of people and you said, 'Oh, Lyuba!'"

I smiled in remembrance. I should have called out all my visitors' names!

Tuesday, 1 February 2011

Guard my life, for I am faithful to you; save your servant who trusts in you. You are my God; have mercy on me, Lord, for I call to you all day long.

– Psalm 86:2–3 (NIV)

Another day of snowflakes hurling themselves at the landscape and covering the roads, the cars in the driveway, the steps to the house that we have to shovel again and again. It's another day of clouds obliterating any hint of the sun and creating a thick, mono-chrome sky that characterizes most of the winter days in Rochester, the second cloudiest city in the United States according to my ninth-grade Earth Science teacher. The toneless sky permeates my very soul and colors my outlook with its bland hue. I wish I weren't so easily affected by the weather—but I am.

Getting out of bed continues to be an acrobatic accomplishment. With the two drainage tubes hanging from my left chest, sitting up is difficult. Normally I don't think about how to get out of bed. But now I lie in bed thinking, planning: I can't use my left arm because moving it is far too painful, so I press the left arm against my side to hold the tubes against my body, then roll to my right and push up with the right arm to a half-sitting position. I thrash like a fish out of water before I find a good angle. Then I swing my legs down over the edge of the bed and sit up.

As I was maneuvering my way out of bed, Alexandra came in with the cordless phone in extended hand. "For you," she said.

It was Joy. I've known Joy, a fellow technical writer and friend, most of my professional career. As we chatted, Joy reminded me that her older sister had been diagnosed with breast cancer at thirty-eight. She also had a mastectomy—then reconstruction about a year later.

"If she'd known what she had to go through, she never would have done it," Joy related. "They used her belly fat—did a 'tummy tuck'—for the reconstruction, but she had complications. In about two percent of the people, there isn't adequate blood flow to the stomach, and that area got gangrene. When it finally healed, there was a hole. It took a year to fill in."

I'm so glad I chose not to have reconstruction.

Wednesday, 2 February 2011

God is our refuge and strength, an ever-present help in trouble.
                                    – Psalm 46:1 (NIV)

A snowstorm was to hit Rochester today, the storm that dropped twenty-one inches of snow on Oklahoma. Supposedly, it was to snow steadily for twenty-four hours, from 10 PM last night until 10 PM today. Our local schools were cancelled in anticipation of the storm.

I can't say that the storm didn't come because snowplows have been roaring up and down Landing Road, producing swirling billows of snow behind them, and the street has been covered in white much of the day. The snowfall, though steady since early morning, was scant and light. But it did keep on coming. Luckily, Jacob had no school today and Tad was home as well. And, of course, the girls are home-schooled, so they're also home.

After breakfast, Larissa surprised me with her offer to wash my hair. I haven't washed it since before I had surgery a week ago. Since I am not allowed to shower or bathe due to my bandages, stitches, and the drainage tubes hanging from my wounds, I had no way of washing my hair. I can't lift my left arm yet—the pain is too great. I wasn't sure how Larissa would do it, but she had a plan: She had me sit on the bathroom floor and lean my head backward over the side of the bathtub. Then she used the hand-held showerhead that detaches from the wall to wet and rinse my hair. Such a servant's heart. I couldn't help but remember how I used to wash her hair years ago, and now she was washing mine.

It's been one week since my surgery. The drainage tubes at the two surgical sites are ever more annoying; the sites where the tubes exit my body are very tender. I avoid even moving my left arm. I can feel a length of tube about four inches long under the skin across my chest. The longer the tubes are in, the more my body protests. My muscles seem to spasm around the tube and ripple along its length in a convulsion. I sit and walk hunched so I don't pull on them. When I accidentally jar the bulbs, which pulls on the tubes, I wince with pain. I can't wait to get them out tomorrow.

Thursday, 3 February 2011

I waited patiently for the Lord; He turned to me and heard my cry.
    – Psalm 40:1 (NIV)

Although a call at 8:14 AM woke me, I unplugged the phone line and slept some more. I didn't get out of bed until about 11 AM. On the one hand, I feel guilty; on the other, why get up from bed when I just lie down in front of the fire on the couch?

When I came into the kitchen and heard from Larissa that today's appointment with Dr. Medeiros to remove my tubes was canceled because she's sick, I was upset. When I called to reschedule the appointment and got a date for next Thursday, a whole week from today, I insisted that they squeeze me in today. "I'm ready to go to Emergency to have these tubes removed I'm in so much pain! Can't someone else remove them?"

They found me a 3 PM slot with another doctor in the practice.

Tad and I had a bit of a wait for Dr. Dynski, but I was grateful she fit us in. She was an older woman with white hair tied up in a bun on the very top of her head. She walked unevenly, supporting her right side with a metal forearm crutch. It begged the question of why or what happened, but I didn't dare ask.

Dr. Dynski was a cheerful woman whom I liked just as much as Dr. Medeiros. She had a detailed printout of my pathology report, which she handed to me. I was expecting her only to remove my tubes, but she sat me down and explained the report, an analysis of the cancer cells removed from my breast.

It's a nuclear grade 3 cancer. "Yes, 3 out of 3, most aggressive," she answered Tad. The tumor was 2.9 cm (more than one inch) wide, and due to its size, my cancer is considered stage 2. The four lymph nodes they removed were all clear. Yes, the final report was that there was no cancer found in them. But due to the size of the tumor and the aggressiveness, Dr. Dynski thinks that the oncologist will recommend chemotherapy for me.

Chemotherapy! This was news to me. I thought if the tumor was cut out and no cancer was found in the lymph nodes, that was the end of my treatment. Done. Admittedly, the thought keeps creeping in: What if one tiny cell escaped and lodged in my bones, lungs, or brain? Especially my brain? It'll grow undetected—until it's too late. So the suggestion of chemotherapy was almost a relief. Almost.

The cancer was not estrogen or progesterone sensitive, but it was sensitive to HER2/neu, a protein. I don't understand what HER2/neu is, but Andrea, the nurse navigator, said this was excellent news. Somehow Andrea managed to show up at this appointment, too, which surprised and pleased me. How on earth did she know about this last-minute change?

The chemo for this type of cancer has fewer side effects than the others. "You can even drive yourself," Andrea said. If I choose this chemo, my hair may or may not fall out.

To take out the drainage tubes, Dr. Dynski had me lie down on the patient table. She snipped the stitches that held the tubes in place and told me to suck in my breath. When she pulled out the tube that was across the top of my chest, it felt odd, and then I knew that the tube was out by the sucking noise it made. Then she removed the second tube, all the stitches from under my arm, and the bandages taped across my long chest incision. Dr. Dynski put just one gauze pad and bandage on the site, covering the places where the two tubes had come out.

"You can take it off later today. If there's no drainage, you can just leave it open." Then changing the subject, she asked, "Are you into hugs?"

"Yes," I replied.

"Let me hug you as one breast cancer survivor to another."

I maneuvered my bandaged left side away from point of contact and hugged Dr. Dynski as she embraced me.

"It'll be nine years," she said, referring to her cancer. Interesting that this surgeon, who was surely performing lumpectomies and mastectomies long before she herself got cancer, can now truly identify with her patients.

The woman at the checkout desk set up a return visit in two weeks with Dr. Medeiros and said she would set up an oncologist appointment at about the same time.

A homeschool mom and acquaintance from our former church promised to deliver supper for us this evening. At 5 PM as stomachs rumbled, different family members asked me, "When is she bringing supper? What is she bringing?" I didn't know.

"She just asked what we'd recently eaten, and I said lasagna," I replied. That lasagna, brought by a very generous couple who support us whenever we go on mission trips, was the most outstandingly delicious lasagna I've ever eaten.

Eventually supper arrived in disposable aluminum containers carried in by the mom and her ten-year-old son. We thanked them awkwardly, almost wanting to invite them to eat with us, then Tad walked them to their car.

Meatloaf with a ketchup sauce, steamed vegetables with potato, lettuce salad, and brownies. It was good, wholesome food, but my cooking is different, and Tad began to criticize the sauce. Alexandra immediately stopped him.

"Don't criticize food brought to us as a gift! You should praise God for it," she said.

It was a good reminder for all of us.

After that, we got into playing an odd game around the table. It went like this: Each wrote his name on a piece of paper. Then we folded up the papers and each of us picked one. For the name that we picked, we had to say three good things about that person and one criticism. The meal around the dining room table was a safe environment in which to give feedback to each other.

Tad pulled my name.

"Works very hard, so hard that sometimes makes me want to cry. Intelligent. Getting better." I suspect he meant at being more humble or submissive. And then the one criticism: "Proud."

Ouch.

Friday, 4 February 2011

He heals the brokenhearted and bandages their wounds.
– Psalm 147:3 (NLT)

Once again I got up late, then after eating breakfast, lay down and wanted to go to sleep. It's so odd that I'm so tired. I spent most of the day lying on the couch, reading.

Today I was to remove the bandage that Dr. Dynski put on the drain site yesterday. It's easier, both physically and emotionally, if someone else does the bandaging or unbandaging, so I asked Tad to take off the dressing. I felt like a child being cared for by her mama as Tad gently peeled away the bandage, but the gauze was stuck on because some fluids had drained and dried. "You can soak it off in the bath or shower," he suggested. I was almost relieved not to remove the gauze just yet. The idea of my mastectomy site being completely uncovered seemed a bit frightening. But in the evening, I took my first steamy shower since the surgery, and the gauze did soak off. Now to heal.

The incision sites where the breast and the lymph nodes were removed still hurt and feel tight. I'm to do exercises, "walk" the fingers of my left hand up a wall and stretch my left arm, which I can't lift freely. When I do the exercise, my left arm and chest feel odd, like there's pulling. I just want to hunch over because where my chest is healing I feel a tugging.

Sunday, 6 February 2011

...the joy of the LORD is your strength.
– Nehemiah 8:10 (NIV)

As I struggled with my aches and pains, I should have done a better job remembering the devotional that I read today in a book that Josie gave me, *Created for a Purpose* by Darlene Sala:

Your body is actually a shell, a 'house' you wear. The real you which is inside your body will someday leave. So if anything happens to your body, it won't affect the real you. Even if you were in an accident and your arms or legs were cut off, the real you would still be intact inside.

So why should I lament when all that I had cut off was a breast? Yet as I stood in the bedroom, I told Tad through tears, "I feel like a cripple." I no longer see myself as an attractive female, no longer appealing to my husband. How can I be attractive when I'm maimed? The bandages are off and my chest is revealed, flat and scarred. My breast—and along with it a part of my femininity—is gone.

"I don't think of you like that at all," Tad cheered me. "Remember Paula? Just her head and her little frail body in a wheelchair?"

Yes, I certainly remembered this amazingly upbeat woman who was a joy to be with despite hands twisted into claws by rheumatoid arthritis and an amputated leg.

My family met Paula when she was almost sixty. We had just started attending Browncroft Community Church in 1999 when I saw Paula in the lobby one day. Slight little Paula, who wore special shoes and shuffled unsteadily, had been my supervisor at the Micro-biology Lab of Strong Memorial Hospital about twenty years before. I had worked part-time B shift in the hospital lab for only two years as I pursued a degree in photography, but she remembered me.

Paula had had rheumatoid arthritis since she was fourteen years old. Eventually she had to have one of her legs amputated due to poor circulation. Even though she was unable to walk or take care of her most basic needs, she was always cheerful. Her faith buoyed her up. After her amputation in December 2005, I visited her every Monday after work to help with menial chores: opening a yogurt container, fetching stamps for a letter, picking up something she dropped. She was too petite and weak for a prosthesis and would be bound to a wheel-chair for the rest of her life. Although I came to help Paula during her rehabilitation, after each visit I was the one who felt blessed. It was her attitude, her faith, and how she never gave up or felt sorry for herself. She never, ever complained. People loved her and flocked to her even though she was disabled. Even my teenaged son had loved visiting her. She exuded optimism.

I don't think of myself a cripple on the same level as Paula—unable to walk. But I feel like a cripple when it comes to intimacy. I don't want my husband to see my maimed body. I fear that this physical defect will mar his attraction to me.

But perhaps worse than my physical pain and visual disfigurement is what cancer has done to my thinking: it's taken away my peace. At night, when I turn off the lights, I wrestle with my thoughts and fears. I know logically that fear is not of the Lord, but the pain in my side, dull but persistent, taunts me, worries me, and shifts around at times. The moving should actually calm me because what cancer moves around? But until I see a doctor, get an x-ray or ultrasound, I will worry that my ovaries or other organs are also affected by cancer. And even if they aren't, isn't it possible that they will be in the future? I've been studying my pathology report: Invasive ductal carcinoma, nuclear grade 3, HER2/neu positive 3+, mitotic count 2 out of 3, overall grade 3 (score 8–9 out of 9)… The numbers are so high!

Emotionally, last night was one of my worst nights since surgery. I can only lie flat on my back. I can't roll over onto my left side because of the painful incision sites on that side; I can't lie on my right side because I have no comfortable position for my left arm. So I lie on my back, stomach up, arms at my sides as if standing at attention.

I feel so out of touch with my body. Even my dreams last night focused on my body. I was traveling somewhere and had to use the rest room, but there was none and I had to squat in public view while heads turned to look at me.

More visitors today. In the afternoon, a couple about our age who attend the Slavic Pentecostal Church on the other side of town came bearing gifts of pizza and cheesecake. None of their six daughters came; they were all sick, said the wife.

"How did you hear about my cancer?" I asked them. They aren't part of our close circle of friends.

"The pastor requested that the church pray for Tad's wife before her operation, so we assumed it was you," said Luda. "We asked around, and found out it was."

In the evening after supper, two more guests came. Sadly, none of Lydia's teenaged children or husband wanted to come with her, so she picked up her Russian friend, Nadia, to come along. Lydia, who lives more than twenty miles away, brought us a delicious homemade torte.

Lydia and Nadia looked through my Haiti photo album, and I mentioned how important it was for children—and adults—to see other ways of life. Nadia shared that she took her daughter to Russia, her homeland, only to have her daughter conclude, "I'm embarrassed to be from Russia. I should be proud of my heritage, but now I don't want people to know where I'm from."

Lydia said that there was always something to keep her family from going to Ukraine: a dog with eleven puppies, a garden to tend, her chickens… I realized that most people don't have my perspective and my goal to raise adults who are aware of conditions in the rest of the world. They don't understand the importance of kids seeing another way of life—a poorer standard of living. Much of the world's population does not have microwaves, washing machines, or even running water in the house.

"Tell me next time you go somewhere," Lydia said. I had told her before, but if you don't make the trip a priority, something will always get in the way.

Lydia and Nadia stayed for devotions—singing and Bible reading. Both wistfully desired something like that in their own homes. Why don't people make an effort to get close to their children? Reading together, traveling together, singing together, praying together, eating meals together builds strong ties. I would rather spend time with my family than with anyone else on earth.

Monday, 7 February 2011

But I trust in you, LORD; I say, "You are my God." My times are in Your hands…
— Psalm 31:14-15 (NIV)

The main event today was the appointment with the oncologist, Dr. Julia Smith.

Oncologist. A few short years ago, I had to look up what the word meant. Now I have my own oncologist, my own cancer specialist.

It struck me how fast this Pony Express of cancer moves. I didn't make this appointment with Dr. Smith; Dr Medeiros' office did. I didn't pick her as my oncologist; Dr. Medeiros' office did. And I didn't set up any medical appointments this month, but when I left Dr. Smith's office, I was handed a printout of tentative appointments—echocardiogram, discussion of mediport with Dr. Medeiros, and chemo and Herceptin treatments—for the next two months! It's as if I had handed over the reins of my life to someone else.

The Lipson Cancer Center is a new medical building, a sign of just how much the medical industry is expanding. Medical buildings seem to be popping up like mushrooms after a fall rain. Stone tiles on the floor and walls, real plants by the window, and a large-screen TV (ugh!) were all part of this modern waiting room. I prefer the calming aquarium of the Elizabeth Wende Breast Care Center to the grating movie that was playing. We heard God's name taken in vain several times before Tad got up and asked them to turn off the movie. Whew. Why on earth would they play full-length movies? Are people really in the waiting room that long? With the violence and annoying audio tracks of most movies, they aren't exactly comforting background for people already troubled by their medical misfortune. After Tad complained, the receptionist put on a video of nature scenes with soothing music—a much improved choice. Filling out forms is challenging enough without the audio portion of a movie barking at me, breaking my concentration and exasperating me.

When I entered Dr. Smith's office, Andrea, the nurse navigator, was sitting in the room. I hadn't expected her, and the smile on my face when I saw her surely gave away how thrilled and relieved I was that she was there. Didn't she have other patients to follow? How is it that she always makes my appointments? Her mere presence was a moral support for me, an anchor in the tempest of my medical appointments.

Dr. Julia Smith is a no-nonsense woman—thick salt-and-pepper hair cut fairly short, blue eyes, and wearing a dress and stockings and sensible shoes. She looked about my age. I liked her intellect and professional manner and the way she made sure that both Tad and I understood the pathology report and its ramifications.

Dr. Smith first asked me to tell her what I know about my cancer. Good approach, I thought. I'd done my homework: I read the report. When stating what I knew of my cancer, I got stuck on HER-2/neu.

Dr. Smith couldn't find the HER2/neu sensitivity on the report, so I pointed it out—middle of page 2. (I was pleased with myself that I knew the report so well.)

"I know that estrogen and progesterone are hormones," I said, "and that some cancers can be sensitive to these hormones—that these hormones make the cancers grow. But I've never heard of HER2/neu before. What is it?"

"It's a surface protein on cells," Dr. Smith clarified. "A growth protein. It's found on the surface of breast cancer cells. The test for the overexpression of HER2/neu is a measure of the aggressiveness of the cancer. In your case, it's three plus."

"Out of three?"

"Yes."

"And that means…?"

"It means that there's a higher probability that the cancer will recur. HER2/neu cancers are twice as likely to come back as the estrogen- or progesterone-sensitive breast cancers. Yours is on the aggressive end of the scale of a cancer that's more likely to recur, to metastasize. The most likely places the cancer would come back are in the bones, liver, lungs, or brain."

Brain cancer.

I teared up when I heard those words. Brain cancer has been my greatest fear. Please, God, not that. Anything but death by brain cancer. I've known too many people who died of it, died after memory loss, personality changes, becoming hostile, mean, not themselves… No, I won't even entertain that possibility. Not brain cancer! I don't want to change into a wrathful, belligerent woman and leave behind that kind of legacy.

"I highly recommend chemotherapy in your case," the doctor stated.

Andrea handed me a tissue.

"Are you a numbers person?" asked Dr. Smith.

"Yes," I sniffed.

"I'll print some numbers for you then."

Another good approach I thought as I blew my nose.

Dr. Smith stepped out for a bit, then returned with a printout of graphs. The graphs showed the survival rates for my type of cancer with and without chemotherapy. With no additional therapy, I have a 30% chance of dying from cancer in the next ten years. With chemotherapy, my chance of dying from a recurrence of cancer would be reduced to 17%. In ten years. I might not live to sixty-five.

We talked a good hour—the doctor, Andrea, and the two of us. In the end, Tad said if it were his decision, he wouldn't do anything. The doctor said that she would go through the chemo. I definitely want to, but also feel that Tad will condemn me for choosing that. In fact, we didn't talk about it for the rest of the day. It should be my decision, but I'm part of a family.

All along, I've been feeling that I have to go through this for a reason—cancer, chemo, hair loss… How else will I know what others have been through?

"God didn't bring this about. But He will borrow it for good." I've heard Andrea say this more than once when talking about her cancer. And my cancer.

Lord, please help me make the right decision, and please, Lord, use my cancer for your glory.

Tuesday, 8 February 2011

Be joyful in hope, patient in affliction, faithful in prayer.
                                          – Romans 12:12 (NIV)

In the morning when I came out of the bedroom, Tad and all three kids were in the living room discussing illness and the reason for illness: Payment for sin. Building patience. A trial or test.

It felt that they were judging me, and though I said nothing, Tad sensed this.

"We're only discussing in theory. It's not about you."

But it felt as though it was a condemnation. Tad also added again that if he were the one with cancer, he wouldn't go through the chemo-therapy. I couldn't help but think that the reason he was so heroic was because his life isn't in the balance. Perhaps if he were the one lying in bed at night, awake, doubts and fears attacking him like a pack of wolves, he might not be quite so brave.

"The odds of me dying of cancer that recurs somewhere else in my body are three in ten over the next ten years. Thirty percent. That's much higher than I expected! If I go through chemotherapy, the odds of me dying of cancer in the next ten years is cut almost in half: 1.7 in ten," I told my family. The kids hadn't heard these stats yet.

I sensed a strong tension, an unspoken pressure not to go through it, to be a hero and rely solely on God. But I don't feel that way. I feel I have to go through the chemo. It's something I need to go through—suffer through—for a reason that God hasn't yet revealed. A miraculous healing would have been preferable, but too easy. An operation with no follow-up would also be too easy. I'd be done. Just exercise those arm and chest muscles, let the wounds heal, and return to work in four more weeks. Chemo will be another "adventure." For someone who doesn't even like to take ibuprofen for a headache, all these chemicals will be a stretch. Shots, IVs, another minor surgery to install a mediport through which I'd get the chemo drugs… I won't be free from this for over a year.

Tad cheered me a bit. "You're in a win-win situation," he said. "If you are healed, you win; if you die, you go to heaven."

What can be better than that?

Wednesday, 9 February 2011

You are my strength, I watch for you; you, God, are my fortress, my God on whom I can rely.
– Psalm 59:9-10 (NIV)

If only my faith would keep me strong and immune to despair! But this was not the case today. I plunged to a new emotional low. I just could not shake the statistic that without chemo three out of ten women with my type of breast cancer die within ten years because the cancer metastasizes. That statistic stood in front of my mind like a neon sign. Instead of focusing on the 83% survival rate after chemo, I was stuck on the negative: I have a thirty percent chance of dying in the next decade. Like Elizabeth Edwards.

All day my appetite was gone, my mood gloomy. I was no longer the person who "went through this as if you had a wart removed," as my mother said more than once. No, today I felt my life was at stake. That the end might be near.

What is that dull pain in my abdomen that I've had for over a month? I finally made an appointment to see the gynecologist next week. What if it's colon cancer? Who do I get to check for that?

Negative, so negative.

When Tad and the kids went to youth group, I called Anne, an elderly woman near ninety whom I befriended during my college years. Her husband answered, but couldn't hear me. "Let me adjust my speaker." He didn't come back on, but Anne did.

Anne has always been a cheerful person, sometimes getting close to annoying me with her bubbly, always optimistic, always positive attitude. She's gotten a little hard of hearing, too, because I had to repeat BREAST CANCER three times before it clicked.

"Oh!" she exclaimed. "Did you know that I had a mastectomy when I was forty-six years old? I was worried that I wouldn't see my children grow up. But I did."

"And your grandchildren," I added. I hadn't known about her cancer.

"Oh, Kathryn, you will be fine. I know you will."

We chatted about twenty-five minutes—about her mastectomy, about Thelma's on Park Avenue, about how hot those prostheses can be in the summer. (Yes, I had heard that before.) Anne didn't even think to ask whether I'd had reconstruction surgery. She obviously hadn't if she's familiar with Thelma's—and knows that insurance covers part of the cost of the prosthesis.

I came away from that call feeling better. Anne had survived almost forty years since her surgery, and she hadn't had chemotherapy.

I realized that I had fallen victim to one of those games the mind plays—that Satan plays with our minds. *For he is a liar and the father of lies* (John 8:44). I need to praise God in all things. God never promised to shield me from hard things, but He is with me and I need to learn to lean on Him more and allow His peace to enter me.

Never will I leave you, never will I forsake you (Hebrews 13:5). I need to focus on that.

Thursday, 10 February 2011

For He will command His angels concerning you to guard you in all your ways; they will lift you up in their hands, so that you will not strike your foot against a stone.
– Psalm 91:11-12 (NIV)

Reading scripture verses like this one cheers me up. Yonnas, the local Christian who was our guide in Ethiopia, read Psalm 91 to our team in Addis Ababa in November 2006. Krysten, a team leader, read these verses to the youth team in the Darien Jungle of Panama last summer. And I read this to our church before our team went on the Haiti mission trip last month. I think of these verses as a protection on mission trips, but today I look to these words as a promise that God will protect me in my illness, too. I long for His protection against harm and against a return of cancer on this long haul ahead of me.

Chemotherapy. What am I getting myself into? Surgery for mediport installation, chemicals flowing through my bloodstream, echocardiograms, hormone injections, blood draws, and surely so much more that I don't know yet.

Yes, I made the decision to go through with it, and today I met with Dr. Medeiros to discuss installing a mediport—a device that is surgically implanted under the skin in my chest. A catheter will run from the port directly into a main vein. IVs will be hooked up to the mediport. Considering my excruciating experience with the IV before the mastectomy, I couldn't possibly go through the searing pain of getting an IV started every week for four months, then every three weeks for another eight months after that. My veins could never tolerate that. Thus the mediport.

My sister Marta drove me to the doctor's office and Tad met us there. Today the doctor's visit was a mini education on the mediport—what it looks like, where it's installed, what the veins and arteries look like in that part of the body, and what could go wrong—bleeding due to a cut artery, collapsed lung, infection… I felt myself getting weak from visualizing this thing going into my body, the scalpel cutting into my skin… Too much information. Way, way too much.

"One slice of pie at a time," said nurse navigator Andrea who, of course, was at this appointment. Knowing too much is not good.

"Your type of cancer tends to recur within five years," whispered Dr. Medeiros. She had laryngitis so what she said was barely audible.

I could see Marta flinch. Or was she blinking back tears?

"So if I live to sixty, I can throw a big birthday party and breathe a sigh of relief?" I asked.

"Something like that," agreed the doctor.

Five years. Yesterday I was struggling with a ten-year survival statistic; today I'm told that I may have but five years to live. Of course, it's not stated that way. In fact, my chances are better than 80% that I will live more than the five or ten years. Still, there are those who are included in that statistic that no one wants to be a part of: those who don't survive. I must not focus on that, but I should be realistic, no?

Dr. Medeiros suggested that I take medical leave for all four months of the chemotherapy to reduce my stress. (After the four intense months, I'll continue on another drug with few side effects for the rest of one year.) Stress, she reminded me, has been tied to cancer.

"You're going to be facing a physical challenge and an emotional challenge as you go through this," coached Andrea.

The mediport installation will be next Wednesday.

Friday, 11 February 2011

He who began a good work in you will carry it on to completion…
– Philippians 1:6 (NIV)

Yesterday Tina, my homeschool-mom friend, arrived with a sausage casserole and a shopping bag full of books that she started to pull out one by one. She knows I'm an avid reader and that I was running out of books to read.

"Have you read *In the Presence of my Enemies*?" Tina asked.

"Yes."

"*Things Fall Apart*?"

"Yes, I didn't like it."

I was surprised by the number of books that she took out of her bag that I *had* read. But there were also eight books I had not read, some of which I had considered buying. They made a nice "to read" pile on the glass coffee table, and by evening I'd already worked my way through the first few chapters of a missionary's adventures in Bangladesh.

I enjoyed Tina's company. I sipped my coffee as we talked about our children, our families, the leak in her bathroom that drips into the kitchen, about my latest medical appointments and her latest challenges with her eighteen-year-old son.

Tina told me about one of her aunts who talked so much that she was a family legend. "I learned never to ask her a question," Tina recounted.

Tina's presence is demure, quiet, and soothing. She's willing to listen and console. But some of my other guests have been more like Tina's aunt.

Although I've appreciated the concerned calls and the visits, guests have been almost constant since my mastectomy. And medical appointments have become all too frequent. The loner in me misses having time to myself.

Today Tad woke with a cough and fever. I know that he feels very sick because he did not go to tune pianos and made an appointment with Dr. Shamaskin without my encouragement. Tad is not one to visit doctors, but he's afraid that it might be pneumonia again, and he doesn't want to go through what he experienced in November.

I'm feeling a bit panicked. With Tad sick, will I stay well enough to have my operation in five days? Tad isn't ultra careful about not spreading germs, and to make matters worse, Alexandra keeps hugging him and cuddling with him. I'm concerned that she might become another germ spreader.

Tad came home a minute before I was to leave for my echocardiogram. "It's not pneumonia," he said with relief. "Not even bronchitis."

I'm finally feeling well enough to drive. It's past the two weeks that Dr. Medeiros told me not to drive. How appropriate that my first solo drive was to a medical appointment.

As I approached the entrance of the Linden Oaks medical building, several elderly people with canes and walkers came shuffling out. A woman with a man's haircut and dressed in jeans scuffled along leaning on a quad cane—a cane with four feet. Two men tottered out, one with a cane in each hand, the other pushing a walker. He'd take two steps, then push the walker, another two steps, then push. The scary thing is that the man with the walker got behind the steering wheel of a car and drove off!

Shuffle, scuffle, totter, sway. Am I now part of this world of people whose lives are extended by drugs and operations, who live just for the sake of not dying, who, like my father, sit and watch TV because they aren't strong enough or creative enough to do anything else with their lives? Am I going to become one of them because I decided not to give in to cancer at fifty-five?

Once again I donned a blue medical gown. "Opening in the front," I was instructed.

Technician Michelle took the echocardiogram, which the doctors need as a baseline. Every two or three months I'll be back for another echocardiogram, and they'll be able to compare these images with the later ones to determine whether the Herceptin is damaging my heart.

"Beautiful!" said Michelle, tossing her curly, dark hair.

"So my heart looks good?" I asked. I could see the ultrasound images on the monitor, my heart eerily beating on the screen.

"Oh, I can't say. Only the doctor can analyze the images and tell you," said Michelle.

But she gave it away with more outbursts of "Gorgeous! Beautiful, like a textbook! A good way to end my week. Nice images, nice patient."

Since I was already in the van, I decided to run errands. Because I haven't had an appetite since the operation, I tend to eat raspberries (a favorite) for breakfast, and then nothing else until suppertime. Today I had a banana and apple as well, but it wasn't enough. While grocery shopping, I crouched down to look at something on a bottom shelf, and when I stood up, my vision started going black. I held on tightly to the shopping cart, determined not to fall or lose consciousness. Suddenly I felt weak, like I shouldn't be out shopping at all, like I'd overdone it.

On the way out of the store, I saw a co-worker, Dan, and greeted him. We chatted outside at least ten minutes. He told me that he'd wanted to stop by my office before my medical leave to tell me that both his sister and his sister-in-law had had breast cancer.

"Seven years later, both got breast cancer again in the other breast. At the same time!" he recounted.

Dan also said that one of them had reconstruction surgery that turned into a nightmare. The first mastectomy and reconstruction had gone well, but the second time one of the doctors (probably the plastic surgeon) was different, and she had to have four additional surgeries to fix the botched job.

I'm relieved that I decided against reconstruction.

Saturday, 12 February 2011

Therefore I take pleasure in infirmities... for Christ's sake. For when I am weak, then I am strong.

– 2 Corinthians 12:10 (NKJV)

I wish I could say that I take pleasure in my infirmity and weakness—and in those of my family members—but today just the opposite happened. It was not a good day. Snow, clouds, cold, sickness, Tad cleaning and complaining about too many things in the house—they did not contribute to lifting my gloom.

Although Tad no longer has a fever, Larissa does. She slept much of the day. I'm terrified that I'll catch this sickness.

But I'm far more terrified of my cancer returning and killing me. HER2/neu sensitive cancers are *the* most aggressive cancers, I read on the American Cancer Society website. They tend to return within five years. That's what Dr. Medeiros said a few days ago. And this information has sent me into a tailspin of fear. I can't seem to even see that statistically I still have more than a 50% chance of living at least ten more years! Article after depressing article discussed morbid prognoses, predictions of doom, and the scary and lethal places where the cancer could spread.

My father's side of the family is long-lived: One aunt lived to eighty-six, another to ninety-eight. Dad's brother died at eighty-nine, and Dad is still alive at ninety-one. But if I reach ninety, it would be a miracle. If I reach sixty-five, it'll be a huge celebration. In the past, I thought I'd still be young at sixty-five.

While sorting through the things Tad wanted me to toss, I started to blink back tears. The black thoughts that clouded my day engulfed me, and I went to my room, kneeled down, and cried into my bed. That was how Tad found me.

"Are you okay?" he asked.

I shook my head.

He consoled me. "I'll have to pray more for you," he said.

I would like my attitude to change completely and for me to use this time off from work productively instead of moping around, but fear tends to paralyze.

I've completely lost my appetite. I ate my raspberries for breakfast, but didn't feel like eating the rest of the day. Not even the sushi that Mama bought me. I was debilitated by my despondency.

When Alexandra heated some leftovers and served dinner along with the sushi, I did eat then, for company's sake. Tad made coffee and brought me cookies that Alexandra had baked this morning— dough wrapped around a cherry from our cherry compote. They were so good that I ate the last five.

I felt blessed that I have the support and encouragement of my family and feel sorry for women who go through cancer alone.

Sunday, 13 February 2011

The generous soul will be made rich…
– Proverbs 11:25 (NKJV)

The profuse generosity of friends, family, acquaintances, and even strangers has overwhelmed me. I received the traditional flowers. Chocolates. Chocolate-covered strawberries delivered to my door. A fruit basket with cheese and crackers and latte mix. Books. Cards.

Then there have been the meals: pizza and lasagna, casseroles and chicken, brownies and cakes, fruit and nuts.

This past Wednesday evening after the youth group meeting, an elderly woman in the church gave Jacob two bags of goodies for the family: chocolate chip cookies, white rice, prunes, walnuts, instant espresso, plus some red socks, a polka-dotted shirt, and a short-sleeved sweater. This woman, whom I barely know, seemed to have opened her cupboards and given us what she had. It was both touching and humorous, and indeed made me smile. A polka-dotted shirt?

Today after the church service, Maria, an elderly widow, gave Tad some homemade pierogies to take home. Pierogies are the traditional dough-wrapped mashed potatoes that I consider the single most popular Ukrainian food. Then another woman whom Tad doesn't even know approached him and gave him a bowl of her own home-made pierogies.

After church, we fried up some onions and had—what else?—pierogies for lunch.

Once again, I had stayed home from church. I slept in, trying to gain back some of my strength.

During the day, Josie called to tell me that she'd be with me on Wednesday morning as I face surgery once more. I need to take lessons from her on how to be a true friend. She ends each conversation with, "I love you." I wish those words came as naturally to me.

Although I started the day with an unpleasant dream that reflects my anxiety about the upcoming operation, I'm ending the day calm and back to my more usual self. "Nothing happens without God's will," I was reminded today. Indeed, God has my situation, my health, in His hands; why should I worry?

In the evening, I wrote a long e-mail[*] that I sent out as a mass mailing to family, friends, acquaintances, and co-workers to update them on my health.

Monday, 14 February 2011

Shout for joy, O heavens; rejoice, O earth; burst into song, O mountains! For the LORD comforts his people and will have compassion on his afflicted ones.
– Isaiah 49:13 (NIV)

Replies to my mass mailing started to come almost immediately. A barrage of responses filled my mailbox from all over the U.S. and from a missionary in Africa. However, it struck me that only one person, a doctor I had met on the mission trip to Senegal almost a decade ago, was bold enough to state that this cancer might kill me. Of course he

---

[*] See Appendix, Date: Mon, Feb 13

didn't express it this bluntly, but he talked about homecoming. No one else dared to broach that subject. Yet we'll all have to face it someday.

Date: Mon, Feb 14, 2011 3:47 pm

Kathryn,

Ana and I are concerned for you. You will be in our constant prayers. There is much to be thankful for, the early diagnosis, the fact that no nodes were involved and that there is a treatment for the cancer.

Many of God's people who have had great faith have not been spared trials, but their faith sustained them through their trials, or helped them die well, with the peace that passes all understanding.

Do not listen to the lies of Satan if he tells you God has abandoned you. He has not and will not, He will be faithful to His covenant. But that covenant promises not eternal mortal life, but eternal resurrection life. I am hopeful that you will have many more years with us and with your family, but if God calls you home, He will raise you up again one day and you will be whole. Trust Him, He loves you and tenderly cares for you and your children more than we could ever know.

You will be in our daily prayers.
In Christ,
Rich and Ana

At three o'clock, I had another pre-op appointment at Rochester General. Suite 350 was filled with people in wheelchairs and walkers, the elderly, and the crooked. Like during other appointments, I looked around and felt I didn't belong. *Why, look at me! Don't I look healthy?*
But am I?
Once again, I was weighed. My heart was listened to. My eyes and throat looked into. Then they wanted blood.
"But I just had blood drawn here three weeks ago!" I lamented.

The nurse thought they kept blood typing records for a month, so I sighed with relief. Then she came back.

"They keep the records only two weeks."

That really surprised me. Nurse Andrea said that they'll keep slides of my cancer forever, but my blood typing isn't on the computer after two weeks? My blood type isn't going to change!

So I had blood drawn by a phlebotomist who thought I was afraid of needles and had a low pain threshold. Her jab did cause searing pain.

"I had a mastectomy three weeks ago and only took Tylenol for the pain one day," I said in my defense.

I'm not a sissy when it comes to pain, but I still have a hematoma from my last blood draw a week ago. And the pain of the IV they couldn't start before surgery is indelibly written in my memory.

"We need an EKG," the nurse said after I had gotten dressed. So it was back down to a gown again.

The pre-op appointment that took one hour three weeks ago took two hours today. I am so tired of medical appointments, yet with chemotherapy still ahead of me, this is just the beginning.

Tuesday, 15 February 2011

You, Lord, hear the desire of the afflicted; you encourage them, and you listen to their cry...
– Psalm 10:17 (NIV)

The smell of the baking apple turnovers wafted through the heating ducts and into my bedroom. Alexandra was baking Tad his special request breakfast. I had set my alarm early so I could eat the freshly baked turnovers, but the warmth of my bed won out. I didn't get out of it for another hour, and by then the turnover was room temperature and Tad had left for work.

Praise God, praise God! My heart sang, the sunshine was even brighter, and hope blossomed in me when I left the OB/GYN office for the second time today. It was a cyst. Just a cyst on the ovarian follicle. Nothing to worry about.

The localized pain in my abdomen was not a figment of my imagination. Oh, praise the Lord it is not a tumor! It is not cancer!! It is just a cyst!

Chaya, the Physician's Assistant who had examined my breast lump, was the one who did my physical this morning. She's very chatty, asking me about myself, about Haiti, offering that she is an Orthodox Jew, and as such, has to have her hair covered. But it's covered with a wig that is so authentic-looking that I'd never have guessed that it's not her real hair. She suggested I could get a wig from her friend, the same place she gets hers.

I'm thinking I probably won't wear a wig at all. I've heard that some women wear theirs once or twice, then opt for less cumbersome headscarves or wraps.

Chaya found the exact location my dull pain was coming from when she pressed a spot and—ouch!

"Could be your ovary," she said. "You'll have to have an ultra-sound exam. I'll see if I can schedule one for you."

I had to come back later in the day for the ultrasound, which was conducted by a technician named Kathy. She was quite talkative as she did the ultrasound exam. Chaya had told her about my mission trip to Haiti; Kathy had been on four trips to East Africa—Tanzania—working with ultrasound.

I've been meeting some very sweet, personable medical people lately. I used to think that doctors were distant and impersonal, but that hasn't been my recent experience at all.

Wednesday, 16 February 2011

And we know that all things work together for good to those who love God.

– Romans 8:28 (NKJV)

The alarm went off in the darkness. Beep-beep. Beep-beep… I got out of bed and walked to the desk to turn it off.

Six o'clock. I had almost an hour to get ready, but there wasn't much to do: just shower and get dressed. I couldn't eat or drink anything, not since midnight. I woke Tad, then took a quick shower.

I put on the hospital shirt that my neighbor Geri, a nurse, lent me because it snaps in front and my gray zippered fleece shirt that also zips in front. I knew from the previous operation that after the surgery lifting arms and getting dressed would be a challenge.

I kissed Alexandra, who was up; Larissa, who was awake but in bed; and Jacob, who was asleep. Then Tad and I went to the VW Golf. It was 7 AM, and the morning rush hour had already started.

I spotted Josie's small frame and blond hair as soon as we walked into the lobby of Rochester General Hospital, and together the three of us followed my instruction card to the OB/GYN surgery unit— the same place where I was three weeks ago. I was even assigned the very same corner stall and chair where I had to change into the hospital-issued gown and socks.

Then came the IV ordeal.

I warned the nurse that the last time it had taken two painful tries to start my IV. Even Dr. Medeiros had heard about it. But the nurse, Nancy, said that she was good at IVs. I didn't argue.

There was a debate over which side to start the IV on. After having lymph nodes removed, the nurse said that I should never have an IV on the left side. But Dr. Medeiros stopped by and clarified that this was so only if all the auxiliary lymph nodes were removed. Mine were not; I had only four sentinel nodes removed. It was okay to start the IV on the left; the surgery was to insert the mediport on the right. An IV on the left would be more convenient.

I gripped Josie's hand. She crouched to my right. Tad stepped out. Nancy injected me with a small shot of a numbing agent then went for a vein in my left hand. My hand shrieked in pain as her needle moved back and forth seeking the vein.

"Breathe," Josie kept telling me. "Breathe, like when you were having a baby." Josie is an OB/GYN nurse.

"I don't remember how! It's been too long," I gasped.

"Then pant like a dog."

My face contorted with pain. I panted. Almost had it, almost had it... gone.

Next, Nancy tried for a vein in the crook of my left arm. Josie again urged me to breathe; I crushed her hand. Josie watched the needle; I shut my eyes and scrunched my face with the burning pain of the burrowing needle. I broke out in a sweat and rubbed my feet together, eager for the fiery pain to end.

Josie dialogued the process while I kept my eyes closed. "Looks good, looks good... oh, there's a bump. Nope. No good."

"I only get two tries," said the nurse. "I'll call the IV team."

"Why didn't they just call the IV team to start with?" I wondered out loud.

"You should have the doctor put that permanently in your record," suggested Josie.

Meanwhile, Dr. Patel, the anesthesiologist, came by and introduced himself. A different nurse stopped in and jabbed my left thigh with a shot of Heprin, a blood thinner meant to prevent blood clots.

It was a bit of a wait before a tough-looking woman approaching sixty showed up with a kit in her hand. She was thin with dyed brown hair and hands as cold as a winter morning. She kept apologizing for her icy hands as she felt my arms and looked for yet another vein.

"Not here or there," I pointed to two hematomas. "I just had blood drawn there two days ago and there a week ago. They still hurt."

The IV specialist found a yet uninjured vein in the crook of my right arm. Josie moved to my left side and held my left hand.

Tad paced just beyond the curtain that was drawn around me. Every once in a while he looked in and his facial expression asked, *Did they start the IV yet?* While he was pacing, I heard a woman's familiar voice greet him by name. It took a few seconds to place the voice.

"Hey, Karen! Come here so I can see you!" I urged when I recognized the voice. I knew Karen from our previous church. She and her husband had been in our small group Bible study for a short while.

Karen obliged and peeked into my compartment.

"You know, I've been praying for you," Karen continued. That was because I was on the Browncroft Community Church prayer list. "I'd also been praying about whom I'd see here. This is amazing that I'm next to you!"

I thought so, too. During the introductions and peeking around curtains and small talk, the IV specialist did what she specializes in: She started my IV. This time I didn't crush Josie's hand; this specialist was so good at her job that I barely felt a thing.

The multiple attempts at starting the IV held up the operation, but now I got escorted into the operating room, the same one as three weeks before. In my socks and tied gown, I walked down the hall as a woman wheeled my IV stand and I protected my right arm—the arm with that hard-earned IV in it.

I lay down on the operating table. The anesthesiologist greeted me. Dr. Medeiros was in the room. The operating lights, all off, stared down at me like a mob of oversized eyeballs. I trembled on the table. I tried to hold back my fear and wondered whether others could see my shaking. I closed my eyes.

The next thing I recall is voices chattering among each other. I knew by the sounds that I was still in the operating room. My eyes were heavy, but I said something to let them know I was awake.

My mind was still foggy as a swamp on an autumn morning when someone wheeled me to the recovery room—right next to Karen. In fact, we were the only two patients in that room.

A technician came to x-ray me, and until they saw the results, which showed where my mediport was installed, I could not drink anything. This was in case I had to go back into surgery. After the x-ray, I heard the results repeated over the phone: "In the superior venous cava." They were talking about my veins. I didn't want to know, didn't want to think about my vein being slit and a three-inch-long tube being slipped into it.

The operation took about an hour. Tad had thanked Josie for coming and walked her to her car, then spent the waiting time talking with Karen's husband.

When I was finally released, I was wheeled down to the waiting car in a wheelchair.

I don't know what I was thinking—that the mediport implant wasn't really surgery? I took a couple of Tylenol at 6 PM. Then two more at 10:30 PM. But my right arm, the incision site, and all through the upper right side were on fire with pain. By 11:30 PM, the Tylenol still hadn't kicked in, and the burning pain was worse—a six out of ten. (The medical personnel are perpetually asking for numbers.) The mastectomy pain never got above a four. I sat on my bed crying, not sure what to do. It felt like a live wire was stuck inside my body and I couldn't even move my right arm because of the inferno. I didn't know whether I was allowed to take Advil; I hadn't been allowed to after the mastectomy. And it was approaching midnight. What should I do?

Although I hate to bother anyone so late at night, I called nurse navigator Andrea's cell phone number. She didn't pick up, and I didn't leave a message. In a few minutes, Tad came to me with the cordless phone in hand. "It's Andrea. Tell her who you are." She had returned my hang-up call, but she didn't know whose call she was returning.

Her sympathetic ear released a flood of tears. I had a hard time forming my sentences.

"I didn't have a mediport installed, so I don't know about the pain," Andrea told me. "You should call Dr. Medeiros."

In the end, I regretted calling since Andrea herself roused Dr. Medeiros, the mother of two toddlers, who called me twice. First, she told me that I *could* take Advil, which I did. Then she called back with phone numbers of 24-hour pharmacies where I could fill a prescription for stronger painkillers.

I didn't want to take the prescription painkillers. Fortunately, after three Advil, I finally slept.

Thursday, 17 February 2011

Have mercy on me, LORD, for I am faint; heal me, LORD...
– Psalm 6:2 (NIV)

In the morning, my right arm movement was severely limited due to pain—something I hadn't expected. It seemed that my vein was protesting the insertion of this foreign body, this catheter, in the only way it knew how: with excruciating pain. I could not use my right arm, could not lift my hand to my mouth to brush my teeth, so I awkwardly brushed with my left hand.

Knowing that it's one of my favorite foods, my mother has been bringing me raspberries, which I've been eating for breakfast. Often I skip lunch because I eat breakfast so late. This afternoon, however, I heated a tiny piece of bread with some brie that Alexandra had bought me for Valentine's Day. Before I could take a bite, the doorbell rang.

"I'm sorry to eat in front of you," I said to Jeanne and Kathy after I invited them into the living room. "I need to eat something with my painkillers."

Jeanne was the one who had visited a couple of weeks ago and brought me the patchwork pillow. Kathy I hadn't seen in years. Both sang in the church choir with me years ago.

Kathy and Jeanne brought a gift for me—vitamins and supplements that boost the immune system. There is a theory circulating that the body always contains cancer cells, but if the immune system is strong, it will kill these cancer cells before they become a problem. I appreciated the gift and the thought behind it. Unfortunately, I am not allowed to take any vitamins or supplements during chemo-therapy.

Kathy shared a few words of wisdom from a friend undergoing chemotherapy: "When handed the sheet of possible side effects, she didn't read it. I don't mean to say that it's smart to be uninformed, but a lot of them will never occur, and it's anxiety provoking to read them."

Earlier in the day when Jeanne called me to confirm that she and Kathy were coming, she asked whether there was anything she could bring. People have been so generous—like the box of groceries that Adelia, an elderly grandmother, gave Tad last night at church—that I couldn't think of anything, and I didn't want to start making up some indulgent requests.

"How about bread?" Jeanne asked.

"Thanks, Jeanne, we have bread." Adelia had given us a lot of bread.

"Juice?" Jeanne persisted.

I sensed that she would continue until I agreed to something.

"Juice would be nice."

"What kind?"

"Oh, any kind," I said.

"How about orange?"

"Orange would be fine."

In the background I could hear her husband's voice, "Ask her if she'd like some chicken Florentine."

"I heard that," I told Jeanne. "I won't turn down John's cooking. He's a fabulous cook!" He made that incredible lasagna a few weeks ago.

In the early evening, John delivered the delectable chicken Florentine—chunks of chicken mixed with ricotta and other cheeses, spinach, a hint of basil, and a generous sprinkling of pecans and almonds over the entire dish. He also brought pesto bread, orange juice, olives and artichokes, a lemon meringue pie from Leo's Bakery, and an eight-pack of Ensure nutrition drinks for me. John even brought a plastic bag of chicken scraps for our cat Mishka. He and Jeanne are so thoughtful.

With temperatures in the fifties today, this mid-February day was a teaser of spring. Water slipped down thinning icicles from the roof, dripping and dribbling onto the uncovered front porch.

In the late afternoon, Alexandra, Larissa, and I took a walk up our street to Ellison Park, as we have done countless times since before they even learned to walk. In an infant carrier, baby backpack, umbrella stroller, double stroller, or on a baby bike seat, they got their fresh air, and Tad and I got our exercise.

The park entrance is just up the street past a dozen houses. This 447-acre park of steep hills and woodlands, ravines and bogs, picnic areas and playgrounds has been the destination of innumerable Sunday hikes, evening walks, and moonlit strolls. Like the woods behind our house, which connect to the parkland, Ellison Park is home to deer, raccoons, possums, skunks, coyotes, foxes, and an assortment of birds, including wild turkeys and the impressive pileated woodpecker.

Many a Sunday we picnicked in Ellison Park on the summit of "our hill," as the kids called it, eating bologna sandwiches on a certain fallen log. We fished here, netted polliwogs, listened to spring peepers, caught fireflies. The kids learned to cross-country ski in this park. We sledded here in the wintertime and hiked in the springtime when entire wooded hills are adorned with white trillium blossoms. This park features prominently in our family memories and traditions.

Whenever we enter the park, we walk by a replica of Fort Schuyler. The original fort, which was really more a trading post than a military establishment, was a log structure built by the British in 1721. Its purpose was to encourage trade with the Seneca Indians and compete with the French for furs. A few decades later, a settler tried to establish a city in this area. A historical marker further up our road states:

CITY OF TRYON
First white settlement west of Canandaigua
founded 1797, abandoned 1818.
John Lusk was the first settler 1789.

Tryon was founded near the banks of Irondequoit Creek, a shallow river not more than forty feet wide, which meanders through Ellison Park in lazy curves. But Irondequoit Creek wasn't always shallow or small. It's hard to imagine this river as it's described in historical documents: deep and wide, with a shipbuilding yard not far from where we live. Forty-ton schooners, which must have made an impressive sight with their tall masts and many sails, floated from this area to Lake Ontario, and then down the Saint Lawrence River all the way to the Atlantic Ocean.

Not a trace is left of the shipbuilding yard. Nor is the river now deep enough to accommodate more than a canoe. Yet in 1669, French explorer Sieur de La Salle sailed his ship up the Saint Lawrence River to Lake Ontario, then up Irondequoit Bay and Irondequoit Creek, and docked at the Indian Landing—a name later given to this spot by white settlers—to meet representatives of the Seneca Indians on whose ancient lands we now live. His trip put Irondequoit Bay on almost every map of the New World until the 1760s.

And to think that when we casually stroll through the park, we walk where La Salle's feet have trod.

In 1687, Marquis Denonville, the Governor of New France (Canada), marched across this region, right through what are now the parklands, and destroyed Seneca villages and their food supplies as punishment for their ties to the British and interference with the French fur trade. Beaver pelts were so popular that beavers were completely wiped out from this area. When I was born, there wasn't a single beaver in all of Monroe County. Thankfully, beavers have now made a comeback.

Our area was also the site of conflicts during the French and Indian War (1754 –1763). And in the 1770s, Butler's Rangers, a military force loyal to King George, are said to have camped in the hills of the current Ellison Park—the hills where we ate our bologna sandwiches. John Butler and his Rangers were Loyalists who fought against the independence of the American colonies.

When I first moved to Landing Road, which is named after the Indian Landing, I had no idea of the historical significance of this spot of land. The Indian Landing was the beginning of an old canoe portage route used by the indigenous Indians of the Iroquois confederacy. They carried their boats and goods seven miles from this point to the mouth of Red Creek on the Genesee River, which connected with waterways all the way to the Mississippi. It was the only overland portion of an all-water route from the Atlantic Ocean to the Gulf of Mexico. Waterways were the only way to transport goods back then; there were no railroads or roadways, and before white man came, Indians had no horses.

The town of Tryon sprouted because of its proximity to this trade route. The growing town boasted a shoe factory, warehouse, blacksmith shop, and a school. A flourmill used the power of Irondequoit Creek to turn its millstones, and a flourishing shipyard launched large ocean-going ships on Irondequoit Creek—although it's hard to believe that anything larger than a canoe could float down this rivulet. Irondequoit Creek was a quarter mile wide in some places back then, but human development of the lands upstream created geological changes that clogged Irondequoit Creek with silt and sand. What now remains is a trickle of its former self.

Today Alexandra, Larissa, and I walked our typical circuit—past the fort, along Irondequoit Creek, across two wooden bridges, and back home, a distance of about a mile. I stepped gingerly along the icy asphalt service road. With each step, that mediport on my right side jabbed me. Every few hours, I continue to take Advil or Tylenol, but I still feel the port. Will I feel it under my skin the entire year that it's in?

The LORD will keep you from all harm—He will watch over your life...
                                             – Psalm 121:7 (NIV)

Tonight the winds are ferocious, tossing the trees, roaring like a speeding train above our home. The springlike temperatures are being forced out, replaced by winter weather: Temperatures in the twenties and snow are predicted for tomorrow.

This evening I reread the discharge instructions, then asked Tad to remove the large gauze pad taped over my mediport site. Part of the gauze was stuck on with a few drops of blood that had soaked through, but when I took a shower, it came off. Now I have a clear bandage taped over the incision site.

I had visitors again today, and several phone calls. Cheri came from thirty miles away and filled our home with her exuberance and her shopping bags, so many of them that it looked like she was bringing in the week's groceries. Indeed, she brought enough food for both lunch and supper, and then some. But what brought a smile to my face was the red rose she brought me.

I sit at home a lot lately, except for doctor appointments, and I don't mind. I have no desire to go anywhere.

Monday, 21 February 2011

I will be glad and rejoice in your love, for You saw my affliction and knew the anguish of my soul.
                                             – Psalm 31:7 (NIV)

The site of the mediport surgery is itchy today. Perhaps that means it's healing. The lump under my skin from the mediport protrudes about a quarter of an inch and is almost as big around as a tea candle. I can now move my right arm without any problem, but across the top of my left hand I still have an impressive and colorful hematoma from the first failed attempt at starting the IV. The top of the hand hurts if I so much as wash my hands or put on hand cream.

I got an e-mail from a co-worker this evening, a graphic designer in our group. She wrote because someone forwarded her my note about cancer—the mass mailing. She responded that she'd had lymphoma, which was aggressive and hard to diagnose. But she made it through—all black and blue at times, and having to give herself injections, but she's back at work. I didn't know that she had cancer. Thinking back, though, I recall her being without some hair—was it that no eyebrow look? But I don't recall anyone talking about it. I see they are talking about me, however, since I've been so open about my cancer, but that was how I wanted it. How else would I have gotten this designer to share her experience? It saddened me that she lives by herself and had to go through her chemotherapy alone.

Tuesday, 22 February 2011

The LORD will watch over your coming and going both now and forevermore.
— Psalm 121:8 (NIV)

When I came to the kitchen after 9 AM, Larissa was finishing making some fresh carrot juice with the new juicer that I had asked Tad to purchase. We've been getting so many groceries, so many fruits and vegetables, but I have little appetite. I have been craving the fruit in the basket I received. However, eating the fruit would be too filling, but if we could make that fruit into juice, I could get all the vitamins by drinking it.

Larissa made me carrot juice twice during the day. It is *so* delicious! Perhaps I like it so much because I'm more of a vegetable lover than a fruit lover. I lived in large cities during the first decade of my life. We didn't have a vegetable garden. But I remember at the cottage in Canada where we spent our summer vacations, someone had planted a row of carrots, one of my favorite vegetables, especially in my childhood when the range of vegetables available in grocery stores was far more limited than today. I was so excited by the pinkie-length carrots that were as thin as a pencil, but sweet, so much sweeter than any store-bought carrot that I'd had. My love of carrots grew stronger that day, and I can't pull a carrot out of the ground without remembering that childhood experience.

I went to Thelma's today. It hadn't been on my list of things to do, but I'd worked my way down my list—write thank you notes, reply to e-mail, pay MasterCard, deposit rolled coins in the credit union. Oh, how I didn't want to leave the house. But the credit union isn't far, and I needed to get the coins off my desk. So half an hour before closing time, I drove to the credit union.

The day had turned sunny—below 20° F, but sunny—and my mood was good, so after depositing the rolled coins, I decided to check out Thelma's, a place I'd driven by innumerable times, but never saw. It's a house converted into a store that sells breast prostheses, specialized bras, wigs and head coverings, and surely much more. I'm not ready for the bra and prosthesis (my chest still hurts; it's less than a month since surgery), but I wanted to buy a headscarf or turban, something that covers my entire head so I'll be ready for the day when my hair falls out.

I spotted Thelma's as I was driving past it and had to turn the car around. A small white banner with a red rose and the word "Thelma's" hung from a two-story gray clapboard house. The building had no window display, no hint of what's inside. I pulled up the driveway and parked in the small lot behind the house. If not for the banner on the porch, this house would have looked like the neighboring buildings.

I felt timid as I walked up the few steps to the back door, which was obviously the entrance to the store. A little sign by the door instructed customers to ring the doorbell. I pressed the button hesitantly as I looked around the parking lot. Was the door locked for privacy? Security?

A woman came to the door and escorted me inside past stacks of boxes and displays of lingerie. It almost felt like a secret society. Or was I imagining things? Was I the one who was guarded and unsure?

"My name is Jill. How can I help you?" said the saleswoman as she escorted me into a room with a chair, dressing rooms, and displays of their products.

"It's my first time here," I stated, then launched into my story of breast cancer and impending chemotherapy and hair loss. I told her that I wanted to buy a scarf.

"Not everyone's hair falls out," Jill said gently.

But I had made up my mind. I wanted that special kind of head covering that isn't just a rectangular piece of material, but covers the entire bald scalp, has an elastic in the back, and long strips of material for tying the head covering in creative ways—a knot on the side, a bow in the back. They're designed to cover the entire head and not slip off. I was looking for one that was brown like my hair. A solid chocolate brown.

"Whenever we get them, we sell out right away," said Jill. But when we rummaged through catalogs, we saw that they are no longer available. That didn't make sense: They always sell out of them quickly, yet the manufacturer discontinued that color.

I settled on a black scarf with white and brown speckles. It was $22.

Monday, 28 February 2011

Know also that wisdom is like honey for you: If you find it, there is a future hope for you, and your hope will not be cut off.

– Proverbs 24:14 (NIV)

The last few days, we've been away. In fact, I postponed my first chemotherapy session until tomorrow so that I could take this trip. From all I've heard, I would not be well enough to travel after the chemo, and it was crucial that I go.

Alexandra, a senior in high school this year, is going to finish her homeschooling in a few months. But in the last year or so, she's been adamant that she will not go to college. My talented, thorough, and hard-working A+ student does not want to go to college. I've struggled with this. I know that not everyone has to go to college. I realize that some people get jobs without a college degree or get married and are contented stay-at-home moms. People do live successful, fulfilled lives without a degree. And loving the Lord and serving Him with your life is far more important than an education. Yet for Alexandra to stay at home and wait for Mr. Right to show up, or for her to work as a cashier or—frankly, I don't know as what—as she waits for her prince would be a colossal waste of her time and talents. The reason for her to go to college isn't necessarily to get a degree and then work in that field for the rest of her life, but just get the education and, well, be educated. Smarter. Learn about something she loves. Or work in a field she enjoys before she meets someone and marries. Or fall back on that degree if something happens to her husband and she needs to support her family. Or what if she never marries? Wouldn't it be beneficial to have an education so that she could get a job more easily?

But Alexandra is stubborn. No college.

So what will she do after June?

While in Haiti, Scott Long had told us about a division of Mission E4 called the Global Training Center, an internship program for young adults that he started in rural Massachusetts where he lives. The program is designed to help young people discover the call of God on their lives. During the one-year program, interns work on the eight-acre campus as well as take twenty-four courses ranging from Apologetics (learning how to defend one's faith), Spiritual Gifts, and Interpreting Scripture to practical courses, such as Marriage and Family, and Life Skills (balancing a checkbook or changing oil in a car). Perhaps Alexandra would consider this program? The only way to find out was to visit the campus, so that's what we did this past weekend.

I wish I could say that Alexandra was thrilled with the program and campus, and she decided to sign up immediately. But that isn't the case.

We left home on Thursday. "We" includes our family of five plus fourteen-year-old Igor, who is often at our house, and sixteen-year-old Ruth, who was in Haiti with us. The van was full.

Hubbardston, Massachusetts is 350 miles from home—a six-hour drive. The first five hours are by the New York State Thruway and Massachusetts Turnpike; the last hour is on the winding rural roads of central Massachusetts, through hilly forests and past fences of piled rocks, by frozen marshes and beaver ponds, through charming villages and past historical stone churches.

We lost our way as the road wound through a parking lot and changed names three times, but eventually the van slowly, tentatively crunched up the snowy drive to Mission E4. We entered what looked like a rustic resort built on a large pond in an evergreen forest. The smell of wood smoke and pine greeted us, as did Scott. He showed Tad and me to our room and the kids to their respective boys' and girls' dorm rooms.

During the weekend, Jacob, Alexandra, Larissa, Ruth, and Igor followed the schedule of the current interns—four young men and three women. They took part in morning exercises at 5:30 AM, attended the classes that Scott taught, and helped fold newsletters and stuff envelopes in the office. We ate with the interns and staff, socialized with them, laughed with them, prayed with them.

The place felt welcoming, like a friend's embrace. The main building and the place we spent the most time is the pool house—a large building with skylights and picture windows and an empty blue pool that hasn't been filled with water in years. The building has a lofty arched ceiling with wooden beams, and wood paneling lines the walls. Built-in planters contain a variety of tropical houseplants. The high windows overlook a picturesque beaver pond with a tiny island that's graced by a single evergreen. The pool house contains the kitchen, a single classroom, and a comfy room with overstuffed couches.

I felt the love and Christian fellowship of the young interns, several of whom I'd met in January on the Haiti trip. These interns knew about my breast cancer, and I talked with some of them about my surgery and upcoming chemo.

"My mother also had breast cancer," shared one of the interns.

We chatted about his mother's cancer, my cancer, and though I can't remember how we got on the topic, my talk with the plastic surgeon and concern about a breast implant possibly popping.

"That happened to my mom!" he exclaimed. "She was using one of those large exercise balls and someone bounced it toward her. The ball hit her in the chest and—pop!"

So I wasn't crazy to consider this possibility.

There was something about the Global Training Center—the Christian camaraderie, Scott's solid teaching, the hush of the wilderness setting—that drew me in. If I were eighteen, I'd want to come here. But Alexandra just doesn't seem interested. She said that she would pray about it. She wants to do what God has planned for her, and she isn't sure what that is.

I hope He reveals it to her before September.

March

Sometimes struggles are exactly what we need in our life. If we were allowed to go through life without any obstacles, it would cripple us. We would not be as strong as we could have been.

I asked for strength, and I was given difficulties to make me strong.
I asked for wisdom, and I was given problems to solve.
I asked for prosperity, and I was given a brain and brawn to work.
I asked for courage, and I was given obstacles to overcome.
I asked for love, and I was given troubled people to help.
I received nothing I wanted, but everything I needed.

– from a forwarded e-mail (author unknown)

It's a week since my first chemotherapy session. The side effects of the chemo felt like severe jetlag and the first trimester of pregnancy combined, then intensified to the point where I was nonfunctional. Nothing I read or heard prepared me for the severity of it.

But now, a week later, my mind has finally cleared enough for me to write another mass e-mail:

Sent: Tue, Mar 8, 2011 5:52 pm
Subject: update after my first chemo session

Last week I went through my first chemotherapy session.

For those who have been through it, I'm sure that you feel my pain. For those who haven't, let me fill you in.

First of all, because of the number of chemotherapy sessions that I will be having over the next year, I had a mediport installed on February 16. The mediport, which was surgically inserted under the skin on my chest, has a catheter that connects the port into a large vein. The port, which now looks like a button-like bump under my skin, has a septum into which chemotherapy drugs can be injected and through which blood can be drawn. If I did not have the port installed, all chemo treatments would have to be through IVs, and starting an IV on me is no easy feat. I have rolling veins, and they do not like to be punctured!

The mediport surgery was unexpectedly painful, but the site has healed well. I now have a fairly large bump under my skin, which still burns at times, but most of the time I no longer feel it.

The day before the first chemotherapy session, my neighbor, who is a stylist, cut my hair to chin length, and I donated my shorn hair to Locks of Love.

I am quite thankful that I did not know what to expect with the chemotherapy.

The session itself was, odd as it sounds, kind of fun. My 17-year-old daughter Alexandra insisted on going to the session with me and sitting with me the entire four hours that it took. I had initially intended to bring a book and read, to block out my surroundings and lose myself in another world. In fact, my nature is to tough things out and to do it alone. I knew that I needed a ride to and from the chemo session, but I had planned to ask for rides to drop me off and pick me up and to spend the time there by myself. But I would have missed out.

What made that chemotherapy session so special was Alexandra's insistence on being there with me. She was there to take care of me instead of the other way around. Although she brought schoolwork to do, I spotted a sign announcing that Scrabble game boards were available and invited her to play a game with me while I waited for bag after bag of drugs to be dripped into my veins through the mediport.

First came the "pre-drugs"—Benedryl and steroids and anti-nausea drugs—meant to curb side effects of the chemotherapy drugs. The Benedryl almost put me to sleep, so I mentioned to the nurse that I was sorry I didn't bring my coffee.

 "I can bring you some coffee," she volunteered. She also brought cookies to nibble on. In fact, all during the four hours I was there, someone came around regularly to offer beverages, lunch, and snacks. The staff was very friendly and helpful, and I had no reactions to the drugs I was given. Since the nurse had to read me a long list of potential side effects in advance (hives, burning sensation, breathing difficulties…), I almost expected to feel something bad.

The Scrabble game was close, but Alexandra won. I came home, delighted to have survived the first session so well. I felt fine all of March 1. All those drugs to prevent side effects that day worked.

Then came March 2. The nausea started to kick in. Despite taking anti-nausea pills, the unsettled stomach persisted. As I had been warned, all I wanted were comfort foods—oatmeal, mashed potatoes, and chicken noodle soup. My usual desire for salads and spicy food vanished. A dull headache settled in. And I had no energy. I lay on the couch in a stupor for three days asking my daughters to fetch me the anti-nausea pills or something to eat to settle my stomach. I couldn't concentrate on anything, couldn't read, and just lay there in a haze existing hour to hour, trying to sleep and wishing the time to go by.

On the third day, I called my nurse. "How long am I going to feel like this? If this is how I'm going to feel all through the chemotherapy for four-and-a-half months, I give up. It's just not worth it. I'll take my chances with the cancer."

"No, no! Don't say that!" the nurse responded. "It'll get better. You won't always feel like this. The worst of it is three or four days after chemo sessions, then the side effects won't be as bad. You won't feel normal, but you won't feel quite like you're feeling. Take it one day at a time; don't think of the entire four-and-a-half months. You'll get through this. In another couple of days, you won't feel quite so awful."

She was right. The worst of it was over in four days, but the lethargy, the dull headache, the underlying nausea, and the metallic taste in my mouth remain. Every day I seem to have a new surprise: One day it's constipation. Another, it's diarrhea. Or my kidneys hurt. Or that burning in my stomach… The list goes on. But I haven't lost my hair yet.

Although I now have a perpetual feeling of malaise, all the cards, calls, visits, meals, fruit baskets, e-mails, letters, flowers, groceries, and gifts have cheered and overwhelmed me. Truly, I am stunned by the generosity and thoughtfulness of so very many. I know I've become an introvert, dedicating myself mainly to my family and to work, and not reaching out nearly as much as I should or would like. I'm moved to tears by everyone's response. I believe that I'm going through this for a reason, and surely one reason is to see just what treasures the people in my life are. How sad that I had to get this sick to make time to see my friends and stop focusing on my little world. How delightful that friends from faraway cities have called. How wonderful to know that friends and strangers and entire churches are praying for my healing as far away as Africa! How reassuring that my fate is in God's hands. *Behold, I have refined you, but not as silver; I have tested you in the furnace of affliction* (Isaiah 48:10). I do believe that God will use this time of illness and trial in my life to refine me and change my focus.

Thank you for the blessing that you have been in my life.
Kathryn

Wednesday, 9 March 2011

I consider that our present sufferings are not worth comparing with the glory that will be revealed in us.
— Romans 8:18 (NIV)

Date: Wed, Mar 9, 2011 2:46 am

Dear Kathryn,

I was stunned to read your e-mail. I am putting you on my prayer chain and will keep you in my personal prayer daily.

My own struggles suddenly seem quite small compared to this challenge you are now facing. Thank you for opening yourself to allow us to understand what you are going through. It is a humbling read and reminds us to be continually grateful for every good thing.

God's Blessings to you and your family.

With love and respect,
Alexsandra

I am so thankful people are praying for me during these gray days.

Monday, 14 March 2011

Humble yourselves, therefore, under God's mighty hand, that He may lift you up in due time.
— 1 Peter 5:6 (NIV)

No one explained to me beforehand that getting Neupogen shots every other day was a part of the chemotherapy treatment plan. Neupogen is not a chemotherapy drug; it's a manmade protein that stimulates the bone marrow to produce white blood cells, the body's primary defense against infections and illness. Chemotherapy kills white blood cells; Neupogen gets the bone marrow to build up their numbers again.

I got my first Neupogen shot at the cancer center two days after my chemotherapy session. I was asked over and over my name and date of birth, and read all the possible side effects, which include pain in my bones, hives, a ruptured spleen, and death. Surely they were reading me this to prevent future lawsuits, not because the symptoms were common.

After the injection, I had to sit for thirty minutes to see whether I had a negative side effect. But I just wanted to sleep. The chemo side effects were intense then, and I felt so very tired and ill. No one had told me that I shouldn't drive myself to the center. In hindsight, I should not have been driving. I was barely functioning. My brain was as cloudy as the sky overhead.

Before I left the cancer center, the oncology nurse brought me a prescription for five pre-filled syringes of Neupogen that I was to inject into my arm every other day. The nurse had suggested that my husband give me the shots, but I thought that for the sake of our marriage (I'm sure Tad didn't want to jab me any more than I wanted to be jabbed), it was better to ask one of my nurse friends to do the honors. They might be a little more graceful at it. Josie and Phyllis, and Geri (a neighbor five houses up the street from me) have decades of experience in nursing.

The next day as Tad was leaving the house for an appointment, I gave him the Neupogen prescription and asked him to fill it. He stopped by our usual pharmacy in a grocery store, but they didn't have any Neupogen. They suggested a hospital pharmacy. Tad drove to Rochester General Hospital where I'd had my surgery. He called me on his cell phone from the hospital pharmacy.

"Are you aware that this prescription costs three thousand dollars to fill?" he asked, incredulous.

"What?! How much?" I thought he might have gotten wrong information. "At Lipson Cancer Center, they said it would be about fifty dollars. Maybe you need to show the pharmacist our prescription insurance card."

Tad didn't have the card with him, so I dictated the information over the phone. Even after that discount, it still cost two hundred and seventy dollars—a little over fifty dollars *per shot.* Tad paid for the prescription out of our Health Savings Account, but couldn't hold back telling me his opinion of me going through the chemo.

Phyllis, who lives close by, gave me my next Neupogen injection on Saturday morning. We talked for a while as her hands warmed up. When she gave the shot, I hardly felt it. It was less painful than at the clinic. Phyllis also prayed with me before she left, which is also better than at the clinic. When someone prays for me, I feel loved.

Over the weekend, I started doing the math. One Neupogen shot every other day. The chemo sessions are three weeks apart. That's ten shots between sessions, so I'd be out over five hundred dollars between each of my six scheduled chemo sessions. During the course of my treatment, the cost for the Neupogen shots would approach $3000. Prescription costs don't go toward the $7200 out-of-pocket costs that our family has to pay before the health insurance company covers one hundred percent of the medical costs. So I got an idea: I called the cancer clinic and asked whether I could come to the clinic every other day to have a nurse administer the shot. The cost of doctor visits or clinic sessions goes on my health insurance card, which means it would go toward that $7200 out-of-pocket limit, and then the insurance company would cover any costs exceeding that amount. The clinic agreed.

Today, another dismal wintry day, I went for another Neupogen shot at the clinic. I, who hate taking ibuprofen for a headache, am getting pumped full of drugs like never before.

Tuesday, 15 March 2011

Cast all your anxiety on Him because He cares for you.
– 1 Peter 5:7 (NIV)

Every winter seems to be a patience test: the frigid temperatures, my incessantly cold hands and feet, the perpetually overcast skies, the monotone landscape, the snow and slush. But this winter has been especially hard with relentless snow, harsh weather, and illness.

Tad had pneumonia. Jacob had a couple of colds. Tad got sick again with a bad cold and cough. Larissa had a fever. And I got cancer—not that cancer has anything to do with the weather.

Because I've been home, I've been noticing the weather more than most years. At Kodak, my cubicle is so far from a window that I don't know what's happening outside during the day. But here at home, that's not the case. Every room has a window, and the grayness outside seems to press in on me inside.

With the snow and cold, I retreat inside—inside the house, inside myself. And with the surgery and then chemo, I haven't wanted to leave the house at all. I once loved to travel the world; now I don't even want to venture to the store or nearby park. I'd rather curl up by the fire with a book. Or nap.

Today, however, the sun came out! I could feel my inner being thawing, glowing with the joy of that warm sunlight. The snow cover that has been on the ground since early December has finally melted, leaving only occasional white patches on soggy brown lawns and sooty piles by the road, piles so black that they are unrecognizable as snow—blackened by car exhaust and by the salt that's accumulated in the roadside drifts all through the winter.

The gold crocuses in the garden on the front hill are about to burst into bloom! Spring, the season of renewal and rebirth, is almost here. The sunshine and flowers have lifted my spirits.

It's a week before my next chemo, and I'm feeling much stronger. I'd even say I'm feeling well. I could work this week, but medical leave is set up in a way that I can't just say today I work, tomorrow I need to chill on the couch because I'm nauseous from the drugs. So I'm doing what the doctor recommended: I'm avoiding stress and not working at all.

In the early evening, I took a walk with Alexandra and Larissa. Even though my lazy body would prefer to remain on the couch, I pushed myself out the door.

We headed first to Heberle Stables, which is at the bottom of our road. Our family has been walking through the stable property ever since the children were toddlers. Bill, the owner and father of four, has always been welcoming, telling us to come anytime and allowing us free access to the stables to pet the horses and feed them carrots. For a few summers, the girls even took horseback riding lessons there.

Because Bear, the Australian Cattle Dog, barked and barked at us as we approached, Bill pulled away from the work he was doing on some machinery to scold him. Bill, who has salt-and-pepper hair and a bit of a paunch, was the school bus driver for all of my children when they attended Indian Landing Elementary School, which is named, of course, for the Indian Landing in the park. Bill is the fourth-generation owner of Heberle Stables. When his great-grandfather owned all the land in this neighborhood, it was a farm and an orchard. During the Depression, however, Bill's grandfather sold part of the property to a developer. Our house was built during that time.

Bill is talkative and friendly, and I enjoy listening to his stories. He told us that due to all the snow, he gave more sleigh rides on Valentine's Day weekend last month (sixteen on Saturday, eighteen on Sunday) than he did all of last winter. I recalled the winter a few years ago when he gave us a free sleigh ride with my mother. One evening during a snow flurry, Alexandra, Larissa, and I had cross-country skied through Ellison Park and were exiting the park through the stable property when we heard sleigh bells. Bill was hitching up a pair of horses to give a sleigh ride.

"My mother always talks about the jingle of sleigh bells that she heard in her childhood," I had told Bill that evening as we watched the horses through the peacefully falling snowflakes. "Back in Ukraine when she was growing up, horse-drawn sleighs were the main form of transportation in the wintertime."

"Where is your mom now?" Bill had asked.

"Here in Rochester, about one mile from here."

"Bring her over and I'll give her a sleigh ride!"

The children and I brought my mother to the stables a few weeks later and climbed into the sleigh with her. Bill took us clip-clopping and jingling through the park, then refused to accept any money for the ride.

This evening Bill shared that his eldest son Jake will be going to Cornell University this coming summer to learn to be a farrier (one who shoes horses). I shared that I have cancer. While we were talking, Bill's wife came out, and then a parent of one of their riding students (the husband of a friend) joined our group. Larissa went to groom a horse while we adults chatted. It was nice to leave the house after all.

Because we stood talking so long, we didn't have time for a long walk before dark. Alexandra, Larissa, and I just strolled through the stable grounds into the park, then up past the fort and back home.

As we walked down our street, Canada geese honked overhead, winging their way back north. And on a neighbor's lawn hopped a robin, its orange breast feathers a contrast to the muted scenery.

Back at home, I walked to our backyard shed to visit another promise of spring—the baby goat born to Mala, the younger of our goats. It was so cold yesterday when the kid was born that Larissa had to blow dry him so that he didn't catch cold.

Wednesday, 16 March 2011

...but those who hope in the LORD will renew their strength. They will soar on wings like eagles; they will run and not grow weary, they will walk and not be faint.
– Isaiah 40:31 (NIV)

The sun was smothered by clouds again today, but the gloominess of the skies was enlivened by the presence of more Canada geese—skeins of them flying in V formations, honking, encouraging one another with their calls. That's why they honk, I read: to encourage each other.

Their honking stirs up some inexplicable longing in me. As they wing northward, calling, calling, it's as if they're speaking directly to my soul. I can hear them inside the house, and I rush out to search the skies for them. And when I see the geese, a spark of hope lights in my heart. Spring! Spring is not far off!

Although the temperature once again did not rise above the forties and the skies were gray, the birdsongs I heard today lifted my spirits. Starlings filled a nearby tree and chattered—and I realized just how silent birds are in the wintertime. *Springtime*, they must be singing. *Springtime is near.*

My patience test this winter has consisted of more than just persevering through the winter weather. It's been patience through my surgery and recovery. Patience through the chemotherapy and its aftermath. Patience as I wait for God to reveal something to me through this experience. I feel like I'm on an emotional treadmill: not going anywhere but exhausted in the process.

However, both my girls have expressed how delighted they are that I'm home with them. Finally, a stay-at-home mom.

Since the outdoor temperatures bounce above and below freezing on a daily basis, it's maple syrup time. In years past, I hadn't paid much attention to this particular time of year, but two years ago during a March walk through our backyard woods, I noticed metal buckets hanging from taps in numerous trees. I was surprised and mystified. Who had tapped the trees? We had lived here many years but had never seen such a sight.

A few days later, we met a middle-aged man walking through the woods. He introduced himself as DJ and said that he'd just moved into a house far up over the crest of the hill behind our home. He owns six acres of the forest that we consider "ours"—ours not by deed, but simply because our family has spent so much time in these woods, and until DJ moved in, no one else seemed to do so.

DJ was delighted to meet us in his woods. His blue eyes danced as he told us about taps and sap and syrup, and how to identify sugar maples by their bark; about his teaching job; about moving to this area to be closer to his daughter.

"You're welcome to take some sap and cook it down for yourselves," DJ offered. "I don't collect until the weekend. Help yourselves to the sap from Monday through Wednesday."

So we did. I hadn't ever cooked down maple sap before, but that winter the kids and I collected many buckets of the slightly sweet liquid and set it boiling in pots on the wood-burning stove and on the four burners of the kitchen stove. All the windows in the house were fogged with steam. We kept adding sap to the pots, boiling off more water, creating more steam. The walls of the house wept with condensation until Tad insisted that we cook no more than two pots at a time. No wonder maple syrup is made in special sugar shacks or outdoors.

That had been my first year of homeschooling all three of my children, and I was pleased that they could have such a practical lesson. Jacob, however, did not appear interested in collecting the sap, and initially wouldn't even go outside to see the taps.

It takes forty parts of sap to make one part of maple syrup. The girls and I collected about twenty gallons of maple sap, and over a period of forty-eight hours, we boiled it down into less than one pot of sweet, golden liquid. That's when Jacob took interest in the project. The children took turns hovering over the pot with a candy thermometer in hand. When the temperature reaches seven degrees above the boiling point of water, the syrup is done and the pot has to be removed from the heat.

Jacob was the one holding the candy thermometer when the temperature of the boiling liquid reached 219°F. He lifted the pot from the stove and did a little dance, carefully holding "his" pot of maple syrup. While all of us like maple syrup, Jacob *loves* maple syrup. Pure maple syrup, not the imitation kind. And he had just helped make two whole quarts of it. He was hooked.

Every spring since then, Jacob has been our main maple syrup maker. He avidly collects maple sap and cooks it down, hovering over the pots protectively. Today he has a large cooler and a five-gallon water jug full of sap. It's Wednesday, and he won't be able to collect any more sap until Monday.

Thursday, 17 March 2011

Create in me a clean heart, O God, and renew a steadfast spirit within me.
> – Psalm 51:10 (NKJV)

It started. When I washed my hair this morning, the shower floor was littered with hair. And when I combed and brushed my hair, large brown wads came out on the comb and brush. For some reason, hair in the shower and on the floor turns my stomach. I think of it as dirty. Disgusting.

I also found my hair on the kitchen table as I ate. After just that one chemo session, I'm losing my hair. That headscarf will come in handy after all.

Friday, 18 March 2011

No man has power over the wind to contain it so no one has power over the day of his death.
> – Ecclesiastes 8:8 (NIV)

In the evening before family devotions, I spent a little time lying down next to Tad in the bedroom, thinking, talking. He mentioned that Oksana, a young woman in our church, had recited a poem during the Sunday evening service last week. Someone had tried to videotape this, but since our church doesn't allow videotaping unless one has special permission, the videotaping had been banned.

"The guy who wanted to videotape her said that it would be a memento—a memory—of Oksana since she has cancer."

I popped up from my reclined position.

"Oksana has cancer again? Since when? When did you hear that?"

Oksana had had ovarian cancer, but the cancer had been in remission for almost a year. And now it's back? She is only in her thirties!

"I learned about a month ago," said Tad.

"Why didn't you tell me?"

"I didn't think it would build you up. You were going through your own issues and surgery."

Tad certainly had a point.

Tad mentioned that Oksana had lost a lot of weight and that the cancer has metastasized everywhere. It's stage four. The doctors offer no hope.

I let this sink in.

I recently saw Rachel, the retired widow next door, for the first time since December. When she asked how things were, I told her about my cancer. Rachel lives alone and doesn't seem to socialize much. She's turned down invitations to dinner at our house. Once when I had searched for her home phone number online, I found a link to her Facebook page instead and some mention of Farmville. How sad when grown people spend their days playing games on the computer instead of having real-life interactions.

Would Oksana spend her days playing Farmville?

We're to live each day as if it's our last—and it might be. I have known far too many people who died suddenly, both in accidents and of natural causes: My brother Alex in a golf cart accident at forty-nine. Co-worker David of a massive heart attack at forty-one. My cousin of a stroke at sixty-four. I used to think that I'd like to die quickly, suddenly, and suffer no pain. But I've changed my mind—not that I have any control over my fate. Dying of an illness like cancer gives the person time to put affairs in order and say good-bye to loved ones. Oh, Oksana…

Saturday, 19 March 2011

And whatever you do, do it heartily, as to the Lord and not to men…

– Colossians 3:23 (NKJV)

Last night I finally finished creating an online album of photos that I took in January of Haitian street scenes. Today I sent out a link to this album to those on the trip who had given me their e-mail addresses.

I received several thank you's, but the note below touched and embarrassed me. I try to live a godly life, but I feel I don't do anything special. In fact, in my heart I feel that I constantly fall short. I imagine it was our family singing in Haiti and my cancer update e-mails that triggered this response:

Date: Sat, Mar 19, 2011 10:39 pm
Subject: Bless you Kathryn!

My Dearest Kathryn,

I am in awe and humbled by your willingness to share all that you are going through. I am blessed to be exposed to your faith. Your graciousness astounds me. If I ever grow up, I would like to be like you! You and your family had a profound impact on me, and while I am sure you all hear that often, it doesn't happen to me often. I take great comfort knowing we will see each other again in Heaven and hope that God sees His way clear to letting us meet again while we are here on earth.

As for your pictures, wow! What a reception they had here in Sheboygan. I walked into Kim's kitchen this afternoon and said "Has anyone checked their e-mail?" and everyone said "Oh Yeah!" They all knew exactly what I was talking about and we agreed we have to get together again so that we can enjoy the next batch. So you are celebrated all over the city here!

Take care my friend!
Love, Katie

The lesson here, I believe, is that I should continue using my gifts and talents, even if it seems I'm not doing anything big or special, and God will direct my efforts. God can use us in ways that we can't even imagine, weaving our small efforts into some greater masterpiece that only He can see.

Sunday, 20 March 2011
First day of spring

*For the L*ORD *your God is living among you. He is a mighty savior. He will take delight in you with gladness. With His love, He will calm all your fears. He will rejoice over you with joyful songs.*

– Zephaniah 3:17 (NLT)

I went to church this morning for the first time in many weeks. Tad gave the announcements. He also thanked people for their prayers for me, their presents and food, and said that I would be undergoing chemotherapy for one year.

The pastor prayed fervently for Oksana and me at the end of the service. Afterward, people surrounded me, greeted me, asked me how I was feeling, inquired about the chemo.

Eventually I worked my way to the back of the church. I found Oksana outside talking with another single woman. I joined their huddle. After a while the topic turned to chemotherapy.

"What drugs are you getting?" Oksana asked me. She was well versed in cancer terminology.

I had finally memorized the names of the drugs. "Taxotere, Carboplatin, and Herceptin," I said.

"Oh, I had the Carboplatin, but I couldn't take it. It made me throw up," said Oksana.

We also discovered that we both go to the same oncologist.

Oksana mentioned that she's turning down the Neupogen shots that stimulate bone marrow to produce white blood cells. I didn't ask whether it was due to side effects or cost.

"My white blood cell count is always low even when I'm healthy," I told Oksana, "so I do get the Neupogen."

Oksana is single. She lives with her younger sister and brother, both of whom are also single. That poor woman is working and taking only two days off after chemo. My heart aches for her.

Naturally the TV was on when we entered my parents' home this evening. My dad was planted in his easy chair, eyes on the ever-changing images. The volume was set a little too loud so that he could hear it.

Inwardly I groaned.

"Zenon! ZENON! Turn it off!" my mother gestured to get Dad's attention as I walked into the living room with the rest of the family.

Dad fumbled clumsily with the remote and muted the TV. Cars exploded noiselessly. Scantily dressed women sashayed across the set without a sound. I averted my eyes. It was only a commercial, but is Dad completely oblivious to violence and sex? He'd never have allowed us to watch that kind of stuff when we were growing up. *The Three Stooges* was considered too violent for us to watch back then.

"Zenon! Turn it off!" my mother repeated. "We have guests!"

Like a young boy who doesn't want to put away his toy, Dad reluctantly turned off the TV.

How sad that the father who had the wisdom to limit his children's TV watching to only half an hour per weekday and one hour on weekends now watches television from the time he wakes up until he goes to bed. He turns off the TV only while checking news on his laptop or taking a nap. Or when Mama makes him turn it off when we visit. Dad knows more about current events and the politics in Ukraine than he does about the lives of his grandchildren. He sneers at us because we got rid of our television years ago. How, he has asked us more than once, are we going to know what's going on in the world? I find this an odd question from a man who grew up in a Ukrainian village not only without a television, but also without running water or a flushing toilet.

I always listen to the news during my commute to and from work. However, these days while on medical leave, I hear or read only snippets of the news. But how is that going to hinder my life? Every day the news changes. Every day it's more murders, shootings, kidnappings, political intrigues, natural disasters. Dad has been a news junkie for decades, yet how has that helped him? If he'd invested just some of the time that he spends watching the news in people, he could have had an influence in other people's lives. Instead, the TV has influenced him.

Watching is addictive and keeps you from doing something productive. It keeps you in isolation. Instead of seeking the companionship of others, you simply turn on the television, and with that as background noise, they don't feel so alone. The TV shapes what you think and how you view the world. It's changing the worldview of an entire society, and not for the better.

"Television is basically teaching, whether you want it to or not," said *Muppets* creator Jim Henson. These days it's teaching that resolving problems with violence is normal, that extramarital relationships are normal, that gay marriage is normal. And Dad just absorbs it all.

Even with the TV off, it's hard to have a conversation with my parents. Mama repeats things that she's already told us dozens of times and doesn't give others much opportunity to speak. Dad interrupts whenever he feels like it since he can't hear our conversation anyway. Mama gets annoyed with his deafness. He gets annoyed that we don't give him one hundred percent of our attention. It would be almost comical if it weren't so distressing. I feel myself getting more and more tense inside until finally it's time to leave.

Monday, 21 March 2011

Keep me safe, O God, for in You I take refuge.
– Psalm 16:1 (NIV)

We've run out of firewood. Although it's spring on the calendar, more freezing temperatures are forecast through the rest of this week. We'll have to switch to heating with natural gas.

Today I was scheduled to have my second chemo session. Josie picked me up at 8:45 AM and took me to the Lipson Cancer Center. I was looking forward to a long chat with Josie, though not to the chemo session itself.

First I had blood drawn through the mediport. No more hunting for veins to draw blood. Then I met with Laura, the nurse practitioner.

I mentioned the nausea I had felt after my first chemo session.

"You shouldn't have to feel that way," she said and prescribed another anti-nausea drug to go with the one I was taking, a steroid that might cause insomnia. I shouldn't take it after 3 PM.

My reaction to the first chemo session was typical: insomnia the first night due to steroids, constipation for a couple of days, then diarrhea. What Laura described was exactly what I had experienced.

As we talked, Laura brought up on the monitor the test results from this morning's blood draw.

"Oh, I should have looked sooner! We can't do chemo today. Your white blood cell counts are too low," she informed me.

I looked at Josie, who was sitting next to me. She had rearranged her work schedule for nothing.

The nurse practitioner decided that all I would get today is Herceptin, which they will give me intravenously, and a Neupogen shot. I'll continue to get a Neupogen shot every other day this week, then return Monday. If my white blood cell count improves, then I can have the next chemo session.

"I don't think I can take off next Monday," Josie said, disappointed.

At this rate, I'll run out of medical leave before the chemo is done. I left a message for my boss Betty: How do I start the process of going back to work part-time?

Wednesday, 23 March 2011

Blessed is the one who perseveres under trial because, having stood the test, that person will receive the crown of life that the Lord has promised to those who love Him.
– James 1:12 (NIV)

"I feel I have to go through this. I'm not sure why. It may not even be for medical reasons. Maybe to understand what other cancer patients go through. Maybe to humble me. I don't tell you all my symptoms—my aches and pains—because I've felt that you don't approve of me going through chemotherapy," I told Tad.

So I keep my pains to myself—my bones that ache, almost burn, from the Neupogen. But I've had rheumatism since early childhood, and the pain is similar.

I'm stiffer, have less stamina, and get short of breath. I don't know why. Probably something to do with red blood cells. Our house is built into a hill, and walking up the sixteen steps to the front door leaves me winded.

My skin is sensitive, cracking, blisters forming easily. After I had raked my gardens last week to gather up dead leaves and spruce needles, I had a blister on my right hand, and I hadn't raked all that much.

My hair is falling out. Every morning I wet my hand and gather the hair from my pillow—a trick Oksana taught me. When I brush my hair, there's as much hair in the brush as there used to be dog's fur when our Belgian Sheepdog was shedding. My hair is disturbingly thin—it's obvious that I have lost a lot. I wear a bandana to keep my hair from littering the house wherever I go. There is hair all over the bathroom. I constantly have to clean it up.

Though it's late March, today was like a winter's day in December—or February. Four inches of snow fell, covering every limb in white, making Landing Road a white slide. And cars did slide. The radio reported numerous accidents. Temperatures will remain below freezing for the next several days, staying in the twenties for the next two.

It's been such a long, ferociously cold and snowy winter. Everyone wants spring. Hard to believe that last week I was raking and spreading compost on flowerbeds, and that the lilies of the valley had poked their little spikes above the ground. Now it's all buried under snow.

At least with this cold weather, the maple sap season is extended.

Friday, 25 March 2011

Praise be to the God and Father of our Lord Jesus Christ, the Father of compassion and the God of all comfort, who comforts us in all our troubles, so that we can comfort those in any trouble with the comfort we ourselves receive from God.

– 2 Corinthians 1:3-4 (NIV)

Late this evening, I found an e-mail from a former co-worker who retired less than a year ago. "Cancer has stricken another" was the subject line, but I had to read the note to understand that the cancer she was referring to had struck her! She has breast cancer. Perhaps she wrote because of my precedent of announcing cancer, not hiding it. Would she have written to her former co-workers, including me, if I had not?

I felt from the beginning—from my diagnosis—that I'm to give moral support to others going through breast cancer. Just how, I'm not sure, but I knew that I had to write back.

Sent: Fri, March 25, 2011 10:21:47 PM
Subject: Re: Cancer has stricken another

Welcome to the club. It's not a club any of us would want to join, not a club we'd volunteer to sign up for. But you'll find some amazing women who are part of this sorority, and some amazing blessings will come your way through this. It's a difficult path, but you've been chosen for a reason.

Mother, daughters, sister, friends
The circle of caring never ends

This was on the door through which I entered to get my MRI. After my mastectomy, I had a follow-up appointment with another surgeon (mine was sick with the flu, but I needed to have my drainage tubes removed), and that surgeon was a breast cancer survivor. She gave me a big hug. I knew I was in good hands; she'd been there.

It will be tough and scary, but I'll tell you what my doc said: DON'T look up info on the Internet about cancer. DO NOT DO IT. I'm not telling you to be ignorant. If you want information, get it from the doctor or a book, but if you start going on the Internet, you will read things that you should not read. It will not build you up, and it's very importat to stay positive. The majority of people get through breast cancer and live a full lifespan. But there was that one weekend that I will probably remember all my life when I started to look at too much information when I had my cancer's pathology report back. I disobeyed my doc and looked up some information about that on the Internet. Big no good. I knew from the report my cancer was quite aggressive, but I spent the entire weekend in a "woe is me" mood after what I read, terrified I'd be one of those who did NOT make it. I cried and moped and didn't eat; I was convinced for those two days that I wouldn't make it.

Then I snapped out of it and stopped reading about cancer altogether. The most important thing in licking cancer is your attitude. The doctors and nurses have all said that. You can think of this as a bump in the road; I look at it as my adventure for 2011. Last year I went to the Panama jungle and Haiti; this year I get the adventure of mastectomy and chemotherapy and meeting many wonderful nurses and doctors I wouldn't have met otherwise!! And I get to be part of this elite club and speak a language others don't know. You bond immediately with other cancer patients and survivors. Instant sisterhood.

My cancer was also in the left breast. I was first told lumpectomy and radiation; I ended up with mastectomy and chemotherapy.

I would love to talk with you. Don't call early in the morning; I've been exhausted and tend to sleep in.

God bless you. I'm here for you!!
Kathryn

Monday, 28 March 2011

When I am in distress, I call to You, because You answer me.
— Psalm 86:7 (NIV)

It's almost April, but temperatures are *still* in the thirties. The high today was 35°F. How can I say "depressing" with a positive spin?

At the cancer clinic this morning, I noticed a basket with several knitted skullcaps on the table in a tiny waiting area.

"You can take one or two," said an assistant. "A woman knits them and brings them in here for patients to take." I chose a light green one.

Today I had my second chemo. I heard that with each chemo treatment, the side effects are more intense, more debilitating. Like the first time, the drugs I received to curb the side effects worked well enough for me to still be functional this evening. While Alexandra and Tad drove to a farm to buy some bales of hay for our Nubian goats, I felt compelled to write my next update to those on my distribution list, which gets a little longer each time:

Date: Monday, March 28, 2011, 7:29 PM
Subject: second chemo

I've received several phone calls asking about my second chemotherapy session, so if you've been wondering but afraid to ask, here's where I stand:

I had my second chemotherapy session in a four-hour session this morning—the session when the nurses give me intravenous doses of various drugs meant to search and destroy any vagrant cancer cells that may have escaped into my body, preventing relapses of cancer in the future. These are the sessions that make me feel ill afterward. (FYI, for some patients, chemotherapy sessions are given to make existing cancer tumors smaller or to destroy them, but in my case, we don't know whether I have any microscopic level tumors; the chemo is a preventative. Even with the preventative, some cancers metastasize and return, but I'm praying and doing everything possible so that my cancer never comes back.)

This second session was actually scheduled for the Monday one week ago, but my white blood cell count was way too low last week. Chemotherapy drugs kill not only cancer cells, but other fast-growing cells, too, such as the white blood cells that protect your body from diseases. The immune system is weakened by chemotherapy and needs time to recover; that's why my chemo sessions are scheduled three weeks apart. Some bodies recover on their own; others need help. Already I'd gotten a series of five Neupogen shots, shots to help stimulate my bone marrow to produce white blood cells. But this wasn't enough, possibly due to the lupus I've had. Last Monday I was told that I would have to wait another week to allow my body to recover, and I would also have to return to the clinic every other day for more Neupogen shots, shots that not only make bone marrow produce white blood cells but also make the bones ache while they're doing so. But I've had rheumatism since I was a toddler, so bone pain is nothing new to me.

I know I'm in for a rough few days ahead after this chemo session today, but now I know what to expect: insomnia the first night due to an overload of intravenous steroids (enough that Olympic drug testers would ban me from sports events); nausea; headache; stomachaches; craving for bland carbohydrate foods the first few days; constipation due to steroids, followed by diarrhea; metallic taste in my mouth; inability to think clearly; exhaustion. But now I also know that the worst of it will pass within a week. Still, although I feel fine at the moment because I've been pumped full of drugs that prevent side effects (and work well the first day), I don't look forward to tomorrow or the next few days. The anti-nausea pills are on my night table.

Last week I had a nurse friend take me to my aborted chemo session. I was disappointed that after she changed her work schedule to accommodate my chemotherapy, we didn't get as much time together as we'd hoped. This week my driver and companion was a woman I hadn't seen in about two years. She was laid off from Kodak and had the time to spend with me, even though she did have to rearrange her commitments a bit. The four hours we spent together chatting weren't enough! How interesting and wonderful to have these long chunks of time to interact with friends. Although I have only four more four-hour sessions of chemotherapy left (but many, many one-hour sessions of biotherapy), I have a lot more than four friends whom I'd like to invite for these one-on-one visits.

During the chemotherapy session today, a volunteer from the American Cancer Society interrupted our chat to offer various services. Kathy was an interesting woman who spent much longer in our "cubicle" than she had intended, sharing her own experiences with cancer—three bouts of it! What she shared really hit home.

"Cancer is the best thing that ever happened to me," Kathy said. "People say that they're sick of the snow; I think snow is beautiful. People honk at me as they drive by; it doesn't bother me at all. Every day I get up and say, 'Thank you, God, I have another day.'"

A friend sent me Lance Armstrong's autobiographical account of his cancer, which was a Stage 4, having spread from his testicle to his lungs and brain. His chemotherapy was far more aggressive and torturous than mine. Yet he wrote these words: "I was beginning to see cancer as something I was given for the good of others." It changed his focus. It changed his life.

I have already had the opportunity to reach out to others who have cancer. It's an instant sisterhood, an automatic bond. No one who hasn't been through it can possibly comprehend. If they had a close friend or relative go through cancer, they can come close to understanding, but they have not walked in our shoes.

I began losing my hair by the brushful a week ago. Combing my hair is like brushing a shedding dog. It comes out in clumps and wads. Hair drifts to the bathroom floor. It stays behind on my pillow. I've been wearing a bandana to keep it from falling in my food, on the table, on the couch, and everywhere I go. I knew it was coming, but living through it is distressing nonetheless. My husband Tad ran his fingers through my hair and got a mass of hair. It's time for that buzz cut tonight. Another cancer survivor said that baldness is easier to deal with than the hair perpetually coming out. So experiencing baldness will be my next adventure. (I still have my eyebrows and eyelashes for now.)

As I lie in bed some mornings and listen to the news on the radio, I think of how my little trauma pales in comparison to the devastation experienced in Japan after the tsunami and ordeal that the Libyan population is facing in its civil war.

So the next few days will be hard, but not that hard when it's put in perspective.

Blessings,
Kathryn

After Tad returned with the hay, I told him it was time. As we stood in front of the bathroom mirror, Tad demonstrated to Jacob how much of my hair comes out when he runs his hand through my hair. Then put these strands on his own thinning hair with a grin.

He got out the hair clippers and shaved my head. I didn't watch. I cringed, though it didn't hurt. It just felt funny. My head feels spiky now, not smooth. It was kind of a nice bonding moment to have Tad shave my head.

I decided to track how I felt each day after this chemotherapy.

CHEMO SESSION #2

Day 1 (Monday 3/28): Got infusion. Feeling a little odd, but generally well. A headache started in the evening. Took no meds.

Day 2 (Tuesday 3/29): Bottom of feet tender when I walk. Foggy headed, tired, general malaise, stomach sometimes burns, sometimes hurts.

Day 3 (Wednesday 3/30): Went to cancer center for Neulasta shot; Jacob drove me. Alexandra is sick—fever, coughing. I retired to the basement to stay away from her germs. When upstairs, I wear a mask. Feet still hurt, double nausea pills, headache, dullness. Tad drilling the house for insulation.

Day 4 (Thursday 3/31): Felt like the living dead. Just lay in bed in the basement in a stupor all day while Tad drilled and with a rented machine blew in insulation. Headache, total dullness, inability to concentrate—can hardly hold a conversation. Can't read. Dying for mama's beef noodle soup, but don't have any. Drinking Ensure that John and Jeanne bought me and taking anti-nausea pills. The worst day. Tad even asked if all was right between me and God. I'm near the point where I wouldn't care if I died. Can't see into the future.

Day 5 (Friday 4/1): Got out of bed. Had half a cup of coffee and half a crepe. Still dull, somewhat nauseous, but made myself go through the day on my feet.

April

But my eyes are fixed on you, Sovereign Lord; in You I take refuge—do not give me over to death.

– Psalm 141:8 (NIV)

The worst of round two chemo is behind me. How can I say "horrible" tactfully? Day four was so bad that I just lay in bed in the basement sweating all day, sweating, knowing I smelled bad and needed a shower, but I just couldn't do it. I felt way too weak, too ill, and too nauseous to get up.

Around four this morning, I awoke and knew that the most difficult part of the horrific nausea and dullness of mind was behind me. The day was still hard, but the horror was over. As I lay in bed, my mediport site ached and burned, and my kidneys hurt—or was it the bone marrow near the kidneys producing white blood cells and aching, as a nurse suggested? I don't know, but for three hours, until seven, I lay in bed, unable to sleep any more (after all, I'd spent two days in bed), yet unable to get up. I drifted off to sleep again, but when Larissa came downstairs and offered me a crepe for breakfast, I didn't hesitate to get out of bed.

"And make me some coffee in that smallest espresso maker—one and a half scoops of coffee," I requested.

I put on my headscarf to cover my baldness, then walked into the kitchen. I felt like I was reentering life. I could only drink half the cup of coffee, but between getting up and eating normal food, I felt so much better. Being able to fit into the family routine also made me feel better. But people who live alone don't have a routine. And if they're alone, who fixes them breakfast and encourages them to get up? My heart aches for those who are alone through chemo. How much more likely they are to get discouraged and give up. Even now, giving up is appealing; going through this personal hell four more times is daunting and seems almost insurmountable.

I did petty things today: caught up on e-mail, printed out Larissa's homeschool schedule for next week, and almost finished getting together information for our income tax return. I fed the goats and rabbits some extra lettuce. I filled the day with little stuff, pushing myself so I did not lie down. Tad spackled all those holes that he had drilled for the insulation. The timing of this home renovation project—drilling holes in the walls and blowing in insulation for the exterior walls—was unfortunate since the drilling thundered through the walls of the house, and all I could do was lie isolated in the basement bedroom in a chemo fog and listen to the nerve-grating sound. But the house will be warmer now.

Last night I called Mama and told her how much I craved her beef noodle soup. She cooked some and brought it over today. I had some of this comfort food for lunch, the rest for dinner. And before bed, I cooked a soft-boiled egg and heated some of Mama's borscht that she had also brought over. I'm already planning tomorrow's meals: sushi for Jacob's birthday dinner.

If I'm thinking about food, I'm getting better.

This evening we loaded little Shishkabob, the baby goat born two-and-a-half weeks ago, into the van. Then all five of us piled in. We took Shishkabob to Mr. Hall, a goat breeder, to get the little buck disbudded.

"How nice to have the whole family go!" Tad commented as he drove the fifteen miles to Mr. Hall's farm. Tad and I both realize that it's rare to have teens come along on such family outings. Jacob will be nineteen tomorrow. I thank God that our family is close, that our children like to spend time with us and are not embarrassed to be seen with their parents, like many teens. Like I was at their age.

Although my immune system is weak and I shouldn't go to public places where I could pick up illness, a farm has fresh air and open spaces, and the only person on Mr. Hall's farm is Mr. Hall himself. He's an old bachelor, a retired schoolteacher with thirty-two hens, half an army of timid barn cats, and more goats than I can count. He gives away the eggs, he doesn't milk his goats, and he doesn't eat goat meat. "I can eat other meat," he explained in his deep drone. "If we had a Depression, well, then I could learn to eat goat." His animals are his hobby and his companions.

Disbudding involves burning the horn buds of a young kid so that the horns don't grow. This is done with an electric disbudding iron. Tad held little Shishkabob as Mr. Hall expertly applied the red-hot iron to the horn buds for several seconds. Shishkabob cried with pain, but not as loudly as I had expected. I could smell burnt hair for quite a while afterward.

It was good to get out, but now I'm in my dungeon. It didn't always feel like this. I like this room that Tad finished in the basement with its curved wall of stones gathered from our yard, a bathroom just a few steps away, and an ancient wood-burning stove to keep the room toasty. But in my illness, this room has become my place of isolation, the place I go to when I'm really ill. And now, even with the fire glowing in the stove down here, it doesn't feel like the friendly place it used to be.

This evening when I took off my headscarf, I noticed a red rash on my scalp. The last time I had chemo, I had hair. A few pimples appeared in my hairline, and even one on my forehead, but now there are more bumps than I can count. At least they are only on my head and not visible when I'm wearing the scarf. Admittedly, I'm worn out by this "adventure." I'm particularly not fond of being bald. My head is often cold! How do bald men manage without skullcaps or headscarves to keep their heads warm?

Sunday, 3 April 2011

The LORD is good, a refuge in times of trouble. He cares for those who trust in Him...

– Nahum 1:7 (NIV)

This morning Tad took our kids and Igor about an hour's drive from Rochester to visit a conservative Mennonite church where women wear flowery cape dresses and traditional white caps as head coverings, and the men come to church in nearly identical white shirts and plain black suits with no lapels. The congregation sings hymns in lovely four-part harmony, and the sermons are often delivered in a quiet monotone. After the service, the people flock around you to greet you. They're very friendly. I know; I've been there several times.

Because my immune system is still compromised, I stayed home. Some alone time is welcome. But by mid-afternoon when my family was not yet back, I began to feel abandoned. I knew that members of this Mennonite church typically invite visitors home for lunch. I understood that I shouldn't expect my family to just hang out with me, constantly entertaining me because I can't be with crowds. They have their own lives. Even so, I wanted them home. I'm in a funk. I wanted the emotional support that their presence provides.

In the late afternoon after the family returned, we went on a long walk with Igor through Ellison Park. My head has not completely cleared and it's hard to concentrate, and the bottom of my feet still hurt when I walk, but I was happy to get out of the house. Fresh air and nature always revive my soul. Even though the temperatures are still in the low forties, the spring peepers are singing noisily in the wetlands of the park. These tiny frogs just over an inch long chirp like a flock of birds, filling the park with their chorus of hope and joy. Even though it's cold and the days have been impossibly dreary, their spring ballad lifted my spirit as if it had grown wings. Like a dry sponge, I wanted to drink in this song, this promise of warmer and better days to come.

Tuesday, 5 April 2011

Every good gift and every perfect gift is from above…
– James 1:17 (NIV)

The Kodak nurse called today to set up next Monday as the date that I'll return to work for twenty hours per week. I will do the work from home, however, because of my weakened immune system.

Tue, Apr 5, 2011 8:12 am
Subject: hope today is a good one for you

Kathryn,
I have been thinking of you every day since I got your e-mail that you are undergoing chemotherapy.

I was remembering when we worked side by side at Kodak on the OLQR*. How we'd shop in the basement recycle store to take a break from the computer screens. And you told me stories of how you fell in love with Tad and had a family together…and would drive to Buffalo for "interrogations" so he could become an American citizen. We would lunch in that gorgeous Kodak restaurant and you would show me dozens of pictures of places in Europe, places I would never see except through your beautiful photographs and stories attached to the image. At the heart of all your life stories was your love of family, acceptance of others, and joy in your doings. My

---

* On-Line Quick Reference

heart aches to think that you are feeling so awful right now and I would like to help you feel better but I'm unsure of what to do. So I am writing to you, melting away the lost years, offering my hand once again in friendship. I smile to think that, knowing you, you are journaling this experience and someday your writing will give hope and strength to another person going through what you now are.

Hope you're feeling better today.
Mary Ellen

Reconnecting with old friends: that's been one of the biggest blessings of this illness. What a gift that Mary Ellen took the time to write to me. But how on earth did she know that I'm journaling?

Wednesday, 6 April 2011

Save me, O God, for the waters have come up to my neck. I sink in the miry depths, where there is no foothold. I have come into the deep waters, the floods engulf me. I am worn out calling for help; my throat is parched.

– Psalm 69: 1-3 (NIV)

The weather continues to be unspringlike, and the days an uninterrupted gray tunnel with no opening in sight. Day after drab day I think, maybe tomorrow will be better. But day after dismal day continues to be cold, overcast, and gloomy. The grayness is seeping into me. Try as I do to keep it from affecting my mood, it has permeated me, penetrated right into my very core. I don't have a gray view of my illness; everything seems gray right now.

It's Wednesday, which means it's time for another Herceptin treatment. I drove alone to the cancer center through the cold and cheerless landscape. It takes about one hour to get the Herceptin intravenously, so I didn't bring along any friends, except a book.

Even as I sat in the chair with the IV connected to the mediport in my chest and the window of my little cubicle behind me, I could sense the grayness outside. I could see it on the nurses' expressions; I could feel it in the mood of the workers.

I removed my headscarf to show Nurse Bonnie my angry red rash. She informed me that it's folliculitis—inflammation of the hair follicles caused by chemotherapy—and suggested hydrocortisone cream for the rash. I hope it helps.

There are days when God seems so close that it feels as if my spirit were singing and I can hardly contain it, like when I was in Haiti. Or when He speaks to me through Scripture and through people, and it feels like He singled me out especially to talk directly to me. Other times He seems so distant, so unreachable, and I feel a void. I know the change is in me, yet I can't seem to keep the fire burning steadily. These days I'm treading water, waiting, though I don't know for what. The waiting is hard. Treading water is exhausting. I don't know what's ahead, but God does. I just have to trust that He is doing what's best for me.

Thursday, 7 April 2011

Now faith is confidence in what we hope for and assurance about what we do not see.
                                             – Hebrews 11:1 (NIV)

God changed the face of the sky this morning, and the sun smiled down on the soggy, winter-dulled earth. The crocuses beamed back—yellow and purple and white—like gifts from God Himself. Sprinkled across my backyard, they cheered my soul.

In the morning, Betty, my boss, called to discuss going back to work twenty hours per week. Two weeks ago she said that I probably wouldn't go back to writing inkjet printer manuals; a contractor had been filling in for me, and a new hire is also working on those. With time off every few weeks for chemo, I wouldn't be able to deliver to deadlines, Betty suspected. I liked working on inkjet printer manuals and could write them quickly; I was sorry that I would have to leave that project. Today, however, Betty asked whether I could start writing today and work through the weekend: they have two BUGs (Basic User Guides) for printers due today, but no one has started them. Could I finish them by Monday?

I pulled new files today, applied templates, and tried to remember how things are done. It's so nice to not to have a foggy brain and to be able to concentrate once again. It's also nice to be needed.

The sun, the flowers, and work—they completely turned around the funk I've been in since my days of isolation in the cold, dark basement in a post-chemo stupor.

Wednesday, 13 April 2011

As you do not know the path of the wind, or how the body is formed in a mother's womb, so you cannot understand the work of God, the Maker of all things.

– Ecclesiastes 11:5 (NIV)

I've seen photos of bald women who went through chemotherapy, their heads beautiful, even elegant, in their startling bareness. Mine is not such a head. A few persistent bristly gray hairs remain, so I look a bit like Yoda from *Star Wars*. And the rash on my head still persists. It's red with many large yellowheads that look like pimples all over my head. The bumps are tender to the touch. They hurt and burn and sometimes itch. Occasionally I bump my head, and a pustule pops and bleeds. When I lay my head on the pillow at night, the contact points are painful. In the morning, the pillow is peppered with spots of yellow (from pus) and red (from blood), plus tiny hairs just a fraction of an inch long with a bulb-like end. The brown stubble on my head is falling out; the gray hairs seem to be hanging on.

This afternoon when I had my Herceptin treatment, Laura, the nurse practitioner, looked at my head.

"It's folliculitis," she declared, just as the nurse had a week ago. "About ten percent of patients who lose their hair get it. Looks like it's gotten infected."

The hydrocortisone had not helped. She prescribed an oral antibiotic.

Before I went to the clinic, Tad had taken out a three-pound can of coffee that he bought for four dollars at a local discount grocery store.

"It's the wrong grind," I had said. "It's too coarse. That's for drip coffee makers. You can't make it in our espresso maker. It'll be like brown water—way too weak. Besides, you get what you pay for." Coffee that's barely over a dollar a pound can't be very good.

Perhaps to prove to himself that the coffee wasn't that bad, Tad made the largest espresso maker full of it. When I came home from the clinic, Tad wasn't feeling well.

"I poisoned myself with coffee," he moaned. He had drunk two cups of it. Normally that wouldn't be a problem, but Tad had been on a long fast, drinking only juices and eating nothing for almost a month. The caffeine, which he hadn't had at all during the last month, hit him hard. He went to bed and tried sleeping it off, but still felt too ill to go to youth group. This wasn't like him. He never misses youth group (except once when I had my mastectomy). He must really feel ill.

For a day or two after chemo, I can't drink coffee. Nor could I drink it when I was pregnant. That makes me wonder just how bad caffeine is for you if the body rejects coffee when it's not well. After such a long fast, Tad's body was ultra sensitive to anything even slightly toxic.

Jacob drove Alexandra and Larissa to youth group this evening, and Tad asked his assistant to lead tonight's activities.

"Sit with me a while," Tad said as he lay in bed after the children had left.

I sat on the bed.

"Would you like me to read you a story?" I joked. But after we had chatted a while, I said, "Wait! I have a story I want to read to you!" It was a story that I had just given to Larissa as a homeschool assignment. She had to write an essay based on this story.

"Elias," by Leo Tolstoy, is a tale of a wealthy man who loses all his riches and ends up as a servant for his neighbor. And that's when he finds true happiness—time with his wife, time to pray, always food to eat, and not a care. The irony is that people seek wealth as a means to happiness, but instead of owning it, the wealth ends up owning them, often causing more distress than happiness.

I spent nearly all evening with Tad. Mostly we talked. It was an unexpected blessing to have one-on-one time like that while the children were out of the house. Spending undivided time with another person is one of the greatest gifts; it's the best way to make a person feel special. That's why I like the late-night walks that Tad and I often take together: we have each other's undivided attention.

We discussed that spending time with our children is *the* most important thing that we can do as parents. Time equals love. If you say that you love someone yet spend little time with him, what does that really say? So we make time for our children—time to talk and time to listen. Backrubs, one-on-one walks, sitting on the edge of the bed at night and listening, family discussion in the living room—these are investments in our offspring and into our own future. If our children see that we care for them, they will care for us. Unconditional love for our children mirrors the unconditional love that God has for us. Love is an action word; it must be lived out. When you spend time together, you show the child, "You are important."

Perhaps that's why I like people coming over to visit me.

Thursday, 14 April 2011

…a sweet friendship refreshes the soul.
– Proverbs 27:9 (MSG)

At one time I had a whole forest of get-well cards on a shelf in the living room. But now the rate of cards and calls and visits has fallen. In some ways, I wish they would stop altogether and I could go back to normal life. But I'm still on half-time medical disability and going through chemo every three weeks, so pretending things are normal is make-believe.

I spent the day trying to catch up on thank-you notes. I'm so behind on the thank-you notes that I almost wish people would not send me stuff anymore. CDs, books, a heart-shaped pillow that a breast cancer survivor I had never met made for me when she saw my name on the church prayer bulletin—all are tokens of love. Today another gift came in the mail—organic papaya moisturizing cream from Meredith in Australia. How odd that twenty years since our chance meeting on the streets of Madrid, we still stay in touch. I truly value the friendships of the many people who have touched my life, sometimes only briefly—a few hours spent together in Madrid, a week together in Haiti. I have almost an obsession for staying in touch. Each person is a precious treasure in my life. Their notes and gifts touch me more than they will ever know.

Saturday, 16 April 2011

The LORD is good to those whose hope is in Him, to the one who seeks Him…
— Lamentations 3:25 (NIV)

After I heard of an art contest for homeschooled students a few weeks ago, I added, "Work on horse drawing for the Regional Art Show" to Larissa's daily school schedule. She had one week to complete the pencil drawing. It would be a good experience for Larissa to compare her artwork with that of peers. She's a gifted artist, but because she's completely self-taught, I don't think that she realizes how well she draws.

Children's gifts are evident from a very young age. Jacob took things apart from the time he was six months old and pushing himself around in a walker. He broke the dishwasher, dining room light switch, car's glove box, and countless other things as he tried to figure out how they work. His preschool teacher said that he's the only pupil she had in twenty years of teaching who took apart a marker to see what makes the colors. It's no surprise that he's studying mechanics.

He'll perpetually be taking things apart.

Alexandra could belt out a tune in perfect pitch before she could even talk. Alexandra plays piano and violin, and has a lovely singing voice. I knew she would be a musician like Tad.

Larissa was fascinated with drawing since she was a toddler. She loved to sit with my mama and watch her grandma draw animals. Now she draws them herself. Larissa's "Windswept Horse" is stunning. When I e-mailed a scanned copy of it to my sister-in-law, who's an artist, Tamara replied, "She has some serious talent."

My hope was that Larissa would get an honorable mention at the art show, which would boost her confidence and encourage her to draw more. But when the honorable mentions were announced at the show today, Larissa's drawing wasn't among them. Next, the judge announced third place. Then second place. Still she didn't place. I knew her piece was good enough to get some award, so I got my camera ready.

"First place goes to... 'Windswept Horse' by Larissa Danylko."

I wish I could have seen Larissa's face when the judge made the announcement. But I had stood in front, securing a position from which I could photograph her. Larissa, being much taller than I am, was about two rows behind me.

I was very surprised—and proud—that she placed first! I'm delighted that others recognize the gift God gave her and that she can appreciate how blessed she is.

Even though it's a couple of weeks since my chemo session, I felt off as I wandered among artwork and picked at snacks. The headscarf over my bald head was like a billboard announcing my illness, but few homeschool parents were comfortable asking me about my health.

After the art show, Larissa and I met several others from our church at the Open Door Mission downtown. It was our night to serve the evening meal to the homeless. I was delighted that it was Captain's night to cook and serve, too.

Sunday, 17 April 2011

The most important things in life aren't things.

– Anthony J. D'Angelo

Through the basement window, I could see colorless sky. Fierce winds roared through the woods like a stampeding train, and with the wind chill, the temperature felt like the mid-thirties. Again.

The rash on my head is still visible, but slowly healing. The pustules, which were all over my head, are now just small bumps.

People see the brutal parts of cancer—my loss of hair, my physical weakness, this rash—but they don't see the gifts. I don't mean the CDs and flowers; I'm referring to the way God has changed my outlook. How much more I cherish another day with my family or the sight of this year's crocuses. And how touched I am by the little things that people do for me out of kindness.

Today I received a note that touched me deeply. I realized that had I acted differently years ago, I would not have had this gift today. I was reminded yet again how important it is not to burn any bridges. My parents taught me this not just with words, but by their example.

Janice was a marketing manager in the same department where I worked in the early 1990s as a contract technical writer. She was known to be tough, to lack social graces, and to say things that came across as downright mean at times. However, I chose to ignore any comments she directed at me, and from time to time I would make small talk. That's how I found out that she had a rough childhood.

Janice's husband David worked for the same department. After two years when my contract was up, I left the company. A little while later I heard that David had died suddenly of a massive heart attack. He was forty-one. He had died alone in the woods when scouting out a piece of land in Tennessee.

When I heard this tragic news, I sent Janice a sympathy card. I had some inkling of what she was going through because I'd lost a close friend in an accident years before. I didn't just sign the card;

I wrote a long note telling her that others consider her a strong person and they cannot imagine the vulnerable woman she is inside and the pain she's feeling underneath that tough outer shell. I told her I understood that feeling of still expecting David to walk in the front door. Or when the phone rings, expecting to hear his voice on the other end of the line.

Janice told me years later that the note really touched her.

One spring, I was hired to do a quick turnaround project for a small company. I was to write some marketing material over the weekend and had to meet the marketing director, Janice, at her house to get the information.

"Janice Engel?" I asked the woman with whom I was discussing the project over the phone.

"You know her?" she ventured. I sensed concern in her voice, and I knew that she was thinking if I'd worked with her, I may not take this project.

"Yes, I know her. We worked together in the past."

"Are you okay working with her?"

"Yes, no problem."

When I arrived at Janice's house, she greeted me like a long-lost friend. It was the beginning of a new relationship.

Janice has since moved to Tennessee. Today she sent me this note:

Date: Sun, Apr 17, 2011 8:31 am
Subject: Re: second chemo

Dear Kathryn,

I think of you a lot, but I guess I've avoided writing you back about your cancer. I was very sad to learn of it – for you, but especially for your family. I seem to be in an avoidance mode too much lately. I'm not sure why. Chicken. Procrastination. Selfishly concentrating on the positive. A myriad of reasons.

Long before this, I thought of you whenever I saw a milkweed or a

Monarch. I loved your Christmas story many years back about them. A few years ago, while visiting a friend in WV, I dug some milkweed up & brought it here for my perennial garden. It gets eaten quickly, but keeps coming back. Somehow the Monarchs have already found it and laid eggs on it! I'm attaching a picture, just taken, of some of the eggs. Nature is so amazing. How the Monarchs find the emerging milkweed. How they make it through the winter & are here so early. It was in the high 30's last night. 40° now (8:00 am).

You and I both know, all too well, that death comes when it does, but I certainly hope it is not your time. Finding a positive way to look at it, like you have (and Lance Armstrong did), is wonderfully amazing to me. The way you put it, it seems so logical, yet so many seem to wallow in self-pity. You will be an excellent survivor and an inspiration to many when you "tell your story," which I'm sure you will. I've loved your stories. Of your visits to the Ukraine. Of your brother.

My friend, Terry, wrote you earlier. She had breast cancer last year. She was back at Jazzercize in 2 weeks, though the chemo continued to knock her back each time for a bit. We met in college & were often lab partners in our engineering classes. It did encourage her to take retirement, though. End of March.

The other picture attached is of a Yellow Swallowtail on my lilac, taken earlier this month. I planted that lilac here just after David died. I wasn't sure when, or if, I'd be back to what was then rough, raw land, but felt the need to mark the spot where he died with something. He liked lilacs; as a child he played in a hedge of them at his grand-mother's in Oregon. And of course, there's the Rochester lilac festival, so a lilac it was. I bought it, a shovel, and a jug of water and hacked in the rocky, dry soil to get it planted. I did it alone, as I wanted to be alone. You probably know that feeling. Now it is a beautiful, ~12' high bush with those wonderfully fragrant blooms that butterflies & people love. Its blooms are gone now, but I know they will be back next year.

I know you will be back, too, with more wonderful stories & lovely photographs.

Love, Janice

I was stunned. Her note was directly from her heart and more precious to me than a gemstone. I also realized that my annual Christmas newsletter, in which I've written about milkweed and Monarchs, missions and my brother, is worth the days and days that it takes to write. It's another case of using the talents that God gave us and allowing God to direct our work. And the newsletter satisfies my desire of staying in touch.

Monday, 18 April 2011

Now may the Lord of peace himself give you peace at all times and in every way.
> – 2 Thessalonians 3:16 (NIV)

Snow. Yes, it's mid-April, and it snowed today. The snow didn't stick to any branches and did not cover the grass; it simply fluttered and gently dropped to the ground where it melted. Odd to think that in Tennessee milkweed is growing, and a Monarch has already laid her eggs on it. Here spring has come to a standstill as temperatures remain in the thirties. The spring flowers have stopped growing like soldiers standing at attention waiting for their next command.

Tuesday, 19 April 2011

There is surely a future hope for you, and your hope will not be cut off.
> – Proverbs 23:18 (NIV)

Oh, for a glimpse of sunlight! I feel like I'm on hold inside just waiting for spring, and that once spring comes, I'll be much better. How I'd love to spend some time outside! I was inside, however, checking my e-mail when I found this from a friend and cancer survivor who lives in Oregon on the other side of the continent:

Tue, Apr 19, 2011 1:26 am
Subject: more chemo?

Hi Kathryn,

I'm guessing you have just had or are due to have another chemo. As time goes on, it will be both harder (longer to recover) and easier (once you know what to expect it won't be nearly as scary as it is in the beginning).

Reconnecting with friends was the best part of the whole experience for me. That, and seeing things around me with a different focus. It really is an intense experience, and unless you are totally self absorbed (some of which is normal, of course) it does change the way you look at what's going on around you.

I think about you often and am sending positive thoughts your way.

Hugs,
Lia

Lia is right. My next chemo is tomorrow.

Wednesday, 20 April 2011

The LORD will vindicate me; your love, LORD, endures forever— do not abandon the works of your hands.
                                           – Psalm 138:8 (NIV)

During the night a crash of thunder woke me. Lightening lit my pillow. Winds whooshed through trees and pelted rain against the window. The storm outside raged and kept me awake. Another windstorm raged inside: Chemo tomorrow. How will I get through another round? How am I going to make it through the aftereffects? And then I battled with a renegade thought: perhaps I should quit the chemotherapy? The numbness in my feet, the strange stabbing pains in my brain, the problems with my vision—could this be permanent damage from the drugs?

Morning came too quickly. My chemo appointment was early, and Cheri, my one-person cheerleading squad, was coming from thirty-five miles away to pick me up at eight o'clock. Just yesterday I realized that today is her birthday, and she's spending it with me in a cancer center. But Cheri wouldn't have it any other way. She, too, is a cancer survivor.

Cheri arrived with an armload of presents for Larissa —canvas, paper, acrylic paints, colored pencils, Prismacolor, charcoal, pastels, and an art textbook. Cheri, though a retired science teacher, is an accomplished artist. She was delighted to hear that Larissa had won first place and showered her with some of her extra art supplies.

"It's a reverse birthday," I commented. "It's your birthday, but you're bringing the presents!"

The cancer center was fairly quiet today. Conversation among the nurses was about the miserable, overcast, wintry weather this spring. The cold and clouds are getting on everyone's nerves, not just mine. The sun came out for an hour or two, and just seeing sunshine melted the grayness inside. Outside the temperature rose to about fifty degrees. But in a couple short hours, the clouds were back, the winds rocked the tree branches violently, and the temperature slumped down like a dog caught misbehaving.

Although the weather outside was overcast, Cheri's cheeriness dispelled the gloom. Her bubbly presence lifts up everyone around her.

My white blood cell count was good, so I could have all the chemo drugs today: Carboplatin, Taxotere, and Herceptin. Laura, the nurse practitioner, met with me for a while to discuss treatment and costs. Because I had needed so many shots of Neupogen to boost my white blood cell count back up, she had switched me over to the single Neulasta injection after each chemo session. A Neupogen shot costs three hundred dollars whereas a Neulasta shot costs three thousand and has to be approved by the insurance company. Fortunately, it was.

"How much does one of my chemo sessions cost?" I asked.

"About ten thousand dollars," Laura responded.

I knew the drugs were expensive, but I had no idea that during each four-hour session I was getting in medication the cost equivalent of a nice used car. I no longer get any medical bills sent to me. We've gone over the $7200 that our family had to pay out of pocket. At this point, the insurance company is covering all the expenses, and I won't see any more bills for the rest of this year. Praise God for that!

What did Cheri and I talk about as I sat plugged into the IV drip? Family, gardening, our children, her three-year-old grandson. It was a good balance of talking and listening. To me that's important in a friend. I don't like to listen to monologues, nor am I comfortable doing too much of the talking. I remember hearing, "If you do all the talking, you won't learn anything new." How true it is.

"Thanks so much for taking time on your birthday to take me to get pumped full of drugs. I'm definitely feeling woozy—but not in a good way," I told Cheri when she dropped me off.

I gave her a photo birthday card I had made, and Larissa put together a bouquet of yellow forsythia, daffodils, and blue scilla from our garden.

This time I felt drugged after the chemo. I was tired when I came home, perhaps from poor sleep due to the thunderstorm or maybe because of the cumulative effects of the chemo drugs. I took a nap on the couch.

Although I want only bland foods during my worst post-chemo days, after I get my appetite back, I crave red meat. I like steak and lamb, but we eat it infrequently. These days, however, I've been obsessed with red meat and buying it to cook for myself. It must have something to do with red blood cells. At least that's my theory.

Alexandra cooked sugar snap peas and tofu in peanut sauce over noodles for supper. It was delicious. But later I grilled some lamb when everyone was at youth group. I probably shouldn't have. My stomach hurts, and now I don't know if it's from chemo or overeating.

Date: Thu, Apr 20, 2011 7:25 pm

I know you are feeling down and out today but eventually you will read this. It was totally my pleasure to hang out with you today. It breaks my heart that you are going through this but I guess God has his plans for us and sometimes they are not clear. I know you continue to come out the other end a stronger person. I'll keep praying for you.

With all on your mind, I can't believe you remembered my birthday. Thank you for the flowers and card but your friendship is a gift enough.

Take good care. Love you.
Cheri

Once again, I want to track how I feel each day after chemotherapy.

CHEMO SESSION #3

DAY 1 (4/20): When I came home, felt drugged. Took a nap in the afternoon on the couch. Had little sleep at night—about five hours—due to thunderstorm last night, which is contributing to me feeling ill. Felt better after the nap, almost normal, but somewhat drugged. Drank three quarts of water. Ate normal food.

And then I wrote nothing for almost a week.

Tuesday, 26 April 2011

I lie down and sleep; I wake again, because the LORD sustains me.
– Psalm 3:5 (NIV)

The last few days passed like a gray smudge. (Is there a synonym for gray?) The cumulative effects of the chemo are really debilitating, and it's taking me longer to recover. Worse than the nausea is the stupor—that feeling of complete mental dullness and apathy. I can't think clearly for days, and each time it's taking longer to recover.

I'm on the verge of giving up. I still face three chemos, and I live in dread of them. With the brain fog, stomach problems, numbness in my feet, and worsening of my vision from the Carboplatin and/or the Taxotere, I worry that some side effects might become permanent. The oncologist can't guarantee that they're temporary (though they probably are). The only thing that keeps me going is thinking how I would feel if the cancer came back in a few years and knowing I hadn't stuck it out. So I plod on. I hope cancer never, ever, ever comes back, but that concern may always be in the back of my mind.

Along with my usual reading fare of biographies and books about missionaries, I've borrowed a few autobiographical accounts of cancer survivors. In one, I read an account of a man who permanently lost fifteen percent of his cognitive function from chemotherapy drugs. I need my brain to continue to work as a technical writer. To be the person I am. I don't want to sacrifice quality of life for longevity. I can't imagine functioning in a fog or with half a cylinder missing. So I vacillate: should I or should I not quit?

Thursday, 28 April 2011

The Lord is my strength and my shield; my heart trusts in Him, and He helps me.
– Psalm 28:7 (NIV)

Spring is in suspended animation—like my life. The snowdrops, crocuses, and daffodils bloomed earlier this month, and then everything stopped as if frozen in time. The cold has kept the open blossoms from fading but prevented any new plants from growing.

My life feels frozen in time, too, as if I've been ill with the side effects (and no hair) forever. Just as the spring that's suspended, my health seems to be suspended as well. With the predominantly gray days this spring and the side effects of the chemo, I was starting to feel like the color of the sky. I've been sick for months, and the people who were going to send a card or gift have long ago done so.

Life goes on. But I'm still sick.

So it was a great mood-lifter to receive a bunny-shaped vase full of flowers from co-worker Lydia a few days ago. And yesterday as I was working on a user manual, the doorbell rang. It was a delivery-man with an "edible arrangement"—a bouquet of fruit from my cousin in Canada. Christine is a breast cancer survivor. Her timing was impeccable.

Now I have to send more thank-you cards.

Friday, 29 April 2011

And surely I am with you always, to the very end of the age.
– Matthew 28:20 (NIV)

Many people have asked me, "How are your children taking it?" I think they expect to hear that my children are terrified that I'll die of cancer. Instead, the children don't seem all that concerned. I decided to find out once and for all.

"I'm used to you being sick and lying on the couch," answered Larissa.

I was surprised. To her, my cancer wasn't much different from the lupus of past years. In fact, when Larissa was just six, I was bedridden and didn't know whether I'd ever be able to live a normal life. But God healed me supernaturally. Perhaps oddly, my self-image is that I'm a strong, healthy super mom. Am I an optimist, or is this pure self-deception?

Saturday, 30 April 2011

Do not boast about tomorrow, for you do not know what a day may bring.
– Proverbs 27:1 (NIV)

This evening I noticed that my cheeks are red. Not red in a healthy glow sort of way, but like a solid rash. And then, almost before my eyes, little blisters started to form amidst the redness.

"Tad, look!" I said pointing to my face.

"Looks like you got some sun today," he noted.

"It might be from the sun, but it's not a sunburn; it's a rash, sort of like I used to get when I had lupus. I didn't put on any sunscreen when we were at the animal auction. But those blisters—I never got those before."

After the interminable cloudiness of this spring, the sun came out today, bright and cheery. It shone without any interference from a single cloud. And I spent half of today outside in that sunlight. I hadn't even thought to put on sunscreen, though I rarely venture into sunlight without it. I have a sun allergy and often break out in an itchy red rash after only an hour of summer sunshine. But it's early spring, quite cool, and when I did think of it, I realized that I didn't have my sunscreen with me. We were at a small animal auction an hour's drive from home.

I had never been to an animal auction before. This auction was for small animals, such as chickens, roosters, partridges, peacocks, goats, pigeons, ducks, bunnies... Alexandra had boxed up and brought all her rabbits. She had been breeding them for two years, but decided to sell off all her stock and even a hutch. The goats and chickens that we have keep the girls busy enough. Besides, the idea had been to raise the rabbits for meat, but it was just too difficult to butcher them. And rabbits breed like... well, you know.

The auction, which was run by Mennonites, was very interesting, and the sunshine was uplifting. But now I'm reaping the result of my carelessness.

May

Sunday, 1 May 2011

*Hear my voice when I call, L*ORD*; be merciful to me and answer me.*

– Psalm 27:7 (NIV)

When the family went to church this morning, I stayed back. The painful rash on my face magnified overnight, and my red cheeks are spotted with pustules. Surely this has to do not only with the sun, but also with the chemotherapy. The pustules on my face are similar to the ones I had on my scalp a few weeks ago.

I walked around the house and had a wrestling match with my thoughts. I've had some strange side effects to the chemo: not just a muddled brain and nausea, but a dimming in my vision. Painful rashes. Abrupt, sharp pangs in my brain that halt me in my tracks. Neuropathy in my feet, which may become permanent—after all, my father can barely walk because of the neuropathy in his feet, so maybe there's a family tendency? (His neuropathy was not triggered by chemo, but came on in old age.) The intensity of these side effects and the risk of them becoming permanent swayed me toward stopping chemotherapy.

But what if there are some cancer cells in my body that the chemotherapy has not yet killed? I can't know that, and perhaps if I stop chemo, they will grow and cancer will return. Maybe I should continue treatments after all and tough it out?

But then again, what if any of these side effects becomes permanent? Do I really want to risk that?

Back and forth I argued with myself, sometimes leaning one way, sometimes the other. Should I or should I not continue with chemotherapy? I prayed. I struggled with my choices. I'm not one to give up easily in the face of adversity, but I'm not sure whether it's God's will to go on. It was time to put the decision in God's hands. I asked the Lord to give me some sign.

A few hours later when Tad and the children came home from church, they brought an unexpected visitor from Massachusetts.

Brother Paul, a widower, was born in Ukraine in the 1930s. He's an eccentric man with a bulbous nose and a habit of leaving behind items when he visits people—sometimes his coat, sometimes his cell phone or wallet. People are always tracking him down to return his lost items.

As Paul was growing up, his education was interrupted because of war, and he finished only third grade. When he was ten years old, God gave him gifts of visions and prophecy and revelations. During his adult years, he spent time in a Siberian prison for his Christian faith. Because of his third-grade education, he is a simple man who speaks with a simple vocabulary—until God speaks through Him. Then his words are eloquent, like an orator's, and you know that it's not Paul speaking at all. Because of God's anointing, Paul has spoken to and advised several presidents of Ukraine. He's a very unusual man.

Tad knew what I was struggling with. "Don't you have something to ask Brother Paul?" Tad prompted me after we'd eaten lunch.

"You ask," I whispered, suddenly self-conscious.

But neither of us brought up the question because Brother Paul said suddenly, "It's time for me to go! Let's pray."

So all six of us—my family of five and Brother Paul—got down on our knees, and Paul began:

"Lord, be glorified so that everyone can see Your glory. To Mother, give strength and health so she would not be afraid that her life will be undercut.

"Banish this illness from Mother so that she is not downcast in spirit or afraid that her life will be taken. You alone are the Commander of life and death. You give the command, and the command comes to pass. For this reason, let Your command be that death not frighten this soul.

"Listen, Mother, do not pay attention to sickness or thoughts of death because I have put into you a spirit of eternity and have assigned you a spot in a heavenly place where there is no death. Death and hell are silenced when I command, and all that has distressed you will also be silenced!"

While Tad drove Brother Paul to the home where he was staying, I thought about what Paul had said: Don't be afraid that my life will be shortened because God will silence—stop—the disease that's distressed me. Or did he mean for me to not be afraid of death because God has prepared a place in heaven for me? I chose the first interpretation. I had asked God for a sign, and I believe that He wants me to trust Him with this illness. I decided to stop the chemotherapy.

Wednesday, 4 May 2011

If you believe, you will receive whatever you ask for in prayer.
– Matthew 21:22 (NIV)

Another printer manual was due today. I worked from home, where it was very quiet. Tad was in a suburb on the other side of town painting a house; Jacob was working; and the girls were away taking some standardized tests required of homeschoolers.

Last night I sat up late talking with Tad. He reminded me: *Again, truly I tell you that if two of you on earth agree about anything they ask for, it will be done for them by my Father in heaven. For where two or three gather in my name, there am I with them* (Matthew 18:19-20, NIV).

"We'll gather people and ask for God to keep the cancer from coming back," said Tad. "But if it's His will that it comes back, no amount of chemotherapy will keep it away."

I had peace with that. Tad is right: if it's God's will, chemo will not keep it away. I don't want to leave my children yet, and I still hope to go on many mission trips, especially to Africa, but if God calls me home, I'm confident that He will give me the strength to get through anything that He sends my way. God has given me the spirit of eternity and assigned a spot for me in a heavenly place. Someday, sooner or later, that's where I will go, and that gives me hope.

Today was Herceptin day. A week from today was to be my next dreaded chemo session. I decided to announce at my appointment today that I would discontinue chemotherapy.

I came in fifteen minutes early so that I could see Laura, the nurse practitioner, about the burning rash on my face, which turned bloody in places. More spots appeared on my chin and the sides of my face.

"I've never seen anything like it," said Laura. She conferred with Dr. Smith. Both of them shook their heads and wanted to send me to my primary care physician. I begged them not to send me away.

"It must be related to the chemotherapy," I insisted. "I've never had anything like it."

Their best guess was that my hypersensitivity to the sun due to lupus combined with the chemotherapy drugs coursing through my body caused this reaction. Laura prescribed prednisone, a steroid.

"By the way, I've decided to stop chemotherapy," I told Dr. Smith. I almost felt justified in my decision just based on this unusual rash.

"There is no magic number," Dr. Smith admitted. "Three, four, six treatments. I'm glad that you had the three. But are you willing to continue the Herceptin?" she asked me. I was supposed to get six chemo sessions, plus Herceptin for an entire year.

The purpose of Herceptin, to the best of my understanding, is to prevent the growth of cancer cells. But the question remained: Do I have any cancer cells in me at all?

In part to please the doctor and in part due to my own doubts, I agreed to continue the Herceptin. Although this drug doesn't cause the dullness of mind or stomach issues, Herceptin may cause serious, even life-threatening, heart problems. But so far the echocardiograms showed that my heart was fine.

During the time I was at my appointment, the co-worker who retired within the last year had her mastectomy in the same hospital and by the same surgeon that I had just a few months ago. As others have been praying for me, I'm now praying for her.

Thursday, 5 May 2011

Then a great and powerful wind tore the mountains apart and shattered the rocks before the LORD, but the LORD was not in the wind. After the wind there was an earthquake, but the LORD was not in the earthquake. After the earthquake came a fire, but the LORD was not in the fire. And after the fire came a gentle whisper.
– 1 Kings 19:11–12 (NIV)

I haven't yet told many people of my decision to stop chemo. I'm dreading the pushback, especially from those who have little faith in God. They may perceive my decision as foolish and risky. In some ways, it may be easier to go through the chemo than to justify quitting when people question my decision, and possibly my sanity, over and over again.

When Josie called me, I shared my battle. I told her about Brother Paul and the fact that I had stopped chemo.

"This is the right decision at this time," she encouraged me. "You're seeking His face. He responds. Stay with it. It would be wrong for you to go back on your decision."

Slowly, slowly over the years, I went from being merely a church attendee to having a personal relationship with God. I went from reciting memorized prayers to having conversations with God. Often the conversations are one-sided—me pleading for my health or reeling off a list of requests or asking God to bless certain people or thanking Him for the uncountable blessings in my life. But when I stop talking and listen with my heart, there are times when God whispers to me in His still, small voice. Sometimes it's in my thoughts. My conscience. My heart. Sometimes someone tells me something, and I can feel that God used that person to speak to me. Sometimes a person repeats something that I thought of, and I realize it is God confirming this idea. Sometimes God sends a person with the gift of prophesy to speak to me. Sometimes He says something to me using a preacher delivering a sermon. Sometimes He uses His Word. And there were even two episodes during times of great emotional upheaval in my life that God spoke to me in an audible voice. Some might say I imagined it, but I know otherwise.

I have learned to distinguish His voice. I know He is with me as I go through this.

Thursday, 26 May 2011

May your unfailing love be my comfort, according to your promise to your servant.
– Psalm 119:76 (NIV)

After Alexandra sold off her rabbits a few weeks ago, she decided to raise chickens. Currently we have six laying hens—one white Leghorn, one black Australorp, and four reds. But Alexandra wanted to add to the flock. She ordered five Plymouth Rock chicks, which Tad picked up from Dick's Country Store three weeks ago. They were just four days old and looked like puffs with legs that seemed to peep without even opening their beaks. "I remember a toy like this," Alexandra said, holding a peeping chick in her hands. Indeed, the children did have a yellow chick toy that was touch sensitive: hold it just so and it peeped, sounding just like these live chicks.

The five chicks that Alexandra bought grew quickly. At first Alexandra kept them in a birdcage in the basement with a light bulb over the cage to keep them warm. In just a few days the smell of the chicks grew so pungent that Jacob and I petitioned to move them out of the basement. They were banished to the garage.

The chicks were soon too crowded in the small birdcage. Alexandra transferred them into the large metal cage that had originally housed a rabbit. She still kept them in the garage, but when they grew enough adult feathers, Alexandra started to take the chicks out on the lawn in the daytime, keeping them under a wire cage topped with a plastic cover for shade.

In a short while, that wire cage where they spent their days became too small. They're nearly half-sized with stiff black-and-white feathers coming in. Alexandra next rigged a small makeshift pen for the chicks by fashioning four sides of an enclosure from a roll of wire mesh. The enclosure was about a foot tall and topped with a square wooden frame with wire mesh to keep away predators and keep the chicks inside.

Yesterday this temporary pen held the chicks well. Today I noticed one chick outside the pen on the grass while the other four were inside. It's hard to corner a chick on the lawn, but when I stopped chasing it, the chick ran back to the pen because she wanted to be with her buddies. Alexandra scooped her up, and then using sticks, rocks, and a chair, she and I propped up the wire wall that had yawned open far beyond the "ceiling" of the wooden-framed wire mesh.

But our work was no deterrent. Maybe the chicks just grew bigger, bolder, able to jump and flap their wings, because when I looked through the kitchen window in the late afternoon, I saw four chicks pecking at the grass, wandering the yard in a small huddle. The pen was empty. But where was the fifth chick?

Alexandra and I searched in our backyard, in the goat pen, in the neighbors' yard, in the front yard. It didn't take long to realize that chicks stay together, and that the chick was gone, possibly snatched by a hawk. Most likely we'll never know.

In the evening, I was thinking about this chick, this tiny life, a life that I strangely miss. There's an emptiness where this chick had been. Foolish chicks were safe in their covered enclosure, but they pushed their boundaries and climbed out of their safe spot the way many children want to push beyond the boundaries given them. When parents put boundaries around their children, it's for a good reason—like Alexandra did for the chicks. And when children push beyond them, Satan, like that hawk, can snatch them up.

Poor chick. Poor silly chick.

Friday, 27 May 2011

Hear my cry, O God; listen to my prayer.
– Psalm 61:1 (NIV)

Rain. Gray skies. Downpour. Mud.

We prayed for the local farmers today. This wet spring, it's hard to bring in hay. It's too wet to cut, or if cut, it will rot in the fields. Ever since we've had the goats and chickens, we're more aware of what local farmers are going through because we buy our hay and feed from them.

Lydia, an acquaintance who visited us in February, called to tell me she was going to bring me stinging nettles she found in her field so I could make some tea. She had heard that tea made from stinging nettles helps fight cancer—or did it prevent cancer?

"Thanks, Lydia," I said, considering how to decline her offer graciously, "but we have some stinging nettles growing in the woods behind the house. Thanks for thinking of me, but it's not necessary. It's a really long drive for you." Lydia lives almost thirty miles away.

Inwardly I sighed. Perhaps I'm being ungrateful, but I'm tired of people telling me various home remedies that are "cures" for cancer—apple seeds, apricot seeds, various teas, flaxseed, assorted health supplements. And then there are all these diets that cure cancer: the no-pork diet, the no-tomato diet, the raw-food diet, the alkaline diet… Some people speculate that these diets and natural remedies really work but that the pharmaceutical industry is keeping them a secret from the general public so that they can make their millions of dollars on chemotherapy and other drugs.

Who knows what's really true? I know that these friends and acquaintances mean well. I know they have my best interests at heart. But I'm worn out by the whole thing. So I halfheartedly eat a few apple seeds and apricot seeds, but really I just want my life to slip back to normal.

Tuesday, 31 May 2011

Are not five sparrows sold for two copper coins? And not one of them is forgotten before God. But the very hairs of your head are all numbered. Do not fear therefore; you are of more value than many sparrows.

– Luke 12:6-7 (NKJV)

Yesterday, on Memorial Day, suddenly it was summer! Right on cue, the temperature soared to the eighties, and the cottonwood trees started their annual blizzard of fluffy seeds that end up in drifts on our driveway.

April's cold weather kept spring in a holding pattern; now spring has fast-forwarded through the gold daffodils, past the pale blue forget-me-nots, and through the heady spring fragrances of lilies-of-the-valley and lilacs. Now the rhododendron has just opened. At this point, all the hostas have leafed out, showing their still unblemished leaves of green, blue, yellow, and white in various combinations.

"My mother doesn't garden. She doesn't even notice my garden when she visits," lamented Cheri when she called me today.

The same is true of my mother. I don't think she sees the beauty. In my family, only my brother Alex was a gardener and could talk plants—what conditions this perennial likes, how beautiful a Sagae hosta is, how grape hyacinths can be naturalized.

I put in a garden for my mother two or three years ago when Laika, her Siberian Husky, died and was buried in her backyard. I brought pink astilbes and hostas from home for this shady area. My sister bought a bench. My brother bought a solar-powered light. I brought stones for a path, then created a little haven in which to sit.

But no one ever goes back there. No one has weeded there. I went there last week, and it saddened me to see the mess the garden has become. I saw a life lesson there: we can make a mess of our lives, too, if we don't watch and "weed" sinful habits out of our lives. We must constantly be vigilant just as a gardener must always weed.

I try to do a little bit in the garden each day. A little fresh air, a little exercise, and a little work daily keeps the chores from becoming overwhelming. Weed a little, rake a bit, dig out the lilies of the valley that have spread too far, mulch a bit. It's soothing to spend time in my garden.

"Did you put makeup on your eyebrows?" Tad asked me when I walked into the living room.

"My hair is growing!!" I shouted, running to the mirror and not bothering to answer Tad's question. I never put makeup on my eyebrows, so I knew it was that five o'clock shadow effect when hair just starts to grow. I took off my headscarf and looked at my head. It too has a five o'clock shadow.

I noticed that on my cheeks, I still have a trace of that rash from a month ago. The prednisone helped a lot for the pain and the intensity of the rash, but touches of it still remain on my face. But, hey, my hair is starting to grow just five weeks after my last chemo session!

June

In the multitude of my anxieties within me, Your comforts delight my soul.

– Psalm 94:19 (NKJV)

Another Herceptin treatment this morning, which means more chemicals coursing through my bloodstream. As summer stretches ahead of me, I feel like I'm in a medical limbo.

The Herceptin treatments, where I get plugged into an IV through my mediport, are now once every three weeks instead of weekly. I have not been to the Lipson Cancer Center for twenty-one days, the longest gap since I began chemotherapy exactly three months ago. I no longer need to have the blood draws because Herceptin doesn't affect the white blood cell count. No more Benedryl. No more nausea. And I no longer need a chauffeur to drive me to medical appointments.

In some strange way, it's like I'm well—but not well. My baldness and the port installed in my chest are visual reminders that I'm not a healthy individual. At this point, all I can do is go for the Herceptin infusions—and wait.

But wait for what?

Wait for the end of the treatment, I suppose. The schedule is for eight more months of the Herceptin, all the way into February of next year. And then what? Surely I'm not going to live my life waiting, wondering. Yet that little gnawing question is there, always whirling in the background: Do I have cancer somewhere in my body? Is it lurking, waiting for an opportunity to strike? Will it be back?

The worst is over, but the Herceptin seems like it's going to go on forever. Eight more months!

Tuesday, 7 June 2011

He has made everything beautiful in its time…
– Ecclesiastes 3:11 (NIV)

Early June is the season for irises. For one glorious week, my gardens are at their peak as hundreds of regal Siberian irises open in tall purple clumps all over the backyard. The dripping pink blossoms of the bleeding hearts are past their prime, but a few persistent blooms still arch over the water garden and stone path. And the lavender rhododendron, which is tucked under the drooping branches of a tall spruce, creates a pastel backdrop for the water garden this week. In the early morning when the sun is low and the water garden is in shadow, its surface is like a dark jewel, still and reflective, as if pondering the day that's about to unfold. When I walk outside with my morning coffee, my eyes are drawn to the glassy surface, which echoes the colors and light above it.

My single peony demands attention today as its full flowers bend under their own magnificent weight. That peony was a gift from an avid gardener, a gift I hadn't wanted because I hadn't liked peonies. But this peony's deep magenta blooms have charmed me. It's the most beautiful peony I've ever seen and has become a garden favorite.

As I walk through the backyard in the early morning, my heart glows at the sight of the sun backlighting the flowers—the colors, the brilliance, the splendor of these plants. The sun's golden rays outline every leaf and petal, accenting each exquisite, glowing detail. The play between the light and colors and green lawn are like a choreographed show of praises to God. It's visual ecstasy of which I cannot get enough.

Gardening is like drawing with God's paintbrush. Yes, I planted these gardens, but I see God's hand in every flower and every leaf. I appreciate this time away from work to enjoy the beauty that's at my doorstep.

Thursday, 9 June 2011

Do not worry about tomorrow, for tomorrow will worry about itself. Each day has enough troubles of its own.

– Matthew 6:34 (NIV)

The phone rang at 6 AM, jolting me awake. Jacob, an early riser, picked up the phone. I heard footsteps in the house, then Tad came to tell me, "Jacob and I are going to grandma's house. Grandpa fell out of his chair and can't get up."

As soon as I heard the phone, I had expected it would be my mother. Yesterday she had related her latest difficulty with Dad: after his hour-long bath yesterday morning, he had not been able to get out of the bathtub. At ninety-one, Dad still weighs well over two hundred pounds. No matter how much Mama and Dusia, who had come to give Dad a bath, tugged and pulled, they could not extract Dad from of the tub. They tried and tried for an hour. Finally, Mama called 911.

A three-hundred-pound male Emergency Medical Technician (EMT) showed up with the ambulance and simply lifted Dad out. But what would have happened had the EMT been a slim woman?

So after yesterday's difficulties, I presumed that this early call had something to do with Dad.

When Tad returned from my parents' house a short while later, he related what had happened: When it was time to go to bed last night, Dad had simply slipped from his recliner in the living room onto the floor. His legs gave out. It was the first time he had tried to get up since toddling over with his walker after his all-too-memorable bath. Because he uses a pee bottle, he doesn't get up and just sits in his easy chair all day long—watching TV, surfing the Internet with his laptop, dozing, eating what Mama puts in front of him. Dad spends his entire days in that recliner, then totters to his bedroom with his walker at the end of the day. That has been his daily routine for years.

But when he tried to get up last night, he sank to the floor. Instead of calling us at 10 PM when it happened, my mother tried alone to lift and prop up and pull Dad to his feet. At 1 AM, she gave up and made him a little nest of pillows on the floor where he spent the night.

Mama could have called us last night instead of struggling alone for three hours. But there's a definite loss of dignity when you can't get up off the floor.

Large-boned and heavyset, my dad is almost twice as heavy as my 5-foot-2 mother. It's not a wonder she couldn't lift him. Dad wasn't much help; his muscles have atrophied from lack of use. He had a sedentary job as a color researcher in the printing industry. Over the years, Dad became less and less active, especially as neuropathy, a loss of sensation, encroached on his feet and legs. I realized just how weak he was when he considered it exercise to sit in his chair and do curls with a two-pound dumbbell. *Two* pounds?

This slide into frailty had occurred so gradually and over so many years that we children had not realized just how incapacitated our dad was until two years ago when Mama was rushed to the hospital for emergency surgery for a perforated duodenum, a condition caused by taking too many pain medications on an empty stomach. Her arthritis is worse in the morning, but Mama never eats breakfast. Painkillers and coffee don't make a good meal.

While Mama was in the hospital recovering from surgery far more invasive and painful than mine, Dad was home alone. But he could barely walk, and he certainly couldn't prepare meals or wash dishes or even bathe himself. So for one heroic week, my sister Marta, brother George, and I tried to take care of Dad in his own home while working at our respective jobs. Marta drove over early and served Dad his standard breakfast of tomato, onion, brie, brown bread, and lox with a cup of instant coffee. Then she rushed off to work. I took a long lunch break and came over to heat leftovers found in his fridge or brought whatever we were eating at home. After work, George stopped by and attempted to please Dad by cooking the perfect soft-boiled egg or serving whatever struck Dad's fancy for supper. Tad or our children drove over around 10 PM to make sure that Dad made it safely with his walker from the living room down the long hallway to his bedroom. They brought iced water and a snack to his bedside.

But we all failed. The egg George boiled wasn't cooked correctly. I gave Dad too much food on his plate. George bought the wrong tomatoes. The children didn't leave him enough iced water in his cup to last the entire night. We came over too early or too late. Criticism and complaints were our reward for caring for Dad, so as the week wore on, we each spent less and less time in the house with him. Dad called Mama at the hospital and tattled on us.

One day I'd heard enough of Dad's complaints about the food and our poor service, so I brought over some photos of Mexicans foraging in a garbage dump. I had taken these photos on a mission trip five years before, but because my dad criticizes photos as well as food, I had never shown him these images. Why does he, the four-teenth child out of fifteen born in a two-room house in a Ukrainian village, think he deserves the best of everything when so many people around the world go to bed hungry? I showed him the pictures.

"That's really dirty," Dad commented about the garbage dump. "It's not safe. You walked on that garbage to get the pictures?"

"Yes."

"You could've gotten sick."

"I would rather get sick doing something I love than stay home and not do anything meaningful," I replied.

"I had a friend in Toronto who had an only son," my dad ventured. "That son liked to do good, like you. He went to India somewhere and contracted a disease while helping others. He died of that disease. You know what his father said?" My dad paused for effect. "'People like him eliminate themselves.'"

Now what do you say to something like that? Normally I'd remain silent, but I was irked and I dove in.

"Mother Teresa did a lot of good in India, and she didn't die of any contagious disease. Dad, I know that you don't enjoy sitting in that chair all day long and would prefer to be able to walk. But I would rather die visiting places like this garbage dump and helping others than to stay home, grow old, watch TV all day, and be confined to a chair like you are."

After that conversation, Dad didn't complain to me again about food. Maybe he was afraid I'd bring my photos of hungry children in Africa next. But he continued to complain to my siblings.

As the days passed, the house began to smell. We realized something that Mama had hidden from us: Dad was incontinent.

That's when Dusia came into my parents' lives. After one week of that frantic schedule, we siblings realized that we could not continue missing work, "disappointing" Dad with our poor service, and maintaining our own sanity while Mama continued to recover away from home for another two or three weeks. We hired Dusia to care for Dad from morning through lunchtime, including meals, baths, and laundry. And when Mama finally returned home, Dusia, who is younger and stronger than Mama, continued to come three times per week, helping Dad in and out of the bathtub, scrubbing him, changing his sheets, and doing his laundry. Dusia was a godsend.

After the Wednesday tub incident and this morning's Dad-on-floor incident came a barrage of e-mails from my siblings.

While I do not want to sound the alarm bells, and it is possible that Dad will get better, I think it's prudent that we look into a nursing home for him. For now, Dusia is planning on giving him sponge baths, but this may be a stopgap temporary solution.

- M

I am not ruling out a nursing home, but I think that it is not a step to be taken lightly. Reason 1: Mama will slide that much more quickly without Dad to cook for and wait on. Reason 2: cost – at 10K per month, they will blow through their life savings possibly before Mama needs her share for her own twilight years.

- P.

Just called home, Dad had a #2 accident (since he can't get to the can). Mama has apparently cleaned him up. She sounded tired; who can blame her?

- M

Power of attorney, male caregivers, increasing the number of days that Dusia comes over, visiting nurses—ideas were thrown out and bounced around like ping-pong balls. I prefer to step back in these situations, and today I had even more reason to do so: I was leaving in the afternoon to drive to Pittsburgh and visit my best friend from fifth grade. I had this trip planned for a while, and I didn't want to miss it because of this latest Dad incident.

This family crisis has taken the focus off me, but I'm still dealing with issues spawned by my cancer. A strange "side effect" of the disease has been intense nostalgia.

I lived in Pittsburgh only three short years during my childhood. But that house on top of a hill and the neighborhood in which it was nestled were my favorite of all the places I had lived—until I moved into the home where I live now.

My early childhood was spent in Toronto. Though I have only flashes of memories from that time, I do recall that our yard was as tiny as a playpen and the houses were so close together that it seemed that I could lean out the window and touch the brick wall of the house next door. In Chicago, where I lived from age six to ten, we resided in a small bungalow on the South Side. Our yard was a small swatch that adjoined an alley, the houses were crowded together, and there were few trees.

But in Pittsburgh, the houses had room to breathe and we children had room to run. Technically, we didn't live in Pittsburgh; we lived in Allison Park, a suburb. Until then, I didn't know suburbs existed. Until then, I didn't know that you could have woods in your backyard. I discovered that those woods could go on and on and on, connecting behind all your neighbors' houses, and curiosity could lead you so far from home that you would never hear your mother calling you for lunch. I saw birds other than sparrows and pigeons for the first time: red cardinals, blue jays, mourning doves, flickers. My sister and brothers and I caught a box turtle on the lawn. We found a praying mantis egg case, which hatched tiny praying mantises all over the dining room window. Since our house was perched on top of a hill, we could watch the sun retire behind the trees and leave a sky glowing improbable shades of orange and pink and red and even purple. I absorbed the nature in our backyard like a thirsty sponge, sought its peace and beauty, its solace as well as solitude.

How I cried when we moved away on my thirteenth birthday and found ourselves on another small, closed-in lot, this time in Rochester.

Nancy had befriended me when I was the new girl in fifth grade of Wyland Elementary School in Allison Park. When I moved away three years later, she wrote letters to me in Rochester. Our friendship continued through hundreds of letters that we exchanged through our teen years, our twenties, our marriages, the birth of our children, and to this very day. Since I moved away from Pittsburgh, I've seen Nancy only five times—twice when she came to visit me in Rochester, three times when I visited her in Pittsburgh. Through forty-three years, our friendship has remained strong. Admittedly, we've taken different paths and have different personalities, and if we met today for the first time, we probably would not click. But Nancy's loyalty and our mutual histories have woven us together, and I feel that Nancy will always be part of my life. But how much life do I have left?

Friday, 10 June 2011

And He said to them, "Come away by yourselves to a secluded place and rest a while."

– Mark 6:31 (NASB)

Although I love to travel with family and friends, sometimes I crave a solo drive. When alone, my mind is free to roam, to unwind, to drift, to soar. Solitude is a time for renewal.

These renewal experiences don't happen if I fly down the interstate at top speed. Had I driven west on the New York State Thruway, then south on Interstate 79, I could have gotten to Pittsburgh in five rushing hours. But a few days before the trip, I got out my road atlas, and with mounting anticipation, sought out the green dotted lines that indicate a scenic drive. I plotted my course down Route 62 through Amish farmlands in New York, and alongside the Allegheny National Forest and Allegheny River in Pennsylvania. Route 62 crosses Route 8 partway down Pennsylvania, and I chose that wandering road through half the state. Route 8 skirts my old neighborhood and goes right into Pittsburgh. Our family took Route 8 to church every Sunday.

The drive yesterday afternoon was long, meandering, and relaxingly picturesque. My soul delighted in the scenery, the farmland, the late afternoon sunshine, the blooming rhododendron and pink phlox. In New York, I passed four horse-drawn black buggies clip-clopping along the road. One was driven by a teenage girl in a black bonnet. Another by a young boy in a straw hat. And still another by a gray-haired Amish couple. I tried to imagine what their lives were like.

Along the Allegheny National Forest in Pennsylvania, the road was a green tunnel enclosed by an archway of branches. Few cars interrupted my reverie. A glowing smile expanded inside my chest as I absorbed the sparkling waters of the grand Allegheny River, the luxuriant leafy trees, the lacy ferns hugging the roadside, the rich light of the low sun. I was alone in the car—yet not alone. It's on these winding rural routes that I can sense God's presence. In the sound of sheer silence, His gentle voice whispers into my soul like a refreshing breeze.

Because of the cancer, I've been thinking more than usual about my childhood. Memories surface uninvited. I want to see old friends, perhaps for my last time; I want to visit places my feet once trod when I was several shoe sizes smaller. Thus this trip to Pittsburgh.

I am so thankful that the "bad" chemo is behind me and I am strong enough to do the drive alone. Not long ago, I got winded just walking up the sixteen steps to our front door. I'm still weaker than I was before all this started, but I've been regaining strength. My slow return to normalcy includes buying myself a special bra and prosthesis before this trip with assurances from the salesgirl that no one will be able to tell. But I still have virtually no hair and continue to wear the distinctive post-chemo headscarf. How would Nancy react to me?

I soon found out. It was nightfall by the time I found her house on top of a hill and parked in front of it. She was waiting for me on the porch and helped me carry my bags inside. An early-summer heat wave swathed the city, so the windows were open, but they barely breathed. Although it had been a dozen years since I was last in Pittsburgh and I had never been to this house before, I was soon sitting on the couch with my feet curled under me, feeling at home as if Nancy and I had just seen each other the week before.

Monday, 13 June 2011

There is a time for everything, and a season for every activity under heaven...
– Ecclesiastes 3:1 (NIV)

Although I'd wandered to Pittsburgh along cheery scenic routes, today I sped home on the solemn interstates, rushing headlong into my work and routine. I was home around noon.

It's interesting to slip into someone else's company and habits for a weekend. Nancy, twice divorced, lives with her younger daughter Hayley, who is twenty-eight and, like Nancy, works at the University of Pittsburgh. They carpool together, they grocery shop together, they take walks together. I was delighted to see how well they got along. I was also amused to see their routine and realize how different Nancy and I are.

Nancy is a meticulous meal-planner and grocery shopper. She makes a precise list, planning for and using everything, like a good steward. In my own home, I stock up on all sorts of frozen meats, canned goods, dried products, and fresh produce from which I can cook meals on a whim without running to the store. When I grocery shop, I have only a vague notion of what I'll cook in the days ahead and usually buy groceries to restock my supplies. I often go to a grocery store with a list of fifteen items and come home with fifty. I got the impression that Nancy would not do that. Although I hate to throw out food, sometimes leftovers go bad or a head of lettuce becomes slimy. But with Nancy's calculated shopping and menu planning, I doubt that her food ever goes to waste.

Not only is Nancy's grocery shopping structured, so are evenings after work. I experienced her routine with her pets while I was there: Every evening Nancy and Hayley take out each of the three gerbils and let them run around on a blanket on the couch. Then they take Tequila, their 8-year-old chinchilla, out of her cage and let her run for half an hour in a gate-enclosed area (with a blanket on the floor) in one of the bedrooms. They give her one raisin at the beginning of the routine, and one raisin plus one peanut at the end. I couldn't help but think that these small mammals are given more time and attention than many children.

Of course we did things that weren't normally part of Nancy's routine. On Friday, at my request, we spent a day at the zoo. I remembered going to the Pittsburgh Zoo as a child, yet the place we visited did not even remotely resemble the zoo that I recalled from the mid-1960s. I might as well have been in a different city. Nothing, not one spot or exhibit at the zoo, triggered any memory. The zoo had been completely redone.

But when Nancy drove me to my old house at 2455 Victoria Drive, what a flood of memories came upon me! I recognized many sites and streets and buildings. Trees were bigger. Houses had been expanded or painted. But the street names were the same, the layout of the land was the same, and there were even a few homes that looked just as they had more than forty years before. They were even the same color.

Our modest red brick house on the top of the hill had been remodeled and enlarged since my family moved away in 1968. On the east end of the house was once an open-air porch where we took all our meals during the summer. My mother used to set out dishes on the picnic table, covering them with food umbrellas made of colorful mesh to keep off flies and wasps. Each year my father strung ropes from the porch railing to the roof, then planted morning glories, which entwined the metal railing, then twisted up the ropes, creating a curtain of heart-shaped leaves and pink, purple, and blue blossoms throughout the summer.

The porch is now enclosed.

Nearly touching the brick wall of the house on the west side was once a sizeable crabapple tree whose branches were wide and sturdy and inviting. In the spring, the tree put on such a dramatic exhibition of salmon pink that I felt my heart leap whenever I saw its enthralling beauty. In the summer, the foliage concealed me as from my perch I listened in on the world through my transistor radio. I can almost see a ten-year-old version of myself, a gawky tomboy with a brown ponytail, climbing that tree, spying on robins feeding their nestlings, or sitting among the branches and daydreaming.

The tree is gone, replaced by an addition to the house.

Kitty corner across the street from us had been a pink house with a steep driveway. Cammie and Christie Ball, twins my sister's age, lived there. We spent our summer days together, Cammie and Christie, Marta and I, swinging on their swing set, playing kickball with their dad, exploring the woods behind our house, sleeping over in their playhouse while their older brother Michael, a redhead with glasses, tried to scare us with noises during the night. Their mother, Betty, was friends with my mama. Betty often took my mother grocery shopping because back then my mother didn't drive. I remember Betty with her pale blue eyes and salt-and-pepper permed hair, a joke on her lips and a cigarette in her hand, its smoke curling upward. In the evenings, a glass of Bourbon on ice jingled in her other hand. Smoking and drinking didn't have the stigma then that they do now.

After we moved away, we stayed in touch sporadically. Mr. Ball died fairly young from a heart attack. Michael married a woman with children from a previous marriage and moved into the city. Christie moved away to Ohio with a boyfriend. Cammie continued to live at home with her mother, working menial jobs. Then one year we heard that Cammie died. She was still in her thirties! The cause of death was not clearly stated. Years later I found out it was from a rare viral disease and her stubborn refusal of medical help.

After Christie gave birth to a son, instead of writing letters, she would call me, but always during the daytime. This mystified me because in those long-ago days before cell phones and calling plans, long-distance phone calls during the day were more expensive than in the evening.

In one phone call, Christie said she'd had a second child, a girl. I had three children of my own. I was happy for her, I told her. But she replied, "This isn't a good situation to bring children into." Unaware of her situation, I naively asked, "Why? Is your apartment too small?"

A long silence ensued. I understood that I'd crossed a line.

Then in a hushed voice, Christie explained that her boyfriend Paul sometimes came home drunk. He was unpredictable, volatile. He beat her. He had even served time in jail for accosting her. She had been hospitalized, then had gone to live with her mother for a while. They were back together now, but she lived in fear of him.

I was shocked. This happened in books and movies or to strangers, not to my childhood friend!

"Christie, why don't you leave him? Why don't you move back to Pittsburgh?" I had urged during that call, horrified by Christie's story of abuse.

"I don't want my children to grow up without a father," she rationalized.

I spoke to her maybe once more after that phone call. I sent her my Christmas newsletter, as I do to dozens of old friends. One January day Paul called me.

"I got your newsletter," he said. "I just wanted to let you know that we lost Christie."

I stiffened. "Lost her?" I repeated as I was processing the information. Lost her like a child at the mall? "What do you mean, 'lost her'?" I questioned, though the ghastly meaning had already sunk in.

"She died in the summer."

"Died? From what?"

"She had pneumonia," Paul explained.

"I had pneumonia last year. I didn't die of it!" I challenged, almost angry at him.

"She was in the hospital. She had kidney failure."

"So did she die of pneumonia or kidney failure?"

"Both."

Pneumonia. Kidney failure. I didn't believe him. I thought for sure that he had killed her, that she had died of injuries from his abuse. But I would never know. I thanked him for calling me. That was the last I heard from anyone from that family. Christie hadn't wanted to leave Paul so the children would have a father, but now they had no mother.

The Balls' house was no longer pink, I noticed when I got out of Nancy's car and walked along the street in front of my former home.

It had been completely redone, the driveway changed, a garage added on, tan vinyl siding covering what used to be pink clapboard. Like the zoo that triggered no memories, this house was unrecognizable.

On the other side of the street next to our dark brick house was the lighter colored brick home where Bobby Ross used to live. He was an only child around the age of my brother Alex—three or four years younger than me. Like Michael, Bobby also had flaming orange hair. He had a dog named Spot who was always tied to the house with a chain. Although we played together, I sometimes teased Bobby because he was a little overweight and a little clumsy and a lot younger than me.

"In high school, Bob Ross was a friend of my brother Steve," Nancy said as we wandered along the street in between my former home and Bobby's.

"Look, there's someone mowing the lawn on the Ross's property," I noticed.

"He's too young to be Bobby Ross," Nancy commented. "Bob would be fifty-one or fifty-two."

I walked up to this man with sandy brown hair tinged with gray and introduced myself as someone who once lived in the house next door. He immediately recognized me. It was Bobby Ross after all, taller, older, and hair subdued with the years. His parents had passed away decades ago, but he, an only child, still lived in his childhood home. He never married. Bob filled me in on all the neighbors: who died, who moved away, who lives in each of the homes now.

"What ever happened to the Balls?" I asked Bob.

"The daughters, Cammie and Christie, both died young."

"Yes, I heard," I said.

"Old Mrs. Ball died a while ago, but the son, Michael, lived in the house. He rarely came out. Sometimes he walked down the road with a knee-length army jacket even in the summertime and waist-long red hair. He was a hippy," claimed Bob. "Never left that hippy stage."

Bob went on to say that Michael died of respiratory failure two or three years ago and the house was left to someone living in Ohio, who put it up for sale. Bob went to see the house because a friend was interested in buying it.

"I came back home, put on rubber boots, rubber gloves, and a respirator," said Bob. "The garage was completely filled with beer bottles. The walls had black mold. A flipper bought it for fifty thousand, but I think he overpaid. He cleaned it up, and it just sold for a hundred and forty thousand."

On Sunday morning, Nancy and I attended services at the First Presbyterian Church, a striking old stone church built in 1903 with arches and woodwork and stained glass. Later we hung around her house, I showed her my bald head, we talked, and we ate outside on her porch, sitting in the dark until the fireflies came out. Nancy lives not far from the zoo, and on a still night, you can hear the roar of the lion echoing from the valley to the top of her hill.

Friday evening, after the day at the zoo, we drove to the Outback Steakhouse to have dinner with Walter, a man in his mid-sixties whom I had met last summer on the Panama mission trip that I went on with Alexandra. He was a recent widower at the time, his wife having died in her sleep from heart failure. Since her death, he has devoted more of his time to missions. Walter, who is completely bald, was always smiling, always exuding a positive spirit. He was the kind of soft-spoken person anyone would enjoy spending time with.

"You know, since I saw you last summer, I got diagnosed with breast cancer," I told Walter over my prime rib.

"Oh, my wife had breast cancer," said Walter as Nancy sampled her salmon.

"I didn't know that," I said. "I thought she died of heart failure."

"She did. The Herceptin she was taking caused that," Walter explained.

"I'm on Herceptin…" I almost whispered.

Tuesday, 14 June 2011

Surely God is my help; the Lord is the one who sustains me…
For He has delivered me from all my troubles…

– Psalm 54:4, 7 (NIV)

Today was the first day that I went to Kodak Office instead of working from home. Usually I call in to the weekly inkjet printer project meetings; today, unannounced, I showed up in person. I needed information to write a chapter on mobile printing—printing wirelessly from a Blackberry phone, iPhone, iPod, iPad, or an Android device. I don't own any of these devices, so I came in to borrow one.

I felt strange walking the halls after being away almost five months. I was a little self-conscious wearing my headscarf instead of a wig, which would have hidden the fact that I lost hair; I'm well aware that with the scarf, it's obvious I'm undergoing something. But the head-scarf was my choice. I *am* going through something; why hide it? Maybe I can even have some interesting conversations about it.

My co-workers welcomed me back warmly. Kodak feels like my home away from home. Yet, I should not get attached. I have struggled over investing too much of my time in technical writing rather than writing from the heart, too much of my soul into a company instead of into God's calling for my life.

But it was nice to be back.

Sunday, 19 June 2011
Father's Day

For those who are led by the Spirit of God are the children of
God. The Spirit you received does not make you slaves, so that you
live in fear again; rather, the Spirit you received brought about
your adoption to sonship. And by him we cry, "Abba, Father."

– Romans 8:14-15 (NIV)

I have heard it said that the relationship you have with your earthly father colors your relationship with your heavenly Father. If your dad

249

is a loving man, one who hugs you and is supportive emotionally, then you will see God as a loving, intimate, compassionate Father. But if your earthly father is a distant and cold man, or worse yet, a violent and angry man, or one who has abandoned you, then you will perceive God as distant or harsh or uncaring.

Through the years, I struggled to have a close personal relationship with God. To me, God seemed powerful, distant, and impersonal. When I recognized the correlation, I understood why I perceived Him as such.

"Abba" in Aramaic is the equivalent of "Daddy"—a name I never used for my own father. God does want to be intimately close to us. Yet it's been hard for me to overcome my perception of fathers as authoritative and unapproachable.

Although I have recollections of close times with my dad during my early childhood—hiking together, pressing flowers and leaves, catching butterflies, listening to him tell stories—the closeness evaporated when I became a teenager. For the majority of my life, my father has been formal and distant, demanding (if not earning) respect, and maintaining emotional distance. He just did not seem interested in his children, not after we went through puberty. He provided for us, he never physically abused us, but he just wasn't there for us. He could be critical and controlling, but most of the time he was simply distant and self-absorbed.

Oh, how I've longed to have a daddy who cuddled and loved me unconditionally. I needed my father's affection and support just as much, if not more, during my difficult teen years and into adulthood. I know that God fills this role for me. He can comfort me supernaturally. Still, a part of me wanted the kind of daddy who would give me a tender hug or even sit me on his lap when life got just a little too hard. And I've always—though perhaps not always consciously—sought Dad's approval.

I recognize that somewhere deep down inside my father loves us in his own intangible kind of way. But he doesn't love his children with actions. Perhaps he doesn't know how.

In any case, it's Father's Day, so I went with my husband and children to visit Dad. He was, of course, sitting on what we have affectionately dubbed his "throne"— the easy chair near the TV. Sadly, the television is his best friend and the easy chair near it is where he has spent literally years of his life.

And now he can't even leave that chair.

My mother was her usual wound-up self, running to the kitchen to bring out food—fruit and ice cream—repeating the same things she told us last week, last month. Mama is hospitable and puts on the air of chatty friendliness, but I wish that she would just sit and converse with us—not continuously be on "send."

Just as I've missed having a father who cares, I've missed having a mother who listens. Mama is generous, genuinely concerned about her children, and I know that she loves me because of actions and deeds. I can feel her love, but I so wish to share my dreams and fears and desires and disappointments with her. If only she'd let me.

When I visit my parents, it's with hope in my heart that this visit will be different. Time after time, though, it's more of the same.

I had to leave to lock up the chickens before dark, but Tad and the girls wanted to stay longer. They would walk the mile back to our house. Jacob came with me. Mama caught up to us on the porch.

"Do you think that Dad looks worse?" she asked me in a low voice as if Dad could hear her. "Do you think he's declining?"

"Yes, a little worse," I admitted.

Mama suddenly seemed so small. I could see she was distraught and a little lost. Dad has dramatically weakened since the day the EMT pulled him out of the bathtub. At this point, he couldn't manage to walk to the car to go to a dentist or a doctor. It just could be that he'll be carried out of the house feet first next time he leaves home.

But that is not something that Mama wants to think about.

Wednesday, 22 June 2011

*Be strong and courageous. Do not be afraid or terrified… for the L*ORD *your God goes with you; He will never leave you nor forsake you.*

– Deuteronomy 31:6 (NIV)

I drove myself to the Lipson Cancer Center, the new brick medical building that I've been visiting since winter, then parked the car in the very back of the lot under some shade trees so the car wouldn't heat up. I remembered how cold and cloudy and miserable it had been the first few months I came to this medical center. And now it's hot.

I walked alone through the glass doors, which open automatically. The receptionist glanced up and perfunctorily greeted me by name, then opened the drawer where she keeps those hospital-type bracelets, and before she snapped it on my left wrist, she said more than asked, "Date of birth."

I answered mechanically.

"Your nurse today will be Bonnie or Mary. Upstairs on the right."

I looked around at the patients and their accompanying families or friends. Every once in a while, I spot a woman with a head wrap like I wear, and I nod and smile. But not today.

I no longer get the Benadryl, and the Herceptin doesn't cause any immediate side effects, so I can drive by myself. I no longer have to trouble anyone. Now I just bring a book.

How long, I wonder, should I continue to do this? Is it really needed all the way through February? My heart is strong and the EKGs support this—but wasn't Walter's wife also monitored?

For now I continue once every three weeks.

Friday, 24 June 2011

The heavens declare the glory of God; the skies proclaim the work of His hands.

– Psalm 19:1 (NIV)

Our local grocery store has a dollar section: items on these shelves are just a dollar. There I found a butterfly net just like the ones that I used to buy for the children when they were still young. Nostalgia swept over me when I saw these cheap nets, and I purchased one as if with that act I could capture the childhoods of my children. Memories of catching not just butterflies, but also fireflies, tadpoles, and the goldfish in our water garden are embodied in that simple net. The longing for those bygone days when I could still sweep up my children in my arms threatened to choke me. How I wished that just for a day I could turn back time and enjoy the innocence and enthusiasm of my children as they were during their single-digit years.

When Jacob, Alexandra, and Larissa were in elementary school, Tad and I started what became a family tradition: On the last day of school, which is near the summer solstice, they stayed up late. There would be no more alarm clocks in the morning, no more school buses to catch. Around ten o'clock, when they would normally be putting on pajamas and going to bed, we fetched our plastic critter cages and those colorful plastic bug nets, and walked up the street to Ellison Park. In the deepening darkness, we would see blinking all around us: in the undergrowth beneath the tall spruce trees, in the grassy field that was once a formal rose garden, in the meadow by the river's edge. It was the magical dance of the fireflies. Tad and I would join the children catching the fireflies, placing them in the critter cages, watching them blink in our hands, in the cage, while flying above our heads. Back at the house we made sure that all the lights were turned off before we brought the critter cages indoors. (If the lights were on, the fireflies stopped blinking.) Then we placed the cages with the blinking bugs next to the children's beds: these were their night lights for that one evening. I would release the fireflies after the children fell asleep.

My father first caught fireflies with me when I was a child living in Chicago. Even on the city streets where there was scant greenery, these amazing insects blinked in the night. Years later I saw them hovering over a field in the Catskills of eastern New York in such fantastic numbers that I stood stupefied, awed by the magnificence of the scene. In the quiet darkness of the night, a giddy number of fireflies floated noiselessly before me like countless twinkling stars. Oh, the majesty of God's creation!

Many of today's children, who spend far too much time in front of a computer and too little outdoors, have never seen more than one or two lightning bugs floating through their yards. So we began asking various friends and neighbors to accompany us on our annual firefly walks. This year we invited Tatiana, Myron, and Michael, the three siblings who came to pray for me the day I was diagnosed with cancer. I brought along the new butterfly net with a green plastic handle and, despite protests from my kids that we didn't need it, the obligatory critter cage.

At thirteen, Michael was the youngest in the group; Jacob, nineteen—the oldest. The two of them romped around and wrestled each other in the dark. They chased one another like high-spirited colts and batted fireflies to the ground with their hands, stunning them, then picking them up, still blinking, from the rain-covered grass.

"Stop acting like a six-year-old," Alexandra complained to Jacob as he loped past.

"Who's out catching fireflies?" Jacob retorted. Indeed, we were all acting like children, chasing fireflies with abandon and filling my "unneeded" critter cage with flashing bugs, so many of them that to find me in the darkness, one just had to look for a high concentration of flashes.

It delighted me that even now, with children on the brink of adulthood, we still take these firefly walks. We still catch the bugs, put them in the cage, even bring them indoors. I know that my children will never forget these nighttime walks. After I'm in my grave, I expect my children will recall these times whenever they see these summertime bugs. I pray that I'm still around to take firefly walks with not just my adult children, but my grandchildren. It's all in God's hands, though. All in His hands.

July

Sunday, 3 July 2011

...so in Christ we, though many, form one body, and each member belongs to all the others.

– Romans 12:5 (NIV)

On Sundays when the girls are not scheduled to teach Sunday school and Tad isn't preaching, we sometimes visit other churches. Yes, it's a little stressful and, yes, it's a bit intimidating to walk into a building where you don't know anyone, don't know where to sit or how to act. Yet each visit teaches us something new, broadens our perspective, and expands our circle of acquaintances. In some churches that Tad and I have visited, people greet us by name when we return!

We thought it would be interesting to visit an Amish Mennonite church. We've visited Mennonite churches in the past—Mennonites who dress conservatively and drive cars. But I didn't know until recently that Amish Mennonites existed. The Amish Mennonites drive horse-drawn buggies like the Amish, but they dress more like the Mennonites, and in their homes they have electricity. I'm sure that there are many things that set apart the Amish Mennonites from the Amish and the Mennonites in terms of lifestyle and church practices, but we went to experience their fellowship and church service, not to study doctrine.

Tad had gotten the phone number of Elvin, an Amish Mennonite friend of a friend, and called him during the week to ask for directions to his church. Early this morning, we headed southeast of Rochester into the rolling hills of the Finger Lakes area where vineyards and farms prevail. The sun was out, golden and merry, its sunbeams skipping across the rich farmland. About an hour's drive from home, following smaller and smaller roads, we found the white clapboard church building.

As we turned onto the gravel driveway, I noticed a cluster of men in nearly identical black slacks, black vests, and black hats. Their shirts were either white or pale blue. They were clean-shaven, like Mennonite brothers. These men were talking in a small group outside, but when our silver VW Golf turned into their drive, all heads turned.

Immediately my stomach tightened. Ours was the only motor vehicle on the premises. We were going to stand out in many ways.

All five of us got out of the car, and while Tad walked over to talk with the men, the rest of us stood awkwardly near our vehicle. We were early, so most of the congregation was still on the way to church.

The plain white church building was set on a rise, so we could see a sweep of dewy green countryside to the south, glistening under the morning sun. Here and there, a black horse-drawn buggy clip-clopped toward the church. It seemed like I'd stepped into the past. Many older children and teens rode their bicycles to church, chasing their elongated shadows along the roads, arriving in pairs or in threes. Boys were dressed like small versions of their dads, but instead of wearing vests, they had on suspenders. The girls and the women wore cape dresses in a rainbow of pastels and dark bonnets that tied under their chins.

Along two sides of the church building was a long, narrow metal building with a roof and back wall; the front was open. This was where the horses, harnessed to their buggies, were pulled in and "parked" so they would be in the shade while their owners were in church. When all the spots in the parking building were taken, additional horses with buggies were tied up under a row of tall, shady maples.

People began to walk toward the church door. I looked to Tad for guidance. He leaned toward me. "Follow the women," he said. Tad and Jacob followed the men.

Alexandra, Larissa, and I went up a few cement steps and into an entry area. This would be the coatroom in the wintertime; today the women hung their dark bonnets on the innumerable hooks attached in even rows on the walls. Under their dark outdoor bonnets, the women had on the white pleated head coverings typical of Mennonite women. I wore the dark head wrap that completely covers my fuzz-covered head. It's been my standard attire for a while.

Seeing us standing self-consciously not knowing where to go, one kind woman showed us inside and suggested a place to sit on one of the hard wooden pews. The rows of pews, which were the same honey color as the floorboards, formed a rectangle. Near the center of the room was a table with cushioned backless benches on two sides. This is where the church leaders sat.

The men sat on the opposite side of the room from the women. Our pews faced one another with that table between us. The pews to the right were perpendicular to ours; that's where the children sat, the youngest in front, older children behind them. Many of the younger children were barefooted, their feet casually dangling in the air far above the floor. I wished that my feet, too, could be free from confinement on this hot summer day.

On the men's side of the building were rows and rows of evenly spaced hooks, like in the women's coatroom. These were for the men's black hats, which hung like dark polka dots against the white walls. Large windows on each of the walls had been opened wide to invite any breeze. There were no decorations, no lights, no electricity in this building. I wondered whether they ever had any evening services after dark, and if so, how they lit the room.

The church service was in German—or rather Pennsylvania Dutch. Occasionally someone would preach in English. Was this for our benefit, or did they preach in English on other Sundays? The hymn singing was in Pennsylvania Dutch as well. Alexandra, Larissa, and I followed along as best we could in the hymnbooks that someone handed us.

Since I didn't understand most of the preaching, I spent much of the two-hour service looking around the room, drinking in this new experience and unfamiliar environment. At one point, a horse neighed outside. From the other side of the yard, another horse responded. As the preaching continued, the horses had their own conversation, neighing to one another from all around the building, back and forth, calling to each other. I tried not to smile. In my own country not that far from home, I was having a foreign-country experience.

When the service was over, Elvin's family invited us to their home for lunch. We could either crawl along in our Golf behind their buggy, or—

"Tad, do you think some of us could ride in the buggy with Elvin and his wife while some of their children ride in the car with you? Could you ask him?"

Of course I was hoping to be one of the passengers in the horse-drawn buggy. To my delight, Elvin agreed, so Larissa and I got to ride in the back seat of the buggy all the way to their home. Elvin's wife sat next to him holding their youngest child. I asked them about the horse that was pulling the buggy; they shared many horse stories with us—including accounts of buggies overturned in ditches—as we clip-clopped along the country roads to their house.

Later Elvin took the rest of our family on a buggy ride while his wife prepared lunch. Elvin showed us his stable, which houses two additional horses, and gave us a tour of his barn, which houses dairy cows. Because he sells organic milk to a local grocery chain, his feed and barn have to meet stringent codes. One example is that he has to trap or shoot rats; he cannot set out poison for them.

The meal was simple; the company pleasant; the family hospitable. Farm life is not easy, but when we visit farms, their life does seem idyllic in a nostalgic kind of way. One thing that stands out in farm families like this one is that everyone works together. Children help with chores, whether it's in the barn or field, or clearing dishes from the table. Suburban families need to learn from them.

Tuesday, 5 July 2011

For where your treasure is, there your heart will be also.
— Matthew 6:21 (NIV)

Today was one of those days that I would like to paste into a mental album so I can take it out from time to time to savor each delightful moment. It was the type of summer day I long for, especially on days when the weather is soggy or the winter has dragged on longer than I can bear. At those times, I'd go to my album of memories to delight in the shimmering sunlight on the lush green lawn; to pick and eat sun-warmed cherries and raspberries right off the plants; to feel the warmth of the sun's rays and hear the murmur of the leaves in the gentle, warm breezes; to drink in the smell of horses and hay wafting up from our neighborhood stable; and to experience, albeit briefly, the life of a farm family on a summer day.

I didn't have any plans for today when I got out of bed. I had the day off from work, a "floating holiday." Perhaps I would weed or dig up some more of the lawn to make room for that new hosta garden I'm putting in this summer; maybe I'd sort some things in the bedroom or garage.

"Are you going cherry picking with us?" asked Alexandra as I ate the biscuits that Larissa had baked for breakfast. "We're going to visit Chad and Michele on the way back and pick up our new milking bucket."

I love, love, love to spend time alone, especially in the mornings when the sunlight frolics across the grass and outlines each blade and leaf with a halo as if each plant was giving off its own aura. I savor the freshness of the new day when the morning air is still cool and my cup of coffee is still hot.

But I also like to spend time with my family. How many more times will I get to pick cherries with my near-adult children? After this summer, Alexandra may not live with us if she goes to Mission E4. Then, of course, there's—but let's not think about it—the possibility that I may not be around to pick cherries at all in a year or two or five. Life is short, too short, and change is inevitable. Picking cherries together sounded far more appealing than even my alone time. Tad, Alexandra, Larissa, and I piled into the VW Golf. Too bad that Jacob had to work and couldn't join us.

The farm where we picked cherries today is farther from home than our usual cherry-picking place, but the prices are far cheaper and, unlike in other U-pick farms, there are few people. Tad handed us buckets, which were stashed in the garage of the family-owned orchard, and we walked thirty paces to the cherry trees. Every cherry I could see was ripe and flawless in color, shape, and taste. Not a fly or wasp, squirrel or sparrow marred the orchard. Although I'm no cherry expert, I have picked cherries before, and I can't recall seeing any fruit trees quite this perfect.

I climbed into the crook of a cherry tree, hung my bucket from the fork of a trimmed branch, and picked every cherry I could reach. All were ripe, every last one. In less than half an hour, the four of us picked twenty-nine pounds of cherries—enough for eating, canning, and giving away.

It was mid-morning when we arrived at Chad and Michele's farm, just a slight detour from the two-lane country highway that leads back home. They sell eggs from their two thousand chickens, which they keep in a barn. Red chickens roam free in that building, their cooing and clucking an overwhelming surround sound when you walk in. Although the chickens have designated nests for laying eggs, brown eggs can be found in the most unexpected places in that barn, like under the staircase.

In addition to selling eggs, Chad sells milk from his thirty dairy cows to individuals and families who come to his farm to pick up the milk in large glass jars. That's how we first met him: we heard of him through the grapevine and came to his farm to buy milk.

The farm has enough acreage to grow the corn and hay that feed the animals. Although they can't afford luxuries on their income, this family's lifestyle of farm chores and homeschooling builds togetherness for the husband, wife, and their seven children, who are eight years old and younger.

When we pulled up next to the barn, I felt we'd walked into one of the storybooks I used to read in elementary school, books about summers at the grandparents' farm, books that made me wish that my grandparents lived in a farmhouse and not on a city lot in Toronto. I know that seven young children provide more challenges and require more patience than I will ever be able to fully grasp, but we arrived at one of those moments when there was harmony. The tumble of seven barefooted children clambered over each other in play like a litter of kittens.

While my children had a sandbox in their childhood, here, under a massive maple tree, was an expanse of sand the area of an entire room with a picnic table at one end and a yellow plastic slide at the other. In between, strewn all over the sand, were heaps of blue and green and red plastic dump trucks and excavators, cars and plastic animals, shovels and naked dolls, and a pair of black roller blades. But the children weren't playing with the toys; they had four kittens tied to one another with a four-ended leash, and these tabby kittens were the center of play. To add to the menagerie, one of the boys took Dusty and Fudge, young bunnies appropriately named for their colors, out of their wire cage on the lawn to join the fun. It didn't look like the bunnies thought it was fun to be sent down the slide or chased in circles around and around the outside of the cage, but the children sure did. An old chocolate Lab lay on the sand, a swarm of little bugs whirling around its head, ignoring all the activity.

This was childhood as it should be with fresh air, a proliferation of animals, rowdy exercise, and unrestrained imagination. No TV or video games here; no organized play dates in fabric-softener-fresh clothes. Just wholesome, old-fashioned play—tugging, laughing, climbing, sliding, running. The girls had on long tee shirt dresses with pantaloons; the boys wore jeans and colorful tee shirts. Their joyful faces were smudged with dirt and the remnants of breakfast. Much of the three-year-old girl's blond hair had come out of the intended braids. One of the boys dumped sand on his youngest brother, who was oblivious to this attack because he was interfering with someone else's play. Those not occupied with the kittens or bunnies were digging caverns in the sand with their hands.

We arrived just as Michele, dressed in a denim skirt and red tee shirt, was clearing the breakfast dishes from the picnic table under the tree. An adult tabby was helping clean up by licking the spilled milk on the table.

"Would you like some coffee?" Michele offered cheerfully. "I have some freshly made in the house."

How could I resist?

"I would love some!" I replied.

Tad, who had wandered off in search of Chad, now returned with the ruddy-faced farmer, and they both joined us at the shaded picnic table. If Chad was annoyed by this interruption of his chores, he never showed it.

Although we had come to pick up a small metal milking bucket for our goats, we spent the rest of the morning under that tree, chatting, sipping coffee, petting the cats that had joined us in the shade, watching the children, pushing them on the swing, and occasionally rescuing a kitten that was being handled a little too carelessly. Before we left, Michele invited the girls into the house to give them the small metal milking bucket that she had ordered for them.

"Sorry that the bucket isn't clean," Michele added. "The children got a hold of it and were playing with it."

I peeked in the bucket and saw sand inside, and smiled.

After we'd driven a little ways toward home, Tad made a U-turn.

"Humor me," he said, and drove back to the farm.

"Did you forget something?" asked Chad as he came up to the car.

"Yes, we forgot to give you these," said Tad as Alexandra handed Chad a plastic grocery bag filled with ripe cherries.

I am so glad that I didn't choose to stay home and have alone time.

Thursday, 7 July 2011

In you, LORD, I have taken refuge...
– Psalm 31:1 (NIV)

Still no rain. The April rains that drowned our yards and our spirits in the early spring would be quite welcome now. The sandy soil in our yard is so dry that it falls apart like flour when I sink a spade into it and turn it over.

I have been digging up an area for a new hosta garden in the front yard. Even if I dig only ten minutes per evening, little by little, the job will get done. I've put in several gardens like that, bit by bit, spadeful by spadeful. The summer I was debilitated by lupus, I put in a lovely hosta garden by working on it only a few minutes every evening. In the same way, each passing day is a small step closer to the end of my cancer adventure.

This evening I didn't dig, didn't work on my new garden. Instead, I spent my outdoor time watering, walking to individual plants with the green hose, letting them drink deeply.

As I wandered from plant to plant, I reflected on each one's history. Each plant has its own story, its tale of how it found its way into my garden. Yes, I did buy some of the plants, both from local nurseries and from online stores, but the majority of my hostas and flowers were acquired at plant exchanges, given to me as gifts, or dug up and brought home from the woods, from a friend, or from my deceased brother's yard.

I watered the 'Sagae' hosta with its blue-green leaves lined with a yellow margin, and recalled how Barb, my brother's supervisor, had commented on this large, stunning hosta.

"Alex once told me that if you have a garden full of hostas, the 'Sagae' will be the one that people notice," she had said.

Indeed, people have commented on its beauty ever since I planted it in the roadside memorial garden that I created with transplants from Alex's yard. So when I see this 'Sagae' on the front hill, I think of my brother, and my heart is sad—sad that he can't see the beauty of these plants that he bought, sad that he died so suddenly and senselessly, sad that he hadn't made peace with God or sought His face.

After soaking the hostas in the new unfinished garden and on the front hill, I went to the 'Remember Me' hosta with its small lemon yellow leaves rimmed with green. I planted one years ago in the front triangle garden by the stairs leading up to our front door. I planted another in the backyard hosta garden under the spruce trees. The second one I dug up from Alex's yard. Think of me, both these hostas seem to whisper to me whenever I look at them. *Remember me!*

"Hosta 'Remember Me' is named in honor of Sandy De Boer, a former employee of Walters Gardens Inc. who died of breast cancer in 2001," says the Walters Gardens website. Who would have thought that a few years after purchasing this hosta, named in remembrance of a woman who died of breast cancer, I myself would have breast cancer? Doubly painful is the fact that my brother also had a 'Remember Me' hosta, and although he didn't die of cancer, I now remember him when I look at it. And I think of my own vulnerability. I wonder whether anyone will think of me when they look at this hosta years from now.

I made my way to the backyard gardens where I have the majority of my flowers. A walk through those gardens is like a visit with friends. The garden is a tapestry of gifts—irises from Joy, a fellow technical writer; lamb's ear from Josie, who befriended me during a medical mission trip to Senegal; blazing star and balloon flowers from Michele, who sang soprano in the church choir with me; forget-me-nots and peony from Joanna, a church friend and avid gardener. These people will never know just how often I think of them.

The flowers are also a scrapbook of memories. The wild phlox remind me of Linear Park where we took the children as toddlers to wade in the river; the red columbine—a camping trip to Buttermilk Falls where our family shared a campsite with the Seeglers and their amazingly well-trained Golden Retriever; the tall magenta phlox under the bedroom window—my cousin's village home in Petryliv, Ukraine, which I visited several times with the children when they were young.

Sometimes I choose plants not because of their beauty, but because of the cherished memories they trigger. And sometimes I bring back plants from special places. Such is the variegated sedum. It was grown from a cutting that I pinched from a sedum that was growing near my grandfather's grave. Today that sedum is not big, and it's not that pretty since most of the variegation has somehow mutated back into plain green leaves, but the plant holds a memory of my family's first trip to Ukraine a dozen years ago and my visit to the cemetery after I dropped them off.

The plane left for Ukraine from Toronto, about three hours' drive from Rochester. Tad and the children flew to Ukraine in late June that year, then after seven weeks, I joined them. The children were only three, five, and seven years old at the time, and other than one weekend when I'd gone to an out-of-state wedding, I had not been apart from them.

"Just don't cry when you say good-bye," Tad had warned me in advance. "You'll get the kids started."

When parting at the airport, Alexandra, then five years old, had asked to be the last to hug me. When her turn came, she began to sob as her little hands clasped around my neck. It had taken all my inner strength not to cry as I parted with Tad, then Jacob and Larissa, but with Alexandra's tears, my resolve broke. With tears streaming, I hung on to my girl until Tad pulled her from me and carried her, still crying and her teary eyes fixed on me, through the barrier where only ticketed travelers could enter. As I turned away, wiping my tears, I wondered what onlookers thought of this scene. Another family splitting up? A divorce case where the father got the children?

After that separation from my family, I felt broken. Incomplete. My most precious treasures and the focus of my day-to-day life had just boarded an airplane and left for a far-off land where I had never been. I drove to a quiet place to collect my thoughts, find some solace, and pray.

I drove to the Parkside Cemetery in Toronto.

I remember that it was a hot June day. Suddenly, for the first time that season, I heard a cicada buzzing, a sound I so love. The cemetery, founded in 1892, has magnificent trees, soothing shade, and impressive tombstones. I have always found cemeteries fascinating, calming, and thought provoking. How can you walk among the tombstones and not contemplate your own eternity, your fleeting presence here on earth? Each of these people buried at my feet once walked and ran, laughed and cried, loved and feared, had hopes and desires. And now? They lie in the ground the way I will someday.

What is your life? You are a mist that appears for a little while and then vanishes (James 4:14, NIV). Even though I know that life is indeed like a vapor and realize my life has come to this point so curiously quickly, yet it's hard to imagine myself there, under the ground. Even now. Most people just prefer not to think of life that way. In fact, when you're healthy and young, it's a difficult concept to grasp. Life seems to stretch out to the horizon and beyond.

That June afternoon, I first visited the grave of my uncle Slavko, my Dad's brother, who was the only relative I had while growing up who was actually interested in me, the only one who always remembered my birthday, who visited our family, who flew kites with my siblings and me. In my early thirties, I had spent hours recording him on cassette tape as he told me stories from our family's history. He had an interest in genealogy, and so did I. But now he is gone. His stories are silenced. His library of knowledge is forever closed.

Next, I drove to my grandfather's grave. Although my mother

tells me repeatedly that my grandfather was a gentle man who never raised his voice to her, a kind doctor who saw patients gratis when they couldn't afford payment, I barely knew him. Oh, I had spent a lot of time in his presence at my grandparents' house, from which I have fond memories, but that isn't knowing him. I remember his toothy smile, his shiny bald head, and his hug when we arrived at his house. But after the initial greeting, he did not show any interest in me, never played with me, nor do I remember ever having any meaningful conversation with him. He talked with adults; I played with the other children. That's how it was with that generation. Grandfather died at ninety after suffering with Alzheimer's for thirteen years. Ironically, he founded a nursing home for aging Ukrainian immigrants, but the family put him in a Canadian nursing home. They were too embarrassed to put Grandfather, a respected physician, into the home that he founded.

It was while thinking these thoughts near my grandfather's gravesite that I found the variegated sedum whose descendent I watered in my backyard. I had pinched a cutting, and after sitting in a glass of water for a few weeks, it had sprouted roots. Since my childhood, I've been fascinated how sedum, unlike daffodils or daisies, sprouts roots when put in a glass of water. I once thought it was magic; I now consider it one of God's little miracles.

Saturday, 9 July 2011

My sheep hear My voice, and I know them, and they follow Me.
        – John 10:27 (NKJV)

Every year as the children grow older it gets more complicated to schedule our summer travels—summer camp, mission trips, camping trips, visiting relatives in Ukraine. Over many weeks and after much discussion and prayer, the plans for this summer have congealed.

Alexandra has decided to commit one year to do the internship program at Mission E4, the mission in Massachusetts that we visited in February. There she will study God's Word and work in a ministry placement. She isn't enthusiastic about it, but feels that is where God is leading her. Alexandra will start at the end of September. Her internship includes a two-week trip to Haiti in October. I will join her in Haiti during her second week there.

Larissa will spend two weeks at Camp Cherith, a Christian camp an hour's drive south of Rochester. It will be her eighth summer at Camp Cherith, a place of campfires and canoeing, of Bible exploration and exploring the woods. This year she'll be in the CILT (Campers In Leadership Training) program to learn to be a camp counselor.

Three days after Larissa returns from camp, my family will fly to Ukraine. But this year I won't be going with them. Even though I have vacation time saved up at work and the oncologist said that I could go away between treatments, a voice inside me says, *Stay. You must stay home this summer.*

"I don't know why, but I'm not supposed to go this summer," I told my husband when he was ordering plane tickets for the family. Tad tried to talk me into going, but the little voice was insistent. *Stay.*

Because they have to start school around Labor Day, Jacob and Larissa will be in Ukraine just under three weeks. But Tad, who is self-employed, and Alexandra, who finished high school this June, will remain there for a full seven weeks, returning only days before Alexandra is to go to Mission E4.

I will stay home with the goats and chickens.

Tuesday, 12 July 2011

But let all who take refuge in you be glad; let them ever sing for joy. Spread your protection over them...
– Psalm 5:11 (NIV)

Another towering spruce gone, taken down by growling chain saws, splintered into mulch. In an hour, decades of growth vanished, leaving a stump and a dusting of wood chips. Another victim of *Cytospora* canker, the disease that is eradicating the magnificent spruce trees that characterize this neighborhood, which was established in the late 1930s. This spruce—actually, two of them—was taken down across the street, changing the character of the neighbors' front yard completely. Soon we'll have to cut down one of the tall spruce trees in our own backyard, a tree well over sixty feet tall. It's been losing needles like rain. It too has *Cytospora* canker.

It's gloriously hot, like a July day ought to be with sun beating down, cicadas joyously singing—and the lawn yellowing under the unrelenting sun and lack of rain.

I'm working from home. Alexandra and Larissa are on summer break. Tad isn't working today. Only Jacob is away from the house, working at the mechanic shop. All of us go to the kitchen at lunchtime and, as is our family's custom, each fixes his or her own lunch. Perhaps it's heating up leftovers. Maybe it's cooking some eggs. Supper we eat together as a family; lunch is a fend-for-yourself meal even if we're all home on a weekday.

Unless my mother has dropped off sushi that day (which she has done often since I was diagnosed with cancer), I make myself a salad for lunch. As I prepare my food, I do the kitchen dance: I sidestep and move out of the way as someone tries to get to the trash bin under the sink, or I bend so someone can reach over my shoulder for a bowl from the cupboard. Four of us in the kitchen is a bit tight, so we shift around each other at the sink, at the counter, at the stove. The kitchen dance. I can't help but think that this is temporary since the children will soon start moving away as they grow up.

I had a two o'clock appointment for Herceptin. I brought my journal with me for company.

When I first started coming to the Lipson Cancer Center, it was wintertime with its endless progression of lake-effect cloudy days. I could hardly imagine summer back then when I was foggy from drugs and coming in every few days for shots, for Herceptin, or for the mind-numbing chemo. I was in so often that the receptionist greeted me by name. She still does.

Although in the main waiting room downstairs there's an annoying large-screen TV bombarding patients with canned laughter or violent explosions of movie scenes, it's pleasantly quiet in the yellow-walled upstairs. No piped-in music or obnoxious videos; just the hum of a refrigerator, the ticking of the IV machine, and the voices and footsteps of the nurses on the beige linoleum—Eva and Mary today.

Eva, with brown hair cut in a bob, knows about my trips to Haiti and other countries, my goats, my children. I'm surprised she keeps the information straight with the number of patients she must see. By forming a relationship with me, coming for treatments is like visiting with friends. I have spent more time with some of these nurses in the last half year than I typically spend with friends.

Saturday, 16 July 2011

The LORD *gave, and the* LORD *has taken away; blessed be the name of the* LORD.

– Job 1:21 (NKJV)

A call this morning notified us that thirty-eight-year-old Ivan, the youngest son of the elderly Omelian and Adelia, who go to our church, died last night about 7:30 PM in a motorcycle accident. Ivan was riding on Route 31 when a drunk driver without a license pulled out from an intersection directly in front of him. Ivan hit the vehicle and flew onto the road. He died at the scene.

The parents are in shock. Ivan had been on his way to their house when he had the accident.

Tad and I visited Ivan's parents in the evening to sit and grieve with them. "I'm old; he was young," lamented the dad, who is seventy-eight. "I'm here; he's not."

And I, who had the dreaded diagnosis of cancer, am also here. Even more than before, I cherish such everyday chores as picking raspberries in our backyard. I'm still here to do these simple things; Ivan is not.

Sunday, 17 July 2011
Baptism service

My soul finds rest in God alone…

– Psalm 62:1 (NIV)

In the morning, our church congregation met on the shore of Lake Ontario for its annual baptism service.

I stood under an umbrella I had brought, hiding from the beating sun. Maria, a short woman near eighty years old, sidled up to me, entwined her arm in mine, and squeezed under my tiny patch of relief from the blazing rays.

The crowd spread across the expanse of green lawn like flower petals scattered by the wind. Our pastor stood in front of the congregation. Behind him—a solemn row of teens dressed in flowing white robes faced the crowd. Behind them—a few trees, a narrow stretch of sand, then glistening water all the way to the horizon.

The service was held in a public park, so while the pastor preached, typical beach activities continued around us: people walking, jogging; motorboats roaring. How incongruous that directly behind the robe-clad youth, as prominent as if just behind the pulpit, a woman in short shorts sauntered along the sandy beach with her dog. And further away on the lake, a motorboat dragged a water skier in a spray of water, the woman with a bathing suit, life jacket, and long hair flying—such a strong contrast to the eight somber individuals pledging to follow Jesus for the rest of their days. The contrast between what we as Christians are supposed to represent versus the self-indulgence of the world struck me during that outdoor service.

After the white-robed youth were immersed in the water, Tad and the children drove to our church building where the service was prolonged and the newly baptized members partook in Holy Communion for their first time. But I went home, ate a quick lunch, then got in the VW Golf and headed west toward Buffalo.

This summer has been a season of reminiscence. Triggered by my bout with cancer and the possibility that I'm in the final phase of my life, childhood memories are especially poignant, vivid, and dear. If life were a circle, I feel close to its starting point; my past seems so oddly near.

Every evening of crickets—memories from vacations at my grandparents' cottage in Canada flood back. Katydids chirping at night—I recall the summer camps near Buffalo. Cicadas buzzing on hot days—I'm again at that beloved cottage, a young girl with a ponytail, my family around me, my grandparents visiting, my father taking us on long nature walks, my mother ever in the kitchen preparing our meals and caring for my younger siblings. I can smell the musty, woodsy scent of the cottage in my memory. I can see the squiggly design on the Formica kitchen table. Friends, family, laughter, campfires, long hikes—they seem so recent that I can almost touch them. The longing to go back to those safe, long-ago days is acutely painful at times.

Today I visited a swatch of land in western New York that is especially dear: Noviy Sokil, the Ukrainian Scout camp in North Collins, a little south of Buffalo. This wooded plot is crisscrossed by a ravine and broken up by clearings for barracks and tents. There's a swimming pool and a mess hall, an office building and a shower building. But for me, the dearest, most enchanting part of the land is the deep, shale-lined gully with the trickle of a creek that runs through it. I hiked there when I was a teenage counselor with my campers. I walked alone in this gully during free time. I caught crayfish there with my three children when they were toddlers. So many memories…

This weekend my sister and youngest brother are at camp—Marta as one of the cooks in the kitchen, Peter, with his four-year-old son in tow, as the head, or "commandant," of the toddler camp. I haven't been to this camp in many, many years, and I wanted to visit, perhaps for my final time.

Noviy Sokil is one hundred miles from home—a two-hour drive if you take the New York State Thruway most of the way, as I did. Only the last few miles are along a two-lane country highway lined with orange daylilies. Then you turn onto School Street, and you're almost there. The final leg of the journey is a long dirt driveway leading onto the camp property.

I arrived in the glaring light of mid-afternoon. When I pulled onto the Noviy Sokil property, I felt awkward. What was I thinking when I decided to visit? Had I made a mistake in coming? As I bumped along the last stretch of road, I had butterflies in my stomach, just like I had as a teenager coming to be a counselor. But today, no one stood by the roadside charging for parking. There were no crowds, no children running, no friends to greet me. There wasn't a single person in the parking lot, which is a field that looks remarkably like it did thirty-five years ago.

How could that much time have gone by? Was it really that long ago that I used to spend summers here?

Indeed, my last year as a camp counselor was over three decades ago—in 1977! Then twenty years later when my children were toddlers, I returned, and for several summers I attended the one-week camp organized especially for parents and their young children. We stayed in tents that we pitched in a field and spent days with our children listening to simple lessons, making way too many craft projects, walking in the ravine, wading in the creek, splashing in the pool, singing around a campfire.

My very last time at Noviy Sokil was in 2000, the summer of rain. Daily drenching rain. I set up our large Eureka tent between downpours, avoiding standing puddles. The rain was not the constant, demoralizing gray showers, but brief, violent thunderstorms that rumbled from afar, hid the sun for a short while, and quickly waterlogged the ground, the tents, and the sleeping bags. I recall how Alexandra, then six, astutely observed, "The weather that is making you adults miserable—we children love it!" All week long parents hung out sleeping bags to dry during sunny periods and grumbled about their kids' sodden and mud-splattered clothes while the children delighted in a bounty of salamanders, newts, frogs, and toads, which they released into convenient puddles near the tents.

Now these memories are like shadows.

I parked the car in the near-empty field and walked toward the buildings. The brutal summer heat had burned the grass into crispy French fries, which crackled audibly as I walked. Voices drifted from the pool area. It was the toddlers and their parents, the camp that Peter was leading. Marta was at the pool as well. I stopped by and greeted them, soaked my feet in the chlorinated water, and briefly made small talk with a few of the other parents, some of whom I knew when they were toddlers themselves. But I hadn't come to socialize; I came to take a walk in the ravine.

I made my way to the building that used to be the old kitchen in the 1970s. Here women cooked meals for fifty or more campers over a rustic wood-fueled stove, their faces glistening from the heat. Although the building was now empty, I could still see these women and the lines of campers, plates heaped with steaming food, the cooks urging me to take seconds, which I nearly always did.

More shadows from the past.

The creek runs past this former kitchen area, and that's where I hopped onto the shale creek bed. Today the creek was dry. No water flowed at all. Yet there were years when this channel contained such a gushing torrent that one would barely be able to stand against the power of the water. I know; I tried.

I wandered upstream, away from the old kitchen, away from all the buildings and into the forest. The shouts and shrieks of children at play receded with each step. A few more steps, and I was alone in the hush of the woods. The whisper of the leaves far above me prevailed. The greenery of the maple and hemlock trees enveloped me; I was surrounded by a world that God, not man, had created.

As I walked upstream, the walls of the ravine began to rise. A cicada droned high above me. Closer to the ground, I noticed how the umbrella-like leaves of the mayapples had yellowed and collapsed on their stalks. This summer has been so dry that even the moss was shriveled.

The layered shale creek bed made a good path. In places, the stone was level and smooth like tiles. In other places it was like stairs leading upward through a narrow channel. Sometimes the gray shale was crushed, and my footsteps went crunch, crunch where water should have flowed. Puddles were infrequent and overcrowded with water striders.

I stopped to take a photo, and memories of my days here with Jacob, Alexandra, and Larissa came flooding back with such force that my eyes grew misty. How I miss those days when everything was a wondrous delight, a discovery: a crayfish, a salamander, splashing in puddles with rain boots, cooking soup over a campfire. I had the joy of reliving childhood through my children. How fleeting are our days on this earth; how quickly the childhood years evanesced.

I kept walking upstream between the steep walls of the ravine, clambering over downed trees and scrambling under others. A chipmunk chirped a warning as I approached. At one puddle, a row of hoof marks indicated that a deer had taken a drink here.

On a bend, I came across an ankle-deep pool of water about twenty feet long. Other summers it might have been deep enough to swim in, but not today. Crayfish. Maybe this puddle contained crayfish? Normally the creek would be full of them. I turned over a few rocks and smiled. A motionless crayfish blended well with the dead leaves in the water. I chased it around the pool like in my childhood years. I caught it and held it triumphantly for a moment. Then I let it go.

I gazed at this brown, shallow pool a while longer. I heard nothing here but the wind—and the echoes of memories murmuring to me. How many thousands of paths have I hiked? How many forests and mountains and seashores? How many cities have I explored and on how many continents? Yet here, right here, this little scrap of land in upstate New York is more special to me than the snow-capped Himalayas, more precious than the Taj Mahal, more beautiful than the Grand Canyon. This place is woven into my soul.

Back at camp, Marta invited me to supper, which she was about to serve. Peter's campers came to eat, so I sat with my brother and nephew enjoying pulled pork sandwiches and camp stories.

Before I left for home, Marta introduced me to one of the women also helping in the camp kitchen.

"Remember Roksolana?" she asked in front of this woman.

I studied her face, but my quizzical expression and my silence answered Marta's question.

When Marta told me Roksolana's maiden name, I was surprised. She and her younger sister had been my very favorite pupils when I taught Ukrainian preschool on Saturdays back in the 1970s. As I gazed at this woman in her forties, I began to sculpt away the years and suddenly, I saw the features of the little blonde girl I once knew.

Roksolana smiled, remembering me for who I had been in her life. A teacher is always a teacher, never a peer.

"I was so excited one summer when I came here to camp and found out you were my camp counselor. I claimed the cot next to yours," Roksolana told me.

Roksolana is now a schoolteacher. I wondered whether I had any role in influencing her choice of career. I, for example, became a camp counselor because when I was young, I had a counselor whom I adored. I wanted to be like her. Today I don't even remember her name, but I do remember her kindness.

Monday, 18 July 2011

The LORD bless you and keep you; the LORD make His face shine upon you and be gracious to you.
– Numbers 6:24–25 (NKJV)

I feel so much better when I work from home. I sit barefooted at my computer dressed in breezy summer clothes, my feet bare on the carpet. Sunshine and flowers, birds chirping and twittering—working from home with open windows and fresh breezes lifts my heart as if it were attached to a helium balloon.

But today I went to Kodak. There the air hints of chemicals. It's breathed and re-breathed, re-circulated and re-cooled. I have to bundle up in layers to endure the unbearable cold of the office building. It's odd to wear fleece during this oppressive summer heat. Winter or summer, I have to wear sweaters and fleece because my cubicle is painfully cold.

Why the company refrigerates the offices in the summertime is a puzzle to me. What a waste of energy and money. What an unpleasant atmosphere for the workers. Even when the city is in the middle of a record-breaking heat wave, as it is today, the bone-chilling cold in my office causes my fingers to hurt and my nose to ache.

At lunchtime I went outside to thaw out. But I didn't just stand outside, even though it was in the nineties; I went to the parking lot and sat inside my car with the windows rolled up. Although it was well above one hundred degrees in the vehicle, I listened to the radio and slowly defrosted. I sat in what's normally a suffocatingly hot temperature, but because I was so cold, I couldn't feel it. I sat in the car until the ache in my hands subsided and my fingers were no longer cold. Then I went back to my office.

No longer is it pleasantly hot and reasonably dry; it's now hot, humid, and stickingly unpleasant to do anything outside—except thaw from the Kodak cold.

When I returned to my office I microwaved some leftovers for lunch. Anna, the administrative assistant for our department, saw me in the aisle carrying my heated container. She hadn't seen me since my operation and kept me standing in the aisle with my warm plastic container in hand.

Anna told me about a family friend who has stomach cancer. He will have to go through chemotherapy and live with a feeding tube for about half a year, have an operation to remove part of his stomach, and if all goes well, in nine months or so he can eat again. That makes my cancer treatment look like a walk in the park.

"My husband has been working insane hours at the post office," Anna continued. She had mentioned this to me before and how hard it was on her and their two young daughters.

"At first, when he got promoted from level 17 to 22, we were elated. But this position meant that he worked from six in the morning until nine at night weekdays, then Saturdays and Sundays as well. I never saw him. The girls never saw him. When they did see him, he was grumpy, and the girls would get annoyed at him. We were all miserable. This went on for years.

"Then he heard about you and this other friend, and he decided that it's just not worth it. Life is too short. So Ken asked for a demotion—for personal reasons, he said. Three weeks ago, he got that demotion. He's now the postmaster of the post office in a small town nearby. He works nine to five, comes home, and spends time with the girls. We're all so much happier. And you know a really strange thing? Because when he was promoted he skipped so many wage levels, his pay wasn't as high as it should have been. He was working salary, so he got no overtime. Now, working nine to five for five days a week, he makes *six dollars* less than what he made before!"

If my cancer helped restore this family, it was worth it. And there are probably many other stories of the ripple effects of my illness that God is using, but I will never know.

Thursday, 21 July 2011

Then man goes to his eternal home and mourners go about the streets.

– Ecclesiastes 12:5 (NIV)

Yesterday while we were at a funeral lowering the coffin containing Ivan, the motorcyclist, into the ground, another drunk driver careened across a double yellow line and sideswiped a van carrying thirteen Amish, sending the van into the path of a tractor, which drove over the van, crushing it. Five Amish died at the scene of the accident.

That's five more funerals this week due to drunken driving. Five more needless and unforeseen deaths.

For many, many years, I feared dying from cancer. I thought that instant death from a heart attack, a stroke, or an accident was better than being bedridden, in pain, and facing death for weeks or months or even years. But I've come to realize that instant death is emotionally far more painful, especially for those left behind. It does not allow you to say good-bye to loved ones. To resolve misunderstandings. To prepare oneself and others for the inevitable. I don't want to die from cancer, not yet, but if that's God's will for my life, I don't fear it so much anymore.

My life is not in danger of being curtailed by cancer in the near future. But when I was first diagnosed, the prognosis was uncertain. As people learned about my cancer, they sent notes and flowers, visited or called, brought meals and gifts. Some of the notes and e-mails were very touching and personal. It was like having my eulogy while still alive. It blessed me profoundly.

This evening I talked with my brother George, who stops at our parents' home faithfully every evening after work. George mentioned that Dad has gone downhill in the last week, and that Mama and Dusia suspect he's had a mini-stroke. Dad sometimes says things that don't make sense. Dusia said that he then has the presence of mind to make a joke out of it.

Today Dad said to George, "So they didn't feed you at the Noviy Sokil camp."

George hadn't been to the camp, so this came out of the blue— but George *is* planning on going there tomorrow to shoot Estes rockets with our brother Peter and his young campers. Did Dad simply confuse the days?

"He no longer goes on the Internet," George elaborated. "You know how he could always tell you what Yulochka (his endearing term for Prime Minister Yulia Tymoshenko of Ukraine) has done? Not any more. Mama had to Google something for him because he couldn't figure it out."

When I suggested he might die while Tad and the kids are in Ukraine, George said, "Not a chance. The nurse said his organs are like a sixteen-year-old's."

Wednesday, 27 July 2011

You will go out in joy and be led forth in peace; the mountains and hills will burst into song before you, and all the trees of the field will clap their hands.

– Isaiah 55:12 (NIV)

"Come outside," Tad urged as I was enjoying my morning coffee at the computer, already online and working on an index for a manual.

I followed him outside.

"Hear that?" he asked, waving his hand toward the back of the yard. He was referring to the cicadas' buzzing. "There must be thousands of them! Where are they all?"

I grinned, and so did Alexandra, who was outside with us. "Dad, there aren't thousands. That's only a few."

"About five or six," I chimed in. "They're just loud!"

Last night Marta called as I was leaving to go to the grocery store to buy twenty-five pounds of sugar. Tad was canning again. This time it was sour cherries. Tad, Jacob, and I had spent the evening pitting the cherries. I was halfway down the front steps when Tad came out, holding out the phone in hand.

"When is the last time you visited Mama and Dad?" my sister asked.

"It's been over a week," I said, "since before we took Larissa to Camp Cherith on Sunday."

"This isn't a guilt trip. I know you're busy and have your own things going on, but Mama needs us to stop by. I went there today, and Mama had tears in her eyes she was so glad that I was there. I think she's scared because Dad sometimes doesn't make sense."

"Like what? Can you give me an example?" I asked. Until recently, my dad had a phenomenal memory, and despite his physical frailty, his mind was sharp.

"Like saying that I was the commander of the camp. I know that he can get confused. I was there at camp, but in the kitchen and Peter was the commander. But it's more like when I was there, he fell asleep. Then he woke up laughing like it was some kind of joke, and he said that I was scared of the three bears."

That was disconcerting. I could picture Dad in the easy chair, guffawing as he sometimes did at *America's Funniest Videos*, but for no apparent reason. And Mama there with him, tied to the house because of his infirmity, having to watch his demise.

There's a feeling of hopelessness in that home. My parents, both staunch Catholics (though Dad hasn't been to church in years), don't find joy in the Lord. They don't read the Bible, don't seek its wisdom, don't have a personal relationship with God. To them, He's a distant all-powerful Lord and Judge, but I doubt that they even think much about Him day to day. I've known elderly couples who prayed together, read the Bible together, and who knew that after this life, they were going to be with Jesus in heaven. Peace emanated from them. Not so my parents. His presence is sadly lacking in their home and in their lives, and a kind of despondency prevails.

Saturday, 30 July 2011

O God, You are my God, earnestly I seek You; my soul thirsts for You, my body longs for You, in a dry and weary land where there is no water.

– Psalm 63:1 (NIV)

Rain! Blessed rain finally soaked the dry, thirsty ground yesterday. After a month of perpetual sunshine, I found the cloudiness a relief, a nice change. Odd how people like variety in weather. When we had constant cloudiness in April, it depressed me. Although perpetual sunshine in July didn't dispirit me, the lack of rain was a stressor in the back of my mind; the gardens were parched. The cloudiness that accompanied yesterday's rain was a reprieve from the brutality of the harsh, hot July sun.

The sun was out again this afternoon when Alexandra and I walked into my parents' house. I glanced into the living room and saw that my dad was awake, but his mouth was open and he didn't have on his glasses. He looked so pale and weak, so frail and confused. His skin was deathly white. It has changed color from last month, and to me it seems like an indication that he is nearing death.

"Do you know who came to visit?" my mother questioned him.

"Yes, it's Al—. You're both going to Ukraine tomorrow."

He was partially correct. He didn't finish Alexandra's name, nor did he say mine, and although Alexandra is going to Ukraine, it's in ten days. And I'm not going with her.

Just how much Dad really knows and understands is unclear. His confusion and slurring of speech came on suddenly. Perhaps he's had a mini-stroke. Maybe he isn't getting enough oxygen to his brain from congestive heart failure. It's distressing to see my father reduced to this state—so pitifully feeble, housebound, and in a chair from which he can rise—with help—only to go to his portable toilet.

I have struggled so much with my relationship with my father. The Bible says to honor your father and mother. I try. My dad is intelligent and until recently could recite epic poems for up to twenty minutes. He had a remarkable memory. He was a researcher, a scientist, an inventor, an author. But he lacked compassion, and though we know he loved his children, he just didn't show it.

It's very difficult to visit there. Such a pitiful scene. My dad used to know the latest details of politics in Ukraine; now politics don't interest him. Being so close to the end of his life, one would think that God, heaven, his afterlife would concern him. But not now. While he could comprehend, he wasn't interested in God; he mocked Tad for reading the Bible and preaching the Word, was annoyed any time God was mentioned in conversation. Politics are irrelevant now, and the most important and precious thing in the world—a relationship with God—well, he missed his chance. He has lived his life as if the end would never come.

Sadly, many in my family don't believe that a relationship with God is important in their lives; they believe that we're all going to the same place—to heaven. But that's not what the Bible says.

John 3:36 states, *Whoever believes in the Son has eternal life, but whoever rejects the Son will not see life, for God's wrath remains on him.* In John 14:6, Jesus says, *"I am the way and the truth and the life. No one comes to the Father except through Me."*

Songwriter LeCrae wrote, "If I'm wrong about God, I wasted my life. If you're wrong about God, you wasted your eternity."

It pains me to think of what will happen to my dad.

Sunday, 31 July 2011

Jesus said, "Let the little children come to me, and do not hinder them, for the kingdom of heaven belongs to such as these."
– Matthew 19:14 (NIV)

Since Larissa is at Camp Cherith, I substitute taught her preschool Sunday school class. Seven children came. All the children were well behaved, but I'm just not sure how much of the lesson got through.

The topic was Moses going to the top of the hill and, *As long as Moses held up his hands, the Israelites were winning, but whenever he lowered his hands, the Amalekites were winning. When Moses' hands grew tired, they took a stone and put it under him and he sat on it. Aaron and Hur held his hands up—one on one side, one on the other—so that his hands remained steady till sunset* (Exodus 17:11–12, NIV).

There was more to the lesson than this, but I focused on that passage. When I asked questions, Lilia's standard answer was, "He went to heaven."

"Where did Moses go when Joshua went to war against the Amalekites?"

"He went to heaven."

"No, look at the picture. He went up the…"

"Hill," someone answered.

"And what happened when Moses held up his arms?" I asked.

"He went to heaven," Lilia answered.

We had gone over this again and again, all of us raising and lowering our arms, then me doing so and the children "guessing" who was winning. No one went to heaven in my lesson.

"No, there was a war, so who was winning when Moses lifted up his arms?"

Silence.

"The Is-----," I hinted.

No answer.

"The Isra----."

Viktor could get it then. "Israelites!"

"And when Moses put his arms down, who was winning?"

I stumped them, even though we had just repeated "Amalekites" ten times. I wonder whether these children remember anything at all! But certainly this is better than sitting in the sanctuary where they would understand nothing. I had thought that playing some kind of game, like a memory game, would be a good activity, but I changed my mind. There seemed to be seven little worlds sitting out there, each one existing in a place that I couldn't reach.

"Will you come visit me?" asked Nathan, which of course had nothing to do with the lesson. (We're friends with Nathan's parents.)

"Yes, but not today."

I taught preschoolers many, many years ago. I suppose they're always like this, but I had forgotten.

I feel lost in the mundaneness of day-to-day living. At first when I was diagnosed with cancer, I was swept away with a flood of appointments. Doctors visits, operations, drugs, visits from friends, a deluge of cards and presents and calls. Now all that has just about dried up.

Drugs are still flowing through my veins and doubts are still trickling through my mind. I do my technical writing and my household chores living what appears to be a normal life, but in the back of my mind the web of worry is never far. Somehow my prayers have been routine; they've lost their urgency and fervor. I'm in the midst of spiritual doldrums, walking on the hamster wheel of life but getting nowhere. When will I be well?

August

Monday, 1 August 2011

Many are the plans in a person's heart, but it is the LORD's purpose that prevails.

– Proverbs 19:21 (NIV)

August. The word conjures images of yellowed fields of tall grass undulating in hot breezes; the brackish smell of crashing ocean waves; the heat of the sun on my bare arms; the magic of moonlight shimmering on a lonely lake; the eerie call of loons… In August, cicadas drone in the heat of day; crickets chant in the dark of night.

August is the month of summer vacations. As a child, I spent August at my grandparents' cottage in Canada, splashing in the lake with family and friends, hiking in the forests and fields with my father, catching butterflies, frogs, and garter snakes. I can still hear the lonely whisper of the winds in the pine forests near the cottage and the wailing train whistle at night as I lay in bed.

As a teenager, I went to special Ukrainian Scout camps in August: canoeing on Stillwater Lake in the Adirondacks, climbing my first mountain in the majestic snow-capped Canadian Rockies, backpacking along remote wilderness trails in the Cascade Range in Washington. Or, if not traveling, I would lie on the grass in my parents' backyard reading a book.

August is the month in which I met Tad and fell in love with him during a walk along the shores of the Atlantic. Several Augusts later, we took our young children back to the same seashore to splash in the whooshing waves and dig in the warm sand. When the children got older, we often spent August in Tad's hometown village in Ukraine, stepping back in time to an unhurried lifestyle, visiting family, walking to the local outdoor market, dropping by at friends' homes and staying for hours over a cup of tea. The children chased chickens, played hide-and-seek in attics with their cousins, rode horse-drawn wagons, and learned to dig potatoes. I watched the wagons overloaded with hay, wove wreathes from wild poppies for my daughter, smelled the acrid scent of burning fields as farmers cleared the stubble with controlled fires, and photographed it all.

The August when the children were eleven, nine, and seven, we took a cross-country camping trip. In the Badlands, the children saw their first bison and prairie dogs. In Yellowstone, we watched Old Faithful propel water high into the indigo evening sky. In the Grand Canyon, we rode mules along the rim of the imposing gorge.

I have more happy memories of August than any other month of the year.

Today I sat alone in a tan recliner and thought about the month of August—Augusts past and August present—while in a cubicle at the Lipson Cancer Center attached to my all-too-familiar IV machine through my mediport. Another one-hour infusion of Herceptin.

Yes, it's a different August this year.

Before that curved needle pierced my skin and slid into the mediport on my chest, I met with Nurse Practitioner Laura. After gathering the usual statistics—weight, blood pressure, and temperature—I sat down in Laura's office as she looked over my charts.

"Do you have any questions?" she invited.

"No…" I started, then quickly changed my mind. "Well, actually, I do. I'd like to know how you're going to track whether the cancer has come back after I'm done with the Herceptin. What tests can you do?"

"For your type of breast cancer, there are no routine exams that can pick up a recurrence of cancer. There's no blood work for follow-up, no CEA marker—an elevated enzyme that shows up for colon cancer, for example. There's nothing like that for your type of breast cancer."

"So how will I know if it's back?"

"You have to pay attention to certain symptoms," said the nurse practitioner. "For example, pain that doesn't go away, even with Advil. If it's bone cancer, you could have relentless pain in your hip, rib, or back. For cancer of the liver, you would have abdominal pain, which can radiate to your shoulder. If cancer spreads to the brain, you could have visual trouble, dizziness, severe headaches, blurred or double vision. If you experience any of these, you should call us immediately."

That was not what I wanted to hear. I wanted a clear-cut test, a definitive answer. But instead, I'll have vagueness and uncertainty stretching far into the future.

Tuesday, 2 August 2011

The LORD will fight for you, and you shall hold your peace.
– Exodus 14:14 (NKJV)

Yesterday the cancer center, today the chiropractor. I'm so tired of medical appointments and grumble in my spirit when I know I ought to be thankful that I have access to all this medical care.

At the chiropractor's office during my lunchtime appointment, Dr. Irene read my spine with her machine. Each appointment starts with me sitting in a chair with a hospital gown open in the back, face in a small bracket, while Dr. Irene runs a little roller up the backbone from my lower back up to my neck. A reading appears on a monitor, but since the monitor is behind me, I never see what it displays. I figured that the machine somehow shows whether I'm out of adjustment.

But after today's reading, she surprised me with, "Have you had any more chemo treatments?"

"I had Herceptin yesterday."

"That explains it," she said, mainly to herself.

"Explains what?"

"Why your nervous system is distressed. Make sure you drink plenty of water to flush that stuff out. I don't know which is worse, the disease or the treatment."

I certainly was surprised that a reading of my nervous system would show that a chemical was coursing though my bloodstream. Maybe those treatments are more harmful than I thought. I've already been wondering whether I should discontinue them.

In the evening, the phone rang. It was my mother. She needed our help to lift Dad back into his chair again.

When Tad and I arrived at my parents' home, there sat Dad, propped up by his chair and surrounded by pillows. Turns out that he had been playing with the power controls of his recliner lift chair and put the chair into a position that dumped him onto the floor. Tad held Dad under one arm, Mama and I under the other, and heaved him up into the chair. Once in the recliner, Dad continued to play with the controls and ride up and down, up and down as our four-year-old nephew might do. Finally Mama scolded him harshly, warning that he'll break the chair.

We stayed and talked with Mama for some time. She's rather distraught by Dad's condition. This man, who was her provider, confidante, and mate, is now but a shell of a person. As we talked with Mama, Dad mumbled, to himself; we couldn't quite make out all the words. "Box... paper," I could hear. Then, "Gold... head." More mumbling. "On the mountain on the cross…"

Could it be he was thinking of Jesus…?

"Why are you laughing?" he slurred to Tad. I turned my head to look at Tad, and indeed he had an uncharacteristic smile on his face.

"You are laughing that I am old and stupid," my dad accused Tad.

"No, not at all," Tad replied.

It would not be like Tad to laugh at a pitiful old man. Tad and I both find the situation piteous, not funny. Somewhere in Dad's confused mind, he must realize that he is old, feeble, and vulnerable. He seemed to have a flash of lucidity, then slid back into a world that none of us could reach.

As Tad and I continued our conversation with Mama, Dad would pipe up every once in a while with some unrelated statement. "Was there a wedding at the credit union?" he suddenly asked Mama.

Mama looked at him. "No, no wedding," she answered. Her tone of voice registered frustration.

While my dad was, well, my dad—cranky and critical—I had little compassion for him. Now in this state, he does call up pity in me. He's no longer mean; he's just helpless now. Perhaps this was God's way of softening my heart toward my father.

Wednesday, 3 August 2011

Hear my prayer, Lord; let my cry for help come to you.
– Psalm 102:1 (NIV)

The mournful cry of the hawk has been a common sound outside the house for many weeks. She circles in the air, sounding that forlorn wail over and over as if calling a lost child. Sometimes these plaintive cries are just above my head in the backyard; other times I can hear them through my open window as the hawk soars over the tall oaks and aspen in the back woods, her doleful cries faint, yet penetrating. Why does she cry?

Surely those desolate wails are just the sound of her song, like the cawing of crows or twitter of sparrows. But unlike the joyful-sounding chirps of the chickadees or the haunting, almost frightening calls of the screech owl at night, this call sounds doleful, like the cry of the bereaved. The sound tears at my heart.

Most days I want the hawk's cry to stop. I'd much rather hear the raucous calls of the blue jays as they fly in groups and land in the spruce trees, seeming to argue with one another before they fly off. Or the cardinal's call, a sophisticated and varied song. But today, the hawk's woeful calls were appropriate somehow.

And the weather today—cloudy, drizzly, somber—reflects my mood. In fact, if it were sunny, that would somehow be inappropriate, completely wrong. Tears from the sky better suit the day's events.

Tad and Alexandra left for Pennsylvania in the morning and will be gone overnight. With Larissa at summer camp and Jacob working at the mechanic shop, I was alone at home getting a taste of how it will be in a week after they leave for Ukraine. I like the solitude, yet it's accompanied with a tinge of emptiness.

When I sat down at my home-office computer, I saw this e-mail from my brother Peter about my sister's father-in-law:

Subject: Bad news x2
Date: Wed, Aug 3, 2011 10:24 am

This is to pass along the sad news that Harry Brewer Sr. had a major stroke today. Marta and Harry are going to be with him.

At the same time, Dusia is now telling us that Dad needs hospice care. He is apparently not drinking today and not taking his pills.

It seems that things are coming to a head. I am sorting out my work responsibilities to see when is the earliest I can come down. I will keep you posted.

Strange that I would find out about my dad's condition in an e-mail from my brother in Toronto. I suspect that because of my cancer, Dusia doesn't bother me. It seems that people consider me frail and incapable of handling anything outside my own needs.

When I talked with my sister Marta on the phone, she said that death is inevitable from the head trauma that her ninety-two-year-old father-in-law sustained in the fall after his massive stroke. (The head trauma is the same type that my brother died from three years ago.) It's a blessing, she said, that he'll go quickly. However, now Mrs. Brewer, who has Alzheimer's, will have to go to a nursing home.

Since Marta is in the hospital tied up with her husband's family tragedy, I drove to my parents' house around 11:30 AM to check on them. By then, Dad was drinking and eating as usual, so this panic e-mail was for nothing. Apparently Dusia started it all with a phone call to Peter, so thinking that Dad is dying, Peter rented a car and is driving to Rochester.

After visiting Mama and Dad, I swung by Gentle's local farm market to buy some sweet corn to go with the grilled lamb for supper this evening. I was within a mile of home when an ambulance sped past me. Then a police car. I was curious where they were going and a little surprised that they continued straight through a main inter-section and down our little-traveled section of Landing Road North. When I caught up to them, emergency vehicles had the road blocked near the park. I couldn't get home. Anything like that near home brings a feeling of unease and apprehension. As I tried to decide how to get home, a woman on a bicycle pedaled up the road, so I rolled down my window and asked her what was going on.

"A bad accident. Really bad," she huffed as she stopped by my car.

"What happened?" I asked, a knot forming in my stomach as I wondered whether it was anyone I knew.

"A car flipped. There was a young man inside. He got ejected."

My heart sank into the depths of my abdomen with the weight of a bowling ball. Could it by some wild chance be Jacob? He doesn't usually come home in the middle of the day, but today was the first day that he was driving the 1999 Acura that he had spent all summer fixing so he could put it on the road. This morning he put plates on that car. Could he possibly be driving around in the day when he's supposed to be at work...?

I backed up and circled through the neighborhood on the hill above ours, then approached home from the downhill side. I parked in the driveway, and with my heart pounding like a mallet, I half walked, half ran up the hill where I could see neighbors gathering, police lights flashing and—oh my!—a gold car balanced on its roof. Jacob's car is gold! I saw a man lying on a green lawn on the opposite side of the street from the car, ambulance workers around him. Then I noticed that this man had on jeans. I then knew it wasn't Jacob; he had been wearing his mechanic's uniform. Relief drained the tension from my body.

The man was lifted and taken away by ambulance. The fire trucks drove off. But I stayed for quite a while talking with several neighbors, and even meeting some neighbors for the first time. One newly met neighbor related that the Animal Control man, who was driving in the opposite direction from the crashed car, was an eyewitness. He said that the driver of the gold vehicle, a forty-six-year-old (not so young, after all), was heading up the hill and just went off the road to his left, crashed through two sets of mailboxes, hit a large spruce tree, then flipped the car onto its roof. No animal ran in front of him. In fact, it didn't appear that the driver even hit the brakes. Was he drunk? On drugs? Had a heart attack? Or had he been texting?

"Too many people speed on our street," sighed one of the neighbors.

"It's a hill," I shrugged.

I chatted with the policeman who stayed behind and found out that the driver wasn't ejected; he had gotten out of the flipped car, walked across the road, then collapsed on the lawn across the street.

Eventually the neighbors dispersed, and I went home. The odd thing is that about ten minutes later, Jacob knocked on the front door. He came home in his gold Acura because when he had been driving it to run errands for his employer, the car started to shake and rattle. Jacob was afraid to drive it, so he came home and took the silver van instead, leaving the Acura in the driveway. He never comes home in the middle of the day—but he did today of all days.

Sunday, 7 August 2011

For prophecy never had its origin in the human will, but prophets, though human, spoke from God as they were carried along by the Holy Spirit.

– 2 Peter 1:21 (NIV)

Although cancer is no longer my first thought of the day, its presence is more like a pesky mosquito. You swat at it and think it's gone, but it returns, persistent and annoying, buzzing around you, tormenting you. Thoughts of cancer are like that.

The medical professionals can't give me clear-cut answers. Nor can they provide a test for monitoring my type of cancer, a test that would warn me of cancer while it's still in the microscopic phase, warn me before persistent pain signifies that the tumor is large—and it's too late.

These irksome thoughts taunt me at times.

How long will this worry of cancer plague me? How much time needs to pass before I can stop thinking about the possibility of cancer cells hiding out in my body like thieves in the night, waiting to steal my peace, my life? How can I have peace of mind that the cancer will not be back?

I don't like to do this. I don't think it's right to go to someone with the gift of prophecy as if he's some kind of fortuneteller, but that is exactly what I did: I asked Tad to call Brother Shtyher in Ukraine, the man who initially had that vision of a deadly illness hovering over me more than one year ago, and ask him whether I was healed—or should I continue taking the Herceptin? Did God have any message for me?

Tad obliged me and called. But Brother Shtyher had no answer for me. He prayed, but had no vision, no definitive word from God; he just said that only through the prayer of the church will God heal me.

Sigh. But *will* God heal me? Is it based on how fervently the church prays? How often? How long? Will I ever know?

Every Sunday, the pastor faithfully ends the service with prayers for healing for Oksana and me, the two women in the church with cancer.

But that constant shadow of worry has not gone away.

　　　　　　　　✼

Last night when my family went to visit my parents, my mother seemed lost, terrified. When Dad doesn't make sense, she yells at him, "Oh, stop it!" or, "Stop saying that!" She can't take it calmly.

Dad said to us, "You're going to Ukraine soon. Are you taking your goats?"

"No, we're not taking them," Tad answered. Mama rolled her eyes.

Monday, 8 August 2011

Commit to the Lord whatever you do, and your plans will succeed.
　　　　　　　　　　　– Proverbs 16:3 (NIV)

Preparations for the trip to Ukraine have reached a crescendo. The flight is tomorrow morning. No matter what our intentions, we seem to do all the packing on the last day at the last minute.

The frantic pace mounted as the day wore on. Tad was still typing up songs for a hymnbook he's putting together for his hometown church in Kopychyntsi, going out to make copies of them, returning home for a hymn he left behind, buying pillows to take to Ukraine, T-shirts. The girls were frantically sewing clothes. Material and threads, suitcases and clothing lay in disarray over beds, floor, chairs. Jacob went to the mechanic shop to inspect his Acura after his final class at Monroe Community College this morning. He didn't even think about packing until sometime during the afternoon.

On top of all that, at 11 AM we attended the funeral of my sister's father-in-law, going first to the church, then to the cemetery, then back to the church for a reception.

By nightfall, I had a stress headache—and I wasn't even packing! I tried to stay out of the way as I waited for the commotion to subside so I could go to bed, but every few minutes someone came to me with another question.

"Mom, should I take my camera in my carry-on or suitcase?"

"Definitely carry-on," I replied.

"Do you have any spare batteries for my camera?"

"No. A little late for that now…"

"Did you order the Sunday school materials for Lily?"

"Yes, I did. They'll be sent to her home."

"Do you have the address for Mission E4?"

"Yes, let me get it for you."

I continued to stress in my corner of the house as far away from the commotion of packing as I could get.

Tuesday, 9 August 2011

In their hearts humans plan their course, but the LORD establishes their steps.

– Proverbs 16:9 (NIV)

Morning was chaos. Tad went through the house weighing everyone's suitcases, stuffing hymnals and other books into them, then weighing them again. We scurried around the house checking suitcases, checking packing lists, then checking suitcases again. Nervous expectation mounted. And then it was time to go.

Whenever we leave on a trip, on the way to the airport we've always stopped at my parents' house to say good-bye. But today we were rushed.

I hesitated at the turnoff onto the expressway. "Are you sure you don't want to swing by to say good-bye to my parents?" I asked Tad. "I don't think that you and Alexandra will see grandpa when you get back from Ukraine in seven weeks."

Tad said there wasn't time to take a detour.

Now it's brutally quiet in the house. So quiet that I can hear the refrigerator engine, the gurgling of the aquarium, the crunching of the cat as she eats her dry food. So quiet that I talk to myself as I do chores around the house—cooking, washing dishes, cleaning counters…

When I'm alone at home, I'm glad for the animal companions that I have—Mishka, our fluffy tuxedo cat; Dodger, the white cat from Heberle Stables who's been visiting regularly this summer; and the goats and chickens. Even the tropical fish in our aquariums and goldfish in the water garden are living things, little pearls of color that surprisingly interact with you, follow your moves, wiggle their bodies begging to be fed. Over the years as I've cared for various animals, I've found that each, even a fish, has a personality.

My sister's phone call splintered my silent reverie.

"Dad has signs of dying. Look them up on the Internet," she suggested.

I did. He's definitely sliding downward.

Wednesday, 10 August 2011

My desire and prayer for you is that your life have a radical flavor. A risk-taking flavor. A gutsy, counter-cultural, flavor to it that makes the average, prosperous Americans in your church feel uncomfortable. A pervasive summons to something more and something hazardous and something wonderful.

– John Piper

So what am I doing at home with the goats and chickens while my family is in Ukraine? While Tad is preaching and visiting churches? While the kids are teaching VBS? While I could be visiting the widows I've befriended there, supporting my husband with my presence and prayers, contributing my voice to the hymns that they will sing in many churches?

Why am I here in this safe, familiar environment working a steady job, secure and comfortable, when my heart yearns and burns to be in Ukraine, in Africa, in an out-of-the-way forgotten corner of this earth with downtrodden people?

Instead, I'm going out to a steak dinner with my friend Josie tonight. A friend who, like me, lives in her comfortable suburban home and works her predictable job and takes annual mission trips somewhere for a week or two, maybe even three, then returns refreshed—but safe.

I have battled this. I want to take more risks for the Lord—yet I'm afraid to do so. I feel that I must hang on to this stable, well-paid job and help provide for my son's education, my daughter's internship, our family's mission trips, and many of our day-to-day expenses. Not only don't I trust the Lord to provide for me, I don't even trust my husband to provide for all of us without my help!

I struggle to let go. I feel like I have to do it all myself, to be in control of my life. That's not what the Lord wants. He wants me to trust, to let go, to let Him lead. But I grapple with that. And I certainly can't have a radical, risk-taking, counter-cultural life while working a nine-to-five job in an office.

Although this afternoon was an adventure of sorts, it was hardly a radical one: I spent fours hours at a neuro-ophthalmologist's office. A decade ago, Dr. David Smith had diagnosed me with an optic glioma, a rare slow-growing tumor along my optic nerve. On hot days when doing physically straining activities, the tumor swells and constricts the optic nerve, causing pain and temporary loss of vision in my right eye. Since having chemotherapy, I've felt stabbing pains not only in that tumor area, but in other areas of my brain as well, so a few weeks ago I convinced my oncologist to send me for a brain MRI. Today's appointment was to discuss the results of that MRI.

Dr. Smith wasn't happy with just the MRI. He put me through a battery of tests in his office: visual field tests and peripheral vision tests, flashing squares and moving dots. After spending half a day in his office, Dr. Smith finally notified me that the optic glioma, which he measured to be 10 mm wide, had not grown much at all in the last ten years, and there were no other areas of concern in the brain.

What a relief!

Tonight the air is unexpectedly cool. Severe rainstorms the last two days have washed away all remnants of the long summer heat wave. The gardens are lush, green, and moist from the rains. I can almost hear them sighing with relief that the drought is over.

I've shut off the air conditioner that ran overtime this summer, and through the open windows I can hear the crickets. Because I've had the windows shut against the heat, I hadn't noticed this nightly chorus.

Thursday, 11 August 2011

Give me relief from my distress, be merciful to me and hear my prayer.

– Psalm 4:1 (NIV)

With the girls gone, my days pivot around the animal chores: feeding and milking the goats at 7 AM and 7 PM; releasing the chickens from their hutch when it gets light; locking them up for the night before dark to keep them safe from prowling predators.

The animals belong to my two daughters, and I normally don't do any of these chores. Alexandra and Larissa share the milking and feeding. But now that they're gone, I'm doing all the chores solo, and it's wearying. I'm finding them more of a burden than I expected.

To milk the goats, I have to put grain in the feed bin, maneuver one goat into the back stall, force her head into a restraint, then lock the restraint and close the stall door to keep the other goat and kid out of my way. Milking isn't hard; it's just tedious. I take the milking stool from the spot where it hangs on the wall, then prop my head against the goat's side as I sit and alternately squeeze—not pull—the teats with a downward motion. Initially the milk pings into the empty metal bucket that we got from Chad's family, but by the time I finish milking, each stream of milk makes a rich frothy sound.

I take the pail indoors, pour the milk through a strainer into a large glass jar, then return with the empty bucket to milk the other goat.

Kluska, the older Nubian goat, has a sweet, calm temperament, but she's harder to milk because her teats are smaller, and it takes longer to milk her. Mala, Kluska's one-year-old daughter, has an attitude. Sometimes she challenges me by lowering her head as if ready to butt me, which doesn't endear her to me. Mala constantly butts Kluska's little kid. She even butts chickens. Although she's easier to milk because of her larger teats, she's jumpy and spooks more easily, sometimes kicking over the pail or stepping into it. Then I have to dump the milk, wash the pail, and start again. When milking Mala, I have to be vigilant and ready to pull the pail out from under her at the first hint of agitation, which is often triggered by insect bites.

Because we don't have a field where the goats can graze, every morning I cut low branches from trees or bushes in our woods for fodder. I scatter grain for the chickens because goats would eat chicken feed if I placed it in dishes. And I fill the goats' manger with feed. Only then do I make myself my morning cup of coffee.

Today, after yet another medical appointment (an 8:20 AM bone scan), I went to Kodak. These days I often work in the office.

When I got home in the early evening, I immediately went to the animals because I had last fed them in the morning. I gave them some day-old bread and filled the water bucket, which had been kicked over. Then I heated up the leftovers from yesterday's dinner out with Josie. By the time I ate, it was milking time.

So go my days.

Monday, 15 August 2011

Peace I leave with you, my peace I give unto you: not as the world giveth, give I unto you. Let not your heart be troubled, neither let it be afraid.

– John 14:27 (KJV)

I didn't want to admit it to anyone, especially not to myself. So I ignored it. The numbness would go away. It always had before, usually around lunchtime. In Panama during last summer's mission trip, I always woke up with a numb right hand. I attributed the numbness to my sleeping position in the hammock or to my age—just one of those things that goes wrong with one's body as you grow old, I figured—and I disregarded the tingling. It was an annoyance, nothing more. It came every morning, but cleared up by the middle of the day.

A little while after my mastectomy (six months after the Panama trip), I noticed that I had no numbness in my hand at all. After months and months, it was gone! What a strange and wonderful result of the operation! Again, I attributed that to my sleeping position, which after the operation was straight as a soldier, arms down, and lying flat on my back. With all the tubes and stitches, I had no choice but to lie that way. My right hand was fine; I had no numbness any more.

Then in early June, the numbness returned, a tingling as if my right hand had fallen asleep and all I had to do was shake it to get the blood flowing again. But no matter how much I shook my hand or what position I slept in, the numbness did not go away. The annoying tingling was always present, and it worsened when I wrote by hand for a while (instead of typed) or when I drove. The vibration of the steering wheel exacerbated my hand so that the tingling turned into painful pinpricks.

For the last two months the numbness in my hand has been unremitting. Mornings it's not just tingly; my fingers feel like sausages that don't want to bend. Milking the goats can be so painful that I have to finish milking using only my left hand.

This past Saturday I had trouble falling asleep because of the pain in my right hand. And left leg. Then left hand. The pain danced around from appendage to appendage, tingling, burning, prickling. The pain alarmed me.

But nothing quite like the fright I got today when Mishka, the cat, jumped on my bed and woke me at 4 AM. Three of the fingers of my right hand felt big as balloons, and my hand had no feeling at all. None. I went to the bathroom, frightened because of my hand, but when I grabbed some toilet paper, my thumb burned as if I'd touched a hot skillet. My hand was on fire, the nerve that runs up my arm stung, and my heart rattled in my chest. I felt profoundly alone.

What was going on? Is my body falling apart? What was causing the firestorm in my hand? Did I overcome cancer only to live my life with appendages that tingle and burn and don't function?

I forced myself to calm down. Whatever was causing the pain wouldn't seem quite so scary in the daylight. I'll get over this hurdle. God, do you want me to spend more time on my knees?

Tuesday, 16 August 2011

When I am afraid, I will trust in You. In God, whose word I praise, in God I trust; I will not be afraid.
– Psalm 56:3-4 (NIV)

I feel lost in the mundaneness of day-to-day living. Work and chores, work and chores, and a murky medical future. I can't see ahead beyond the next few days.

My family has been gone for one week, and it's rained daily since they've been gone. No more drought. With the severe thunderstorms and torrents of rain, now we have flooding! Roads are submerged under muddy runoff; the river in Ellison Park has swollen beyond capacity and formed a great lake. More rain is predicted for this week. We are now breaking records for amount of rain falling within twenty-four hours.

And all the mud! What a mess in the chicken and goat yard. The water bucket overflows, the goats churn the mud with every step, and the chickens drink out of puddles.

The rain keeps me indoors, except for chores. I called my mother in the evening instead of visiting. She said that Dad is worse, that he doesn't make sense much of the time.

"I would just like to talk with him. I don't ask for much," my mother murmured. I imagine that she is quite lonely—and afraid.

Thursday, 18 August 2011

*He will cover you with His feathers, and under His wings you will
find refuge; His faithfulness will be your shield and rampart. You
will not fear the terror of night...*

– Psalm 91:4-5 (NIV)

I dread going to bed. The numbness in my hand is worse day by
day, but it's the searing pain that comes in the dark of night that I fear.

I know what it is now: a symptom of neuropathy. But knowing
doesn't keep away that intense pain that wakes me night after night.

Once again I awoke in the solitary darkness of nighttime, my
hand burning, scalding, silently shrieking with pain. It felt like I was
holding a hot coal in the palm of my right hand, but couldn't drop it.
I rose and paced the vacuous darkness, my right hand cradled in my
left, praying for relief. Everything is amplified in the nighttime: I'm
more frightened, and I'm acutely alone. How I wished that Tad were
here to console me, to share my pain and help calm my fear.

I sat in the easy chair by the bow window in the living room with
the lights off, rocking and pleading with God to take away the burning pain. But in all things praise God, I remembered, so I thought of
things for which I could be thankful: That I don't have it as bad as
many millions of people who are hungry, who are in jail, who are
persecuted, tortured, or sick without medical care. That my family is
alive and well in Ukraine. That they call me often. That it's peaceful
and safe in my home. That I have a cat who keeps me company when
I'm distressed at night. That I can still use my hand, at least partially,
despite the pain.

"Lord," I got down on my knees and stretched my right hand out
to Him, "I want to serve you and use this hand to do Your work for
years to come. Please, Lord, *please* heal my hand!"

Eventually I fell asleep again, but in the morning I slept through
the alarm. I ran out to the animals at 8:30 AM feeling guilty that I'd
kept the hens locked up in their small hutch under the warm sun and
the goats imprisoned in their shed unfed, not milked. The hens were

clucking, the goats were restless, and I was worn out from another sleepless night.

Milking this morning was excruciating. How I wish Larissa were here to do the chores. I'm afraid I don't take as good care of the animals as the girls do.

After chores, I called the Lipson Cancer Center to tell them about the burning neuropathy. "You're the third person who called today who finished Taxotere in April." Yet the doctor said that because the neuropathy is in my hand, not my feet, to see my primary care physician. Instead, I made an appointment to see my chiropractor tomorrow.

Friday, 19 August 2011

May the God of hope fill you with all joy and peace as you trust in Him, so that you may overflow with hope by the power of the Holy Spirit.

– Romans 15:13 (NIV)

Why hadn't I thought to see my chiropractor for the neuropathy in my hands sooner? Even though I had just been there a few weeks ago, all it takes is one bump on the head as I stoop to enter the goat shed or one awkward lifting of a hay bale for my back to go out and put pressure on the nerve that runs to my hand. But I'm a skeptic by nature. Although a few years ago Dr. Irene had healed me of back pain so severe that sixteen Advil pills per day didn't even dull the pain, I still hesitated to go to her because I was not convinced that it would help. And when I arrived at the office, I wanted to see whether she'd find the misalignment herself, so instead of telling her my problem, I distracted her with small talk.

"How was your vacation?" I asked as she did the reading on my back. I got her talking about camping, her camper, a camping spot she and her husband are now renting.

"How's the reading?" I asked after she ran the machine up my back.

"Not too good. What's going on?" she asked.

So I relented and told her about the hand that burned like flames. She assured me that it was from a misalignment of the neck and head, and that within five days that fiery pain would subside. The numbness, however, would take much longer to go away.

The NUCCA[*] procedure that Dr. Irene practices is to adjust the alignment between the upper neck vertebra and the head to "get your head on straight." Today I needed a big adjustment.

When I returned from the chiropractor, I found this update from my sister:

Sent: Fri, Aug 19, 2011 2:07 pm
Subject: Dad Update

Today I noticed a measurable decline in Dad from the state he was in last week. He did not recognize who I was, and when I finally got through to him that I was Marta and that he was my dad, he looked a bit bewildered and pleased at the same time. Mostly, he sleeps.

For anyone who is up to it, I think that Mama could use a lot of phone calls, e-mails and moral support.

He woke Mama up in the night several times... She told me that Dad was even more confused (that seems to be what bothers her the most) and was speaking in German and English to her.[**]

Marta

After locking up the chickens, I stopped by my parents' house but Dad was asleep the entire time so I don't know whether he would have recognized me.

---

[*] National Upper Cervical Chiropractic Association
[**] He normally speaks Ukrainian at home.

Saturday, 20 August 2011

For God does speak—now one way, now another—though no one perceives it.

– Job 33:14 (NIV)

My friends think that I'm lonely or bored because my family is away, but in reality I'm agonizingly overwhelmed—overwhelmed by the demands of the animals, by the nightly inferno in my hand, by my much-too-frequent medical appointments, by the situation with my dad, by the calls that interrupt my meals. I battle with the demands from outside and my desire to retreat into myself and work on my new hosta garden or sit and read a book. The outside pressures win, and I feel stressed.

Yesterday I met Nadia for coffee at Tim Horton's. Nadia is a chatty and cheerful woman, mother to Tatiana, Myron, and Michael, who are friends of my children. Nadia and I meet for coffee every few months, usually in the evening before she starts her late shift as a medical technician. While I drink decaf in the evening, she drinks high-test to carry her through the night.

We talked about the usual—our kids, family, recent events, church. Nadia mentioned that a Christian co-worker had gone to a service at a local church when a visiting preacher was speaking.

"He had the gift of prophecy," Nadia shared. "He told her that she would soon have a baby, but she hadn't been able to conceive for years. Within a year, she had a baby! And her husband had been out of work. This preacher told her that he would soon have a job, and within two weeks, he did!"

Interesting. My heart burned with desire to have God speak to me through someone, too. If only God would tell me that my cancer is gone for good.

"If you ever hear of this preacher coming back to Rochester, let me know. I'd like to go see him," I said.

"My co-worker said he comes every year."

Monday, August 22, 2011

*In the morning, LORD, You hear my voice; in the morning I lay
my requests before you and wait expectantly.*
– Psalm 5:3 (NIV)

Last night I came across a box of prints that I made in the 1980s
from slides that I had borrowed from Dad. Among them was a photograph of my dad dressed in hiking boots and a canvas backpack, sitting on a rock high above the surrounding Alps and gazing toward the
distant mountains. The photo was taken in the 1940s in Germany
after the war. The color photo was faded and stained; my father was
virile and fit.

Seeing Dad when he was younger somehow comforted me. I find
it painful to watch my dad sitting in his chair, unable to get out,
hardly able to communicate. Today when Marta and I came to lift
him back into his chair yet again he said, "Marta, save me!" It really
got to me. It was like watching a wounded deer trying to get to its
feet, but knowing the animal will die. Seeing him so feeble is heart
wrenching, which is a good thing considering how much anger I've
had toward him over the years. The anger melts away when I see
him so frail.

Only one more week of being home alone. Every other summer
when the family has been away, I've enjoyed the solitude and free-
dom of being temporarily single. But this year it has not gone well.

I find myself annoyed at the animals. They're perpetually under-
foot—chickens scampering under my feet when I walk into the pen,
goats blocking my way compelling me to push them, which makes
me feel cruel. Even the cat in the house often weaves under my footsteps to such a point that I accidentally stepped on Mishka's paw
yesterday. She yowled in pain and then lifted her white-slippered
paw and held it up protectively. I apologized and she seemed to
understand.

This evening I was milking Mala and counting the squirts ("When
you reach one hundred fifty, you're done," Alexandra had said) when

Mala somehow managed to get not one, but both hind feet into the milk bucket. She jumped around trying to get out of the bucket, all the while spraying milk like a blender with the lid off—on my face, my arms, my shirt, and all the rest of me. I had to take the pail to the kitchen, dump the milk, wash the pail with soapy water, then go back and finish milking her.

Sometimes Mala body slams me. Other times she nips me. I know that she's trying to establish dominance over me, but Larissa is the goat behavior specialist and I'm not sure what to do. I'm counting the days until she's back.

Tuesday, 24 August 2011

Man is like a breath; his days are like a passing shadow.
– Psalm 144:4 (NKJV)

Hospice. That's what the nurse in Emergency at Strong Memorial Hospital recommended. Clearly there is nothing the doctors can do for Dad, even if he hadn't signed his do not intubate, do not resuscitate form many months ago when he was still lucid.

Mama and Marta and I huddled in the Emergency room corridor trying to ignore Dad's protesting bellows as three hospital staff members wrestled Dad to remove his street clothes and dress him in hospital garb. He was beyond reasoning, beyond reach.

"We have a tough one," said one of the men.

Dusia and Mama hadn't been able to feed Dad this morning or sit him on the toilet. Dusia, who'd worked for years in a nursing home, could tell it was time. I drove over to my parents' house to confer. We knew that once we called an ambulance for him, he would never return home.

My brother George left work to loiter in the hospital with us. Dad had only a few days, a week. Two weeks at most, said the nurse. But until a room in a hospice facility opened up, they would keep him at the hospital. Fortunately, a room in the palliative care unit became available late in the day.

The day was long. A lot of waiting. A lot of wondering. A lot of wandering the halls.

It was almost night by the time Dad was cleaned up and settled in his room, and we were allowed to see him. The room was spacious and well lit. Dad lay in the center of it, unconscious and sedated. The nurse pointed out that his hands were clammy and his left leg was swelling from congestive heart failure; the right side of his heart wasn't working well. I peeked under the sheet and was shocked that his left leg had blown up to twice its normal size. I quickly covered it. It was so grotesquely large that I couldn't imagine he could live that way for very long.

Thursday, 25 August 2011

Fear God and keep His commandments, for this is the duty of all mankind. For God will bring every deed into judgment, including every hidden thing, whether it is good or evil.

– Ecclesiastes 12:13-14 (NIV)

I was gathering the things I'd need to be with Mama at Dad's side for a few days—books, Bible, laptop, flash drive, cell phone—when the call came. I was almost out the door; must be Mama calling to ask when I was coming for her.

"Dad died..." said Marta. "Would you tell Mama when you pick her up?"

Since Marta works at the hospital, she had come to Dad's room early in the morning to check on him. But already he was gone. He had been alone when he slipped away.

I now knew why that inner voice had told me not to go to Ukraine. Surely that had been the Lord's still, small voice. I was glad I obeyed.

We knew it was coming, but it's still disconcerting to lose a family member. Marta, Mama, and I sat in the room with Dad's unmoving figure, absorbing the news, making phone calls, making plans. In a short while Marta's husband, Harry, arrived with a basket of flowers for my mother. Mama teared up, and so did I. The flowers wouldn't change anything, but that touching act communicated compassion.

After a while, the priest from Mama's Catholic church arrived to perform the last rites on Dad, a man he hadn't met, a man who hadn't attended church for well over a decade. After praying over my father, the priest said to the now-cold body, "Your sins are forgiven." I was taken aback. Forgive a corpse sins he never confessed?

I bristled inside. This unbiblical ritual was purposely misleading to give the family false peace.

Then the priest turned to us and said, "Pray for his soul."

I had prayed for Dad's soul countless times while he was alive. I had prayed for him to be transformed by God's grace. But Dad had remained staunchly…Dad. And now the priest implied that he's in purgatory, a place where Catholics believe souls go for purification. No amount of prayer by the living can atone for the transgressions of the dead; each of us is responsible for our own salvation. The burden on my heart was that it's too late now. But those around me appeared not to think so.

"Now he's in heaven meeting with Mr. Brewer," Marta said cheerfully, "and they don't need their hearing aids."

It's just so hard for me to listen to such fantasy.

Peter arrived from Toronto in the afternoon. George had come earlier. Of our siblings, only Alex was missing. But he's been missing almost three years now; Dad would be buried next to him.

I should feel sadness. I wish I could feel sadness. But what I feel is not exactly relief. It's just… well, I'm not sure how to put it into words. In some ways I miss him—not the relationship as it really was, but the idea of him, the idea that I still had a father and that perhaps someday, somehow, our relationship *could* change.

We sat on the couch in Dad's hospital room, mother and children, in a rare moment of togetherness without the interference of our own children. My mother sighed. "When something went wrong, he always found someone to blame," she shared.

"And it was usually your fault, wasn't it?" I asked.

Mama nodded. "He was so charming when we dated, so attentive and polite," she recalled.

"Really fooled you, didn't he?" teased Peter.

But now that Dad is gone, we can begin to weave a myth of the man. He's no longer here to counter our fantasy of the dad that we wanted.

As we sat on the couch, George got a text message from a friend, which he read to us: "The world is a lesser place without him. He gave to the world."

The myth begins.

Saturday, 27 August 2011

...for your love is more delightful than wine.
– Song of Songs 1:2 (NIV)

I spent the day going through albums and scanning old photographs of my father for a slideshow that will be given at the funeral home. Pages and pages of pictures of a lifetime, snapshots of happy moments. A view through a tiny peephole into what was and what my mother surely dreamed would be. Dad in the 1950s when he just married my mother—slim, debonair, attentive. Dad hugging my mother affectionately as they sat on a park bench, both grinning at the distant camera. You can see the love between them in that photo. Dad hovering protectively by Mama when she's pregnant with me. Dad with his arm around Mama.

When I look at those early photos of him smiling, I almost miss him. But what I really miss is the dad I wish he was, the dad I wanted him to be. I miss the dad he was when I was four or seven.

These photos aren't the true portrayal of life, but the polished version of it: the pleasant moments, the family gatherings. It all seems a little fantastic, this peek into a bygone age. And all of them such happy times. The unpleasant moments, which were never recorded, are gone, like chaff.

Sunday, 28 August 2011

Cast your cares on the LORD and He will sustain you; He will never let the righteous fall.
– Psalm 55:22 (NIV)

I almost lost it today. I was close to an emotional breakdown when Kluska, the older goat, couldn't get to her feet. I feel that I'm not up to the challenge of caring for the farm animals; my girls are the ones with the practical experience and book knowledge. I can do the basic chores, but I don't know what to do when something goes wrong.

Today Kluska was walking in the pen when her hind legs simply gave out. She sank to the ground and lay there. When I urged her to get up, she looked at me as if embarrassed by her infirmity but made no effort to stand. After several minutes she struggled to her feet, and walked off wobbly as if drunk. There is definitely something wrong with her. But what?

Last night while I was milking her, Kluska slowly dropped into a sitting position. I pulled out the bucket in time to rescue the milk. She often leans on me—her full weight—when I milk her, and it's hard to milk with that weight on my head and shoulder. But I hadn't realized that she was leaning on me because she was having trouble standing on her own.

I had noticed that Kluska has skin issues, but I chose to ignore them. Larissa will take care of it when she returns, I reasoned. Kluska rubs against the doorframe and beams, and scratches herself with her rear leg like a dog. She's growing bald in several areas and was bleeding by her ear. Although I know she has a problem, I don't even know where to research what it is. It would be one additional task to put on my list. One more assignment after helping with funeral arrangements and visiting Mama and scanning photos and caring for the animals and cleaning house, shopping, cooking, mowing the lawn… Larissa will be home soon; she'll research the problem and cure Kluska. I'm too overwhelmed. Too exhausted. Too stressed. But I am worried about her. I hope nothing serious happens to the goat under my watch. One more day, thank God, just one more day until Larissa and Jacob are home!

I called the goat breeder who disbudded our kid. He's owned and bred goats for decades, but he had never heard of a goat simply sinking to the ground. I decided not to milk Kluska anymore. I'm not sure what she has, if anything, and whether it's transferable through milk. Maybe it's just arthritis. Or old age.

I feel so inadequate to take care of the animals. It's not just the goats; one of the red chickens is limping. By nightfall, she was hopping on one foot, so I carried her into the coop. Perhaps a goat stepped on her foot.

Between Kluska's illness and the red chicken that limps, I was on the verge of tears with these critters. The bright spot of the day was unexpected visitors in the late evening: my children's teenage friends—Tatiana, Myron, and Michael. I don't know what prompted them to stop by (perhaps their mother Nadia?), but I really enjoyed our time together sharing laughs and stories about pranks that each of us played on our siblings. In this aspect, my generation is no different from theirs.

Monday, 29 August 2011

So we fix our eyes not on what is seen, but on what is unseen, since what is seen is temporary, but what is unseen is eternal.
– 2 Corinthians 4:18 (NIV)

I am *so* happy that Jacob and Larissa are returning home tonight. It's like a song in my heart, and the day is different somehow, sunnier.

In the afternoon, I drove to Harris Funeral Home. I reached the front entrance at the same time as another woman with long, disheveled hair who looked about my age.

"Are you here together?" asked the receptionist.

"No," I replied. "I'm here to drop off a CD of photos of my dad."

"And how may I help you?" the receptionist directed her inquiry toward the other woman.

"I'm here to pick up my cat."

Did I hear that right, I wondered? My cat? Do they embalm cats? Or just cremate them?

"And what was your cat's name?" asked the receptionist.

"Spice."

"Come this way," the receptionist directed the woman, then picked up the phone to call someone.

"…is here to pick up her cat, Spice," I heard her say.

How odd. I had no idea. We just buried the deceased members of our menagerie in our backyard.

September

Thursday, 1 September 2011

I sought the LORD, and He answered me; He delivered me from all my fears.

– Psalm 34:4 (NIV)

The bouquet of garden flowers I found on the kitchen window as I was making my morning coffee put a smile in my heart. Yes, Larissa is home.

Larissa and Jacob still get up very early because their bodies haven't yet readjusted to our time zone. Larissa lets out our chickens and floppy-eared goats at dawn, so in the afternoon she's a little tired. I found her resting in the hammock in the backyard with Kluska tied up nearby enjoying some grass. Although goats typically live about as long as dogs do, it's sad that at six years old Kluska is already so feeble that we'll have to put her down. I don't want to think about that. She's always been an affectionate goat, nudging Tad the first time he met her in a "pet me" sort of way. Her amicable manner is why Tad bought her and why I favor her.

Even though I no longer have to get up to milk the goats and feed the chickens, I'm feeling unusually tired. The last two days by nine o'clock at night, I'm so exhausted that it feels like midnight. This tiredness worries me. I was drained when the kids were in Ukraine, but I wasn't this exhausted. This is an abnormal kind of tired.

A worn out kind of tired. A hint of lupus kind of tired. Is it age—or illness? Always in the back of my mind is, *Has it spread?* When any little thing goes wrong with my body, I wonder, *Could it be cancer?*

Why am I so tired?

In the late afternoon, I told Larissa about my exhaustion.

"Go lie down," she told me.

"It's such a waste of time," I protested.

"Then I'll lie down with you. We can talk."

What a wise child. So we lay in bed for about half an hour, sharing.

"Before you fall asleep, what do you think about?" Larissa asked.

"All sorts of things. Plans for the next day. Review what I did that day. Maybe I think about what I'm going to plant in a new garden or how I'll design it. Lots of things—it's always different."

"Do you ever make up stories in your head?"

"Stories—like fiction? I don't have that kind of imagination!" I admitted.

"Maybe it's odd, but I think of all sorts of stories. Sometimes they don't have a beginning or an end. I often think, 'If only I could write this down,' but I'm too tired. It would take too long. Sometimes I'm in the stories. Sometimes not. And then I think, 'It's getting late. I'd better stop this and sleep.' I think Alexandra also thinks up stories. Did you use to read us bedtime stories?" Larissa asked.

"All the time! Or Dad would make up stories. Or I'd lie on the floor of your bedroom in the dark and start a story and have each of you add to it in turn so that we were all making it up."

"I guess I tell myself bedtime stories now," Larissa suggested.

I'd never heard of such a thing before. Interesting how we're all so different.

Saturday, 3 September 2011

...and the dust returns to the ground it came from, and the spirit returns to God who gave it.

– Ecclesiastes 12:7 (NIV)

If I could capture memories of my dad, it would be when I was a child. Nature walks. Teaching me to catch a garter snake. Demonstrating how to find caterpillars on plants and raise them into butterflies. Showing me how to put a worm on a hook. Fishing. Identifying wildflowers. Pressing leaves. Making candles. Story time.

I would like to wipe away all other memories of my father and keep only these. In fact, at my father's funeral today, all the speeches my siblings delivered were of how he once was. The happy times. The view through rose-colored glasses.

"I was born in the wrong family," our cousin Helen said to my sister after these talks.

The day was sunny and warm and beautiful, just as it had been when we buried Alex at the same gravesite three years before. After the funeral service in the church, we drove behind the hearse to the cemetery and had a small outdoor service before my father's body was lowered into the ground. Earth to earth, ashes to ashes, and dust to dust.

Perfumes mingled and clung to my skin as family members from Canada and Pennsylvania, New Jersey and Connecticut hugged and kissed me and offered condolences. When a person as old as my father dies, the funeral is not a sad occasion, but more of a family reunion. Relatives I hadn't seen since the last family funeral arrived and shared meals and caught up on news. Since I'm still wearing a headscarf that covers my entire (rather bald) head, one obvious topic was my health. Two of my cousins—one a half-cousin, the other a step-cousin—are breast cancer survivors.

By late afternoon it was over. The guests left. We went home.

We found Kluska lying in the shed and the other goats stepping over her. Now what do we do?

Sunday, 4 September 2011

*"For my thoughts are not your thoughts, neither are your ways
my ways," declares the* LORD.

– Isaiah 55:8 (NIV)

Kluska is not getting up. It's been heartbreaking to see our dear
mother goat so helpless, and although she eats and drinks, she just
can't stand. She is lying in her excrement. We so want to help her,
but other than continuing to feed her, give her water, and clean her
up, we don't know what to do.

I called my friend Nadia and asked whether her husband, a hunter,
could come and shoot Kluska, but when we read on the Internet that
maybe dewormer and vitamins will help her, we wanted to wait another day to give her a chance.

Monday, 5 September 2011
Labor Day

*For great is your love, higher than the heavens; your faithfulness
reaches to the skies.*

– Psalm 108:4 (NIV)

Today marks the end of the summer season according to American
tradition. Already it is rainy, cold, and dreary. We stayed home. I
spent time at the computer typing up a homeschool schedule for
Larissa, writing the IHIP (Individualized Home Instruction Plan)
required by New York State, and trying to sort some things on my
desk to make room for new books and new assignments. Larissa starts
eleventh grade tomorrow.

There has been no improvement in Kluska's condition. Larissa
read that you should put a towel under the belly of a goat that's down,
then lift the goat and place a hay bale underneath to prop it up
because the leg muscles of goats that can't stand atrophy after two
days—or was it one? Jacob and Larissa tried to lift Kluska and put her
over a hay bale, but her legs would not bend that way. Kluska could

barely protest. Her voice was so quiet compared to her foghorn cry when she was healthy.

It's time.

Somewhere in the woods near the circle of stones and ostrich ferns that mark our Belgian Sheepdog's burial site, Jacob dug a new grave. By the time Nadia's husband Stefan came over with his rifle, night was falling. Jacob and Stefan loaded Kluska into our old blue wheelbarrow and wheeled her into the woods. Larissa and I couldn't bear to witness this, so we went inside. We heard one shot, then another, and then the skies opened up like a faucet. The guys ran to the house, shielding the rifle from the deluge, leaving behind the wheelbarrow and dead goat. An hour after Stefan left, Jacob and I donned raincoats, and with shovels and flashlights went back to the woods. I felt like a criminal burying a body during a rainstorm under cover of darkness while holding a flashlight with my mouth to see what I was doing (although I didn't really want to see what I was doing). In the distance, Mala started a lament. It became louder and louder.

"She sees the flashlights," Jacob suggested.

"I think that she misses her mom," I said. "They've never been apart." And it occurred to me that since the day Mala was born, Kluska has been at her side. Always.

When I entered the goat shed to close its windows and dampen the sound so the neighbors wouldn't hear, Korovka (Kluska's kid from this year) chimed in. They cried in unison, a loud wail and a softer, baby lament. I hope that these two half-sisters bond to one another.

Wednesday, 7 September 2011

I can do all things through Christ who strengthens me.
                                        – Philippians 4:13 (NKJV)

As Larissa and I loaded our shopping cart with fifty-pound bags of chicken feed and goat pellets at Tractor Supply Company, a gnarled farmer in jeans and baseball cap started a conversation with us. Standing in the aisle among various types of goat feed, this old farmer described at length his fifty goats—what he feeds them, how much milk they produce, what awards they've won. Listening to him was like opening an encyclopedia about goats. So I decided to ask. I described Kluska's symptoms.

"Do you know what it could possibly be?" I wondered.

"Sounds like blood-sucking lice. They're not visible to the naked eye, and they make the goat so anemic that it has no strength."

That would also explain Kluska's scratching and her increasing feebleness. If only we'd known. Such tiny insects, such catastrophic results. But the same is true of bacteria invading our bodies. Or sin infecting our lives.

The old farmer picked out medicine for us to put on the other goats to prevent their downfalls. If only we could just apply some medicine to prevent a downfall from sin.

Friday, 9 September 2011

Blessed is the man who trusts in the LORD, and whose hope is the LORD.

– Jeremiah 17:7 (NKJV)

I keep drinking coffee, but it doesn't help. I'm so tired that it's hard to get through the day. I keep pushing myself from one chore to the next, forcing myself to not lie down because there's so much to do. Even when I've lain down for an hour I haven't felt any better, so there's no point to it. Sleep doesn't help. The feeling of fatigue resembles how I felt with lupus—a tiredness behind my breastbone, a tiredness that reaches through my body and to my shoulder blades. I'm concerned that it's a recurrence of lupus, triggered by the combination of poisons (drugs) in my body, the strain of the animal responsibilities while the family was away, the death of my father, and the stress of starting homeschooling. Oh, I pray it's not that autoimmune disease!

Last night I was glad when I heard Larissa was tired, too. That meant that I was not alone in feeling weary. Today she has a fever. Most likely my body is fatigued because I'm battling the same illness.

Sunday, 11 September 2011

...whatever you did for one of the least of these brothers of Mine, you did for Me.

– Matthew 25:40 (NIV)

After church, fifteen-year-old Igor came home with us. We hadn't had him over for some time, and in Tad's absence I felt I should extend the invitation to lunch and fellowship.

Igor's company is always a challenge. He has not known normal family life because of his parents' substance abuse problems and mental disorders, so at home he isn't supervised or disciplined. Although Igor is polite with us, he's not that way with his family. Nor does he use his time wisely. After lunch, Larissa, Jacob, Igor, and I had a lengthy discussion about morality, godliness, and life before I decided to lighten things up with a trip to the local fish hatchery at Powder Mills Park.

At the hatchery you can feed the trout, which are divided into separate cement pools based on size and species. Throw them some pellets, and the fish swirl around and splash in a feeding frenzy. As usual, there were mallard ducks at the hatchery trying to eat the food thrown to the trout. When Jacob, Alexandra, and Larissa were little, I would catch these human-acclimated ducks so the children could pet them. Apparently I've passed on the tradition of duck catching. Today I was amused to see both Larissa and Jacob catching ducks using my technique of feeding them from the palm of the hand, letting them get closer and closer and—gotcha!

We didn't stay very long. Thunder rumbled in the distance and rain began to dot the water surface. Back home we sat down to yet another discussion with Igor about life, godliness, and what he does with his time. His dark eyes challenged us and he smirked impishly as he talked. He said that we wouldn't like his answers. He doesn't do homework; he thinks that it's OK to copy other students' assignments. He watches TV—shows that don't build up and have profanity—and plays violent games on the computer. In going through his daily schedule, Larissa noted that he didn't mention making any time for

God, no time for prayer, no reading the Bible, yet he still says that he wants to go to a Bible college. For everything that we said, from why one should drive the speed limit to being honest and faithful in doing homework, Igor would play the devil's advocate and challenge us with, "Why?" It got a bit wearying in the end, though Jacob and Larissa did a great job defending the godly point of view.

As Jacob drove Igor home, he told him to save the date next Saturday because we were going to take him on another outing.

Monday, 12 September 2011

O LORD my God, I cried out to You, and You healed me.
                                          – Psalm 30:2 (NKJV)

I felt *much* better today, like a weight of stone had been lifted from my sternum. I'm no longer overwhelmingly tired. Thank you, Lord!

With Tad gone, my relationship with the children has become closer. While I'm often in my home office at night correcting home-school assignments, Tad sits on the children's beds in the evening, giving them a backrub, and getting the children to relax and open up. Since Tad is still in Ukraine, I'm the one sitting on the edge of the bed and listening. It's a delight and a privilege to be part of their worlds.

In the past, I've had some intimate conversations with the girls, but not with Jacob. He shares with Tad. But these days Jacob has asked me to rub his back, or I've come in and massaged his feet. During that time alone at the end of the day when Larissa is already in bed and the house is quiet, that is when we have our best conversations. The darkness and the late hour promote closeness.

Touch is such an important human need. Yet lack of touch is rarely talked about, unless you're discussing the tragic case of the neglected orphans in Romania under Ceausescu's rule. Hugs, holding young children in your lap, backrubs—they are so vital to children in a healthy family environment. If parents don't give their teenage children appropriate forms of physical touch, then they will seek it from inappropriate sources. Yet how many fathers stop hugging their daughters when they become teenagers for fear of being misconstrued? And in how many homes do children get backrubs from their parents?

As I sat on his bed, Jacob shared about his challenges at work. As is often the case, it's not the job that's difficult, it's either the people or the environment.

Ours is a quiet house. Even guests comment on how peaceful it is in our home. We got rid of our television years ago, and the music in our house is from someone singing or playing the piano, violin, or guitar. The TV is not on. The radio is not on. We are accustomed to tranquility. But in the mechanic shop where Jacob works, a radio is on all the time. The incessant sound is like drumbeats on his nerves. One day Jacob told the owner, "If I talked to you an hour or two, you'd probably want me to stop talking already. What if I talked to you all day long non-stop? That's what it feels like to me when that radio is on." But the owner admitted that he doesn't like the quiet because then he's alone with his thoughts.

I take pleasure in being alone with my thoughts. Those raised in peace seek peace, those raised in noise and chaos are more comfortable in that. When I am silent, I can hear God speak to me. How can you hear someone in a noise-filled environment?

Saturday, 17 September 2011

Is anyone happy? Let them sing songs of praise.
– James 5:13 (NIV)

"The last time I was in Niagara Falls was when Cousin Ivan was here in 2005. I was only nine years old!" said Larissa.

I organized today's day trip to Niagara Falls for fifteen-year-old Igor. He'd dreamt of going to Niagara Falls, just two hours drive from Rochester, but his dysfunctional family wasn't capable of organizing such an outing. However, Igor wasn't the only one excited by the trip; we were all excited: Igor, Larissa and I, and Nadia's daughter Tatiana whom we'd invited. Perhaps even Jacob, though he didn't show it.

"My family went to Niagara Falls last summer," said Tatiana. "We enjoyed it so much that I wanted to go back again this summer, but we never got the chance. Thanks so much for inviting me!" she smiled. Her two brothers, Myron and Michael, were disappointed that they'd made other plans for the day.

We took route 18, a country highway alongside sparkling Lake Ontario. The blue sky made the waters a deep indigo. Orchard after orchard displayed its produce in roadside stands. At one such stand, we bought a basket of succulent peaches.

When we arrived in Niagara Falls, I found a free parking spot on a city street. The time limit was two hours.

"We should make it," I said confidently, "as long as the line for the Maid of the Mist isn't too long."

It wasn't.

No trip to Niagara Falls is complete without the thrilling half-hour ride on the Maid of the Mist. These diesel-powered double-decker boats, which accommodate hundreds of passengers at a time, take you into the middle of the thunderous Canadian Horseshoe Falls.

Donned in the disposable blue plastic ponchos we were provided, our group boarded the boat and rushed up the stairs to the open-air top deck. There we had a 360-degree view of the river, gorge, and waterfalls far upstream.

The ride started out mild enough. The boat's powerful two engines grumbled into gear, labored against the current, and pushed us up the Niagara River slowly past the American Falls. The top deck was crowded with tourists young and old chattering in numerous languages and snapping pictures.

Nothing can prepare you for the ride as you approach the Horse-shoe Falls. The waves get rougher, the light spray becomes a shower, the boat bucks and lurches in the turbulent, frothy waters. It feels so incredibly wild and thrilling, so wonderfully perilous that you can't help but smile even as a cold blast of water drenches you. In that tumultuous epicenter with nearly a half-mile arc of massive thundering walls of water surrounding you, soaking you, churning under you, if you can pull your eyes from the seventeen-story avalanche of water, you would see everyone on the boat grinning as if their smiles were imbedded in their faces. I was grinning until my face hurt. I glanced at Jacob, my most serious child, and he was grinning, too.

The impossibly majestic waterfall, the deafening wild roar, the raucous ride, the soaking spray—they were all so gloriously untamed. A marvel with God's signature on it.

"You paid $13.50 for this shower?" Jacob joked after the boat docked.

"It was worth every penny," I said emphatically.

Whirlpool State Park and a hike into the Niagara gorge were next—after a picnic lunch that included the peaches we bought. From the rim, we walked down, down to the riotous river. Igor sprinted from boulder to boulder climbing them like a gazelle. I had not been on any long hike all summer, not since I started the chemotherapy, so it was both exhilarating and strenuous to hike the paths and jump the rocks by the fast-flowing Niagara River. Perhaps the most rewarding part of the whole day was climbing out of the gorge up the hundreds of steps—and keeping up with the teenagers in my group. I'm far from having my full strength back, but my body has recovered much since the days when I got winded walking up the sixteen steps to the front door of my house.

Friday, 23 September 2011
first day of autumn

Delight yourself also in the LORD, and He shall give you the desires of your heart.
– Psalm 37:4 (NKJV)

As I went out the front door, I almost walked face first into an orb web that a large spider had spun overnight across the entrance to the house. The only thing that saved me from this spectacularly unpleasant experience was the fact that opening the screen door destroyed most of the web, and the hideous spider hung vulnerably on the few remaining strands.

I removed the remains of the web with a broom.

Around the house are many orb webs, like flattened parachutes, some big, some small, each reflecting the size of its weaver. Although I'm not a fan of spiders, I leave these delicate webs alone if they aren't in a place where I might walk into them. Orb-making is a late-summer phenomenon; I never see orbs in the spring or early summer, but I know that summer days are ebbing when the intricately-woven orbs begin to appear.

Little flashes of red dot the foliage. When I looked out the back window as Larissa went out to the goat pen, golden leaves fell like a gentle rain from the trees in the forest. Most of the trees are still green, a dull green, but the coverage is thinning. The enormous burning bush that drapes our green metal shed like a cloak has turned pink and red at the tips, like the beginning of a blush.

In the backyard, a flock of robins flitted through, six or ten of them moving as a group, gathering to make their way south. On Wednesday when we drove to Larissa's math tutor, we saw Canada geese lifting up from a pond, the swarm of geese gradually rearranging themselves in the air to form the familiar V-shaped skein that is so typical in the fall and spring skies.

Signs of fall are everywhere.

I always count the chickens whenever I'm near the pen—three red, three speckled, one black, one white. One, two, three, four, five, six, seven, eight. I count them twice, just to make sure. It's a habit. I always count them whenever I feed them, when I call them, or when I close them up for the night.

Yesterday as Larissa headed to the backyard woods to take some photos, she noticed a red-tailed hawk flying from our yard into the woods. When it landed on a tree, Larissa took some pictures of it, thinking how odd that the hawk landed so close to her. Then instead of going on to the woods, she checked on the chickens. One, two, three, four, five, six, seven… Where was the eighth? She scanned the pen, and by the back fence saw the missing red chicken, its feathers plucked and scattered, its body badly mutilated. It had been the hawk's lunch. Too big for the hawk to carry off, it had fed on the chicken inside the pen probably while the other chickens watched. How frightening that must have been to see their friend being killed and eaten.

This morning Larissa went to hang a net over the pen so the hawk can't get in. Shortly I saw her running from the back of the yard down the stone steps two at a time. I met her at the door.

"What's up?" I asked.

"The hawk! It got the white chicken! I didn't think that it would come so early! I went out and as soon as the chickens saw me, they all came running toward me, squawking. I counted them, as I always do, and one was missing, the white one. Then I heard a fluttering from the pen, and saw the hawk flying away. But I'd spooked it, and it flew into the wire fence—it didn't have enough room to take off—and one foot got stuck under the fence. It kept flapping with its foot stuck in the fence, so I ran around the outside of the pen and stepped on its entangled foot so it couldn't get away. I wanted to frighten it. It lay there on its back with its beak open, wings spread, helpless, not even struggling. It's not really that big, and its talons aren't that big either. Then the neighbors' white cat came walking by and scared the hawk, and it struggled and got away."

Wildlife is so lovely—as long as it's in the wild. We realize now that the goats' presence in the pen had kept away hawks in the past. With mama goat gone, we've kept the other two goats locked in the shed because they cry and cry whenever they're outside alone.

Larissa fenced the chickens in a small corner of the pen and draped netting overhead. The chickens aren't happy and seem quite lost; the white chicken had been their leader. The mama goat had been the goats' leader. All the animals are in a time of transition.

So am I.

Tuesday, 27 September 2011

No eye has seen, no ear has heard, no mind has conceived what God has prepared for those who love Him.

– 1 Corinthians 2:9 (NIV)

The bustle in the kitchen reminded me that the whole family is together again. Now there is a traffic jam when I prepare my coffee and breakfast, and I have to shimmy around family members at the counter.

Tad and Alexandra arrived last night. Jacob went with me to the airport just before midnight. We didn't have to wait long; the plane was early and we could see Alexandra coming toward us.

With all five of us in the house, life is returning to our somewhat chaotic normal.

Since spring, I've had weeks of "normal" living interrupted by medical appointments that shock me back into the reality that I'm still a cancer patient under treatment. Today: an echocardiogram to check again whether the Herceptin is causing any heart damage. Once more, I lay on the table, blew out all the air from my lungs and held my breath while on the monitor I saw my own heart beating. The whoosh, whoosh, whoosh sound was freaky. I don't often think about my heart beating, but there it was on the screen, throbbing, pumping, whooshing.

I also had an appointment at the chiropractor. My adjustment is holding, but my right hand is still numb, the nerves still frazzled, ultrasensitive, tender whenever I touch anything, sometimes burning, like when I was cutting up tomatoes for salad. But pain no longer wakes me in the night.

Music now fills the house much of the day—Tad playing the keyboard and piano, singing, doing voice exercises; Alexandra playing and singing as well; and each of them singing, singing as they walk around the house, while cleaning, cooking, taking a shower. Jacob and Larissa both play the piano and keyboard too, and they both sing, but not without musical accompaniment. I'm keenly aware that Alexandra's sweet voice will echo in the hallways for only a few days because she is soon leaving for her year-long Christian internship program.

October

Monday, 3 October 2011

*The eyes of the L*ORD *are on the righteous and His ears are attentive to their cry.*

– Psalm 34:15 (NIV)

I walk through the automatic doors of the Lipson Cancer Center infrequently now. The receptionist who once greeted me by name asked for my last name today. Perhaps I should rejoice.

I came alone. As I waited, I observed the clusters of people in the waiting room and inside the cubicles where we receive our drugs intravenously. Each group has its own world of troubles that brought them here. Although most have no outward signs of cancer or chemo, some women wear baseball caps set low on their foreheads. Others wear a headscarf like mine. I make eye contact and nod to these women.

Before I went to my own cubicle to receive my Herceptin infusion, I met with Dr. Julia Smith in her office. Her friendly blue eyes and smile put me at ease.

"I've been thinking," I said to her. "If my treatment extends all the way to February, that will be in the next fiscal year. Currently insurance is paying for one hundred percent of my treatments, but if I go into the next year, I'll again have to cover the first seven thousand dollars out of pocket. I'd like to stop the Herceptin and get the port removed before Christmas so my treatment doesn't go into next year."

"We can arrange that," the doctor agreed. "In Europe, they give Herceptin for only six months, not the twelve months like we do here. You've already been on it for six months."

I appreciated that Dr. Smith didn't give me any pushback.

Back at home, I began to gather kitchen items—an 8 x 8 and 9 x 13 baking dish, some noodles, a few spices—for Alexandra to take to Mission E4. Her moving-in day is Wednesday. Hard to believe that my middle child is leaving home at seventeen. I'm excited—and sad.

Wednesday, 5 October 2011
Moving-in day for Alexandra

For this God is our God for ever and ever; He will be our guide even to the end.

– Psalm 48:14 (NIV)

Since we are leaving the silver minivan for Alexandra to use during the year that she's an intern at Mission E4, we drove to Massachusetts in two vehicles—the minivan and the VW Golf.

Tad insisted on driving the minivan. Crammed in the back was a small upright piano that he had just purchased to donate to Mission E4 so that Alexandra would have an instrument to play. Alexandra without a piano would be like me without my camera.

Alexandra rode with me in the Golf as we drove east on the New York State Thruway. Conversation was slow to start. Alexandra had been away in Ukraine with Tad for seven weeks. Just as I was wondering how to get Alexandra to open up without seeming like I was prying, a scene straight out of Europe helped stimulate conversation: a herd of cows walking across a thruway overpass, a man with a stick following behind them. Because of preparations to move to Massachusetts, Alexandra and I hadn't had time to talk about her trip, and the hours in the car allowed her to share about visits with family, singing in churches, teaching VBS, traveling to villages.

The Massachusetts border is two hundred and fifty miles from home. Hubbardston is another hundred miles beyond that. On a rural road soon after we exited the Massachusetts Turnpike, we found a grocery store that sold sandwiches and rotisserie turkey breasts. We took our purchase outside, and under the shade of tall leafy trees at the edge of the supermarket parking lot, we sat on some large rocks and ate our bittersweet last meal together.

The wooded Mission E4 campus by the beaver pond was idyllic on this golden fall day. As Alexandra unpacked her belongings and Tad (with a couple of helpers) wrestled the piano into a small room, I went to the office to speak with Scott. In just ten days, I'll be meeting Alexandra and Scott in Haiti.

"I can't do anything very physical on the mission trip," I told Scott. "I was thinking: everyone wants photos of themselves in the mission field, but they don't always have time to take these photos. Perhaps I can be the group photographer on this trip," I suggested.

"I have something even better planned for you," Scott informed me. "We're going to do a calendar of the orphan girls as a fundraiser, and I want you to take the photos."

I beamed. Yes, it was better than I'd hoped for.

We couldn't stay on campus very long; we had a six-hour drive back home. With a kind of emptiness tugging at my heart, we prayed for Alexandra, hugged and kissed her good-bye, and with just an hour of sunlight left, we got into the Golf and drove west, leaving Alexandra to make new friends and a new life.

I had felt a cold coming on, but in the flurry of activity preceding Alexandra's move, it hadn't taken hold. However, it hit me hard on the drive back—sore throat, coughing, fatigue. I felt ill, so Tad drove the entire six hours back home, entertaining me with story after story from his seven weeks in Ukraine.

Friday, 14 October 2011
Rochester airport

The righteous cry out, and the LORD hears them; He delivers them from all their troubles.

– Psalm 34:17 (NIV)

Rain, heavy rain bounces on the tarmac, flows in curtains from the seething sky, races down the plate glass windows of the airport. I sit at Gate B3 and watch the sudden storm that has delayed my 2:37 PM flight from Rochester to Atlanta, severely shrinking my layover time. Will I make my Miami connection? Will I be able to meet up with the rest of the Haiti team at the Miami Airport Hotel where we're to spend the night before tomorrow's early morning flight to Port-au-Prince?

Even though little prickles of worry nibble at me, I relish this time at the airport, this time alone reading, observing, thinking. Praise God for His mercy! Earlier this year I didn't know whether I'd ever travel again; now I'm at the exhilarating start of another mission trip. Tomorrow, Lord willing, I'll see Alexandra in Haiti where she's already been for one week with Scott, the President of Mission E4, and Lynn, the Director of Child Services.

I've been rushing for days. At work, I had to prepare four user manuals for translation, and as always, there were pagination issues, problems with the index, illustrations linked to wrong files. I worked frantically and late. I finally went to Walmart last night to buy a few presents for the Haitian children I sponsor—granola bars, shirts for the boys, bandanas for the girls. I packed them into Ziploc bags with stuffed animals and toy cars, plus the less exciting beans and bouillon. Then I finished writing up the list of Larissa's homeschool assignments for the week that I'll be gone.

I did the majority of the packing this morning. My suitcase is lighter than usual. On this trip, I didn't have to bring food or relief supplies, organize or train a team. I feel so free traveling solo!

While in Haiti, I'll miss the peak fall foliage in Rochester. At the end of summer, the trees became a dull green as if autumn were sucking in her breath, inhaling the colors of the leaves, preparing to exhale a crescendo of colors—cream and pink, orange and yellow, crimson and scarlet. This morning when the sun rose and the low, rich orange sunbeams lit up the neighbors' maple trees, it was like looking into a golden temple of God's exquisite handiwork.

But in Haiti, a different world awaits me.

Saturday, 15 October 2011
Haiti

The LORD is my light and my salvation—whom shall I fear? The LORD is the stronghold of my life—of whom shall I be afraid?
– Psalm 27:1 (NIV)

"In case you haven't been in a car since 1972, watch to see how you fasten a seat belt," flight attendant Tom said during one of yesterday's flights.

"Now here's a question for you," he continued. "First person to answer wins a small package of cookies. Your seat cushion can be used as a…"

"Flotation device!" answered a quarter of the passengers.

"Looks like we'll be running out of cookies on this flight."

Tom finished the announcements with, "If there's any way we can serve you, feel free to call Emmanuel." He pointed to the other attendant.

I so enjoy flight attendants who don't just methodically do their jobs, but add a little creativity and humor.

I did make my connection yesterday because my second flight was also delayed, and I arrived in Miami after nine o'clock. I located Jane, the leader of the Wisconsin group, by asking for her at the airport hotel desk. Jane, who was on her ninth trip to Haiti, joined me as I devoured a slice of pizza at an airport eatery that was about to close. I appreciated that she came down so I didn't have to eat alone.

I roomed with redheaded Linda, also from Wisconsin, who had recently retired from a factory job. It was her first trip to Haiti. She was nervousness and excitement wrapped into one boisterous bundle.

The night was short; we rose before the sun. After I showered, Linda complimented my haircut. I cringed. Perhaps because my inch-long hair is just a bit shorter than Linda's, she thought a stylist cut it to this length. Tad said I now have a "modern" cut, but I feel like a shorn sheep.

"I've never cut my hair this short," I told Linda. "It's like this because I lost my hair during chemo last spring and it's starting to grow back."

The new hair is coming in soft as a baby's and undulating like waves on an ocean, some clumps growing this way, other clumps that way. At first there seemed to be a lot of gray hair, but now that it's longer, the brunette color predominates. However, it's still so short that I continue to hide it under a head wrap.

After check-in, security, a short flight, more lines, customs, and then baggage claim, I was back in Haiti. Back in the steamy heat, the poverty, the disarray. Back where life isn't plastic-wrapped or ultra-pasteurized.

I could see that Alexandra thrived since we dropped her off at Mission E4. "She is delightful. I didn't think that she'd enjoy spending time with an old lady," said Lynn of their week together in Haiti.

"Tad used to take the kids everywhere. He did a lot of visitation. My kids are quite comfortable with adults," I said.

Alexandra told me about sleeping on the lowest berth of a bunk bed in the Léogâne orphanage while the orphan girls still chattered, eating in a restaurant under an open roof as a deluge began, riding in the back of a pick-up in the rain. I was delighted that she was going places and having her own adventures, delighted that she had fledged from the nest and seemed comfortable spreading her wings.

Sunday, 16 October 2011
Haiti

...call on me in the day of trouble; I will deliver you, and you will honor me.

– Psalm 50:15 (NIV)

Scott has been battling a stomach ailment, so with only a few hours' notice, Paul, who led my team in January, flew in yesterday to lead this trip until Scott recovers. It's a much smaller group than in January. I already memorized the names of the sixteen women and nine men.

As during the January trip, we are staying at the Villa Ormiso guesthouse. I'm rooming with four others: my daughter Alexandra, Lynn (the Director of Child Services), Jane (who met me at the Miami Airport), and Chelle (a friend of Lynn's and a professional photographer). All the women are close to my age, pleasant, and easy to get along with.

Last night Paul announced that the morning devotions would be led by volunteers. "If anyone has a word to share, please see me."

I felt a little nudge inside. But what could I share?

This morning we attended a lively service in a church in Léogâne. We sat on green and red and blue school benches under a corrugated metal roof that shaded us from the tropical sun. There were no walls. As the preacher delivered his message in Creole, I furiously scribbled in my notebook. Although it may have appeared that I was taking sermon notes, I was taking dictation from the Holy Spirit. God gave me a word as I sat on that church bench. I filled page after page. As often happens when I step away from my daily routine and the comfort of home, God directs my steps more easily because I'm not bound by my daily schedule and habits.

After the service, we walked next door to the girls' orphanage where Madame Bazile, the pastor's wife, set out a feast of a lunch for our team. She and the older orphan girls had worked since dawn to prepare the variety of Haitian foods: chicken and rice, noodles and vegetables, fried plantains, pikliz (spicy Haitian coleslaw) and some dishes that we had to guess. Conch? Goat? All were delicious; I'm especially fond of the *pikliz*.

We start the real work tomorrow. Today we practiced skits that we'll perform at each of the schools and got acquainted with the other members of our work teams. The teams include light construction (painting, shoveling gravel), heavy construction (building projects, such as framing walls at the new boys' orphanage), food and water (making lunches and filling water bottles; Alexandra is on that team), and special projects. I'm assigned to special projects with staff member Lynn and veteran missionary Jean. My role includes taking portrait photos of the orphan girls, photographing sponsored children with the gifts sent to them by their American sponsors, and going with Lynn to off-the-beaten-track locations to photograph newly built homes financed by child sponsors so that the sponsors can see what their donations funded. I'm excited!

In the evening, during supper back at the guesthouse, I sat with an elderly couple from Canton, Ohio who aren't part of the Mission E4 group. Manning, who is seventy-eight, and his wife Pat have been coming to Haiti on short-term trips for twenty-eight years. Something about Pat was different. She and her husband traveled alone serving in various Haitian churches. I shared with Pat the many things that God had done in my life, such as healings and giving me a message for our team during this morning's church service.

"I feel that you are a special sister in Christ," Pat said to me. "I'm so happy to meet you."

I, however, felt that she was the special one. Pat took my hand and prayed over me, prayed and prophesied that I would travel and speak in many places and that God would use me for His glory.

The prayer was powerful and made me weep—me speaking in many places? Tad had said this, too. Oh, that I may leave this cancer journey behind me and serve the Lord on a different journey for many more years!

I wiped away my tears as we gathered for the evening devotions. Scott, who is still not well, delivered the message. He talked about exercise. Spiritual exercise. If you don't exercise spiritually the way you exercise physically, you'll stagnate or atrophy.

"True evidence of our salvation is the lifestyle we lead," Scott reminded us. "James 1:27 says, *Religion that God our Father accepts as pure and faultless is this: to look after orphans and widows in their distress and to keep oneself from being polluted by the world.* It's easy to forget those in greatest need when you're polluted by the world. The world creates a greater hunger for more—more stuff, more of what the world considers normal. We pray, 'Give us today our daily bread'—not mutual funds, not big savings accounts. When we end up pursuing them, it takes away the ability to follow God's purpose."

I'm challenged by Scott's teaching. It's very difficult not to be ensnared by the world. Who doesn't want a well-paid job and a comfortable retirement?

But being polluted by the world means other things to me, too. I couldn't help but think of the money that Christians spend on their hair. During my recent period of baldness, I became even more keenly aware how much emphasis people put on their hair—cutting and styling it, dyeing it, streaking it, primping it. In the churches, we're taught to consider WWJD—What Would Jesus Do? We put it on bracelets and key chains, teach it in our Sunday school classes. We give WWJD lip service, yet how many people actually contemplate what Jesus would do as they make decisions in their daily lives? Would He dye his hair when it became gray? Would He have tattoos on his neck and arms? If He were a woman, would He have His nails done? How much money would He spend on his hair or tattoos or nails? How much money do Christians spend on these frivolous things? Does my conscience allow me to spend that kind of money on my outward appearance—my vanity—while fifty percent of Haitians go hungry? What right do I have to spend God's money (all money is God's money) on such frivolity? Who am I trying to impress with my outward appearance? Why am I trying to impress people and not the Lord? What's more important, perfectly coiffed hair and fingertips covered in nail art—or sponsoring another hungry child?

Scott's sermon broke into my thoughts. "The Lord is looking for obedience," he said.

Maybe we should question things that we consider normal and sincerely examine our motivation behind our actions. WWJD?

Monday, 17 October 2011
Haiti

This is the day the LORD has made; we will rejoice and be glad in it.
– Psalm 118: 24 (NKJV)

I sang this psalm in a church service in Senegal. French and English and Wolof voices melded into one joyous noise to the Lord that day. I also sang this psalm atop a truck in Haiti during my post-earthquake trip. I remember the euphoric wave of joy as we rode through the countryside after a baptism service, wind in our faces, singing at the top of our lungs and waving to Haitians we passed.

And today is another lovely day that the Lord has made. I'm rejoicing being in Haiti, rejoicing being with my daughter and with sisters and brothers in Christ, rejoicing being well enough to travel!

Alexandra and Linda (the animated redhead) are in charge of making our lunches at the work sites all week. It's odd for me to let go of Alexandra and not work alongside her. She has matured considerably since the beginning of summer. She's so much more independent. Gone is the child that clung to me and asked what color paper she should choose for her craft project. Because Scott has been sick, leading worship has fallen to Alexandra. She was once shy about playing piano and singing in front of people; now she seems unruffled by it. I'm delighted to see the self-confident young woman she's become. I can hardly believe that she'll be eighteen in less than two weeks. She holds up well to Scott's teasing and gives some back. Scott and Paul have both expressed how impressed they are by her.

I feel that I've sent them my jewel, a solid Christian who knows the Bible well, is studious and thorough, and a gifted musician, gifted in languages as well. I see by her relations with the older orphans—the smiles, hugs, holding of hands—that they like her, and she them. Sending her to Mission E4 feels something like giving my best to the Lord. Not that Jacob or Larissa are worse; they aren't. But in this season in her life, Alexandra has completely given herself to serving God, and God is blessing her.

After devotions and breakfast, we piled into our bus for the sobering hour-long drive to the girls' orphanage. The hills are clothed with poverty, the roadsides with heartache. To Haitians, suffering is part of daily life. Some days they have enough food to feed two children, but not the other two. I can't imagine having to decide which of my children go hungry.

This morning Jean and I helped Lynn coordinate meetings between our team members and their sponsored schoolchildren. I met with Pierre, my mother's sponsored child, who is ten. My mother bought him a dress shirt, size ten, but it was a good size too large. In Haiti, children are often much smaller than their American counterparts.

Herlie, the three-year-old preschooler I sponsor, was next. Through a translator, I found out that Herlie lives in a tent with her mom and dad. When I handed her the Ziploc bag full of little gifts, she honed in on the granola bar and ate it greedily. She was more interested in the granola bar than the stuffed animal or clothing. She ate so voraciously that it surprised me. Then I realized that it was a Monday morning and the children had not yet had their school lunch. Considering half of Haitians eat only one meal per day or less, who knows when her last meal had been?

Wednesday, 19 October 2011
Haiti

For we are God's handiwork, created in Christ Jesus to do good works, which God prepared in advance for us to do.

– Ephesians 2:10 (NIV)

During mission trips, I try to have a one-on-one conversation with every person on the trip so I can find out a little about each individual. Jerry has an adopted two-year-old Haitian son. Angie is a foster mother with two children of her own (her daughter is on this trip with her); her husband is a chef who dreams of opening a soup kitchen someday. Paula, who has an autistic son, raises cows and sheep. Everyone has their own story, and listening to them is like opening a new book. How I wish I could also hear the stories of the Haitians I meet.

I've been photographing the orphan girls between other assignments. I spot a girl I haven't photographed, lead her to a different background (by a bunk bed, a blackboard, or on a chair in her school uniform), and I mime how I want her to pose. But my main task today was sorting schoolbooks by grade level with Angie and her daughter Shyanne, putting them in suitcases, and then distributing them in a school in Laquil. The rest of the team had taken our small charter bus to work in construction at the boys' orphanage in Fauche. To get around, Angie, Shyanne, Lynn, and I took a tap-tap—one of those gaudily painted covered pickup trucks—from the girls' orphanage to the school, then to join the rest of the group at the Fauche boys' orphanage. Mission E4 had hired the tap-tap as a private taxi, but generally tap-taps are public transportation vehicles that follow set routes, and people jump on and off them as needed, paying a small fee for the ride.

It's thrilling to travel the Haitian way, bumping around on a hard bench in the colorful tap-tap. A modern bus is so tame in comparison. When it was time for the entire team to go back to the girls' orphanage, some team members rode in the tap-tap. Instead of a routine bus ride, it would be an adventure.

Dawn and Peg, both first-time visitors to Haiti, claimed the two best seats, the ones nearest the open back end. There they got a breeze and a view of the Haitian scenery behind us.

Part of the drive back is through a village where traffic always slows to a crawl. An open-air market comes right up to the roadside. Pedestrians wander on the street; there are no sidewalks. Bicyclists and overfilled trucks, motorcycles and buses, dogs and hawkers all share the dusty road.

As we inched along past rickety wooden market stands, a young Haitian man in bright yellow sneakers jumped on board our tap-tap. He happened to touch Peg's arm as he boarded. She screamed; we all screamed in response, and the young man, shocked at finding a public transport vehicle full of screaming white people, jumped off. We all laughed and laughed at ourselves after the incident. How silly we must have seemed to that Haitian.

Thursday, 20 October 2011
Haiti

Do not merely listen to the word, and so deceive yourselves. Do what it says.

– James 1:22 (NIV)

Another day in Haiti unfurled before us like an offering to the Lord. As befits a mission trip, we start the days with a personal quiet time of reading, praying, and journaling, then come together for devotions.

Once again Alexandra played the piano and led worship. Afterward, it was my turn to give the morning devotional. I stood in front of the group and delivered the message that the Lord had put on my heart on Sunday. Pat and Manning sat behind our group, offering silent support as I spoke:

"I want to share a burden God put on my heart ever since I traveled outside the U.S. and saw poverty firsthand.

"In America—and in Canada and Western Europe, too—we live in the Disney World of the planet, a place of leisure and entertainment. In fact, the media and our society have brainwashed us, convincing us that we deserve the best—fancy cars, expensive restaurants, cruise vacations, big houses.

"We also deserve to be entertained, says society. Sports, movies, TV shows, amusement parks, jet skiing, downhill skiing, eating out— we deserve it. We earned it.

"In our bubble of wealth, our refrigerators are full, we have electricity and hot showers, indoor toilets (often more than one), washers and dryers, microwaves and dishwashers. These are considered normal. Necessities. Not luxuries as they are here in Haiti or even in Ukraine where my husband grew up—or in much of the rest of the world. Many people on this planet have less in their homes than I take with me on a camping trip!

"You've surely heard that forty percent of the world's almost seven billion people live on two dollars per day, or less. That's over *two-and-a-half billion* people who live on two dollars per day. Or less.

"Stalin said, 'A single death is a tragedy; a million deaths is a statistic.' The death is a tragedy if it's your father or brother, your husband or son, your uncle or cousin, your neighbor or friend. It's a tragedy if it's someone you personally know. But if it's a million people you don't know? It's just a statistic. The same is true of the two-and-a-half billion poor. An overwhelming statistic. You don't know them. They're not part of your life.

"I want to share with you some of these individual tragedies that I saw and people I met on different mission trips.

"In 2006, I went to Kenya on a mission trip visiting African churches and ministries that were helping the poor, reaching out to the community. Africans know how to help other Africans. They have good ideas and good programs, but they don't have the funds. We Americans have funds, but often don't know how to best put them to use helping the poor. So I went on a kind of scouting trip with another woman so see which programs and ministries were worth supporting.

"Our first day in Kenya, a Sunday, we were taken about two hours from the capital of Nairobi into a village up in the red earthen hills. We went to a church service there. In a small building of corrugated metal and earthen floors, the pastor asked his congregation to bring up to the altar any clothing that they had brought to give to the poor people in that church. To me, they were all poor people. It was a case of the poor giving to the poorer. If only I'd known, I thought, I could have brought with me an entire suitcase of clothing and not even missed it!

" 'And next week,' announced the pastor, 'anyone who has extra blankets, sheets, mattresses or beds, bring them with you. There are those in this church who have nothing to sleep on.'

"No mattress? Nor a hammock? Not even a blanket? Sleeping on an earthen floor with nothing? I couldn't imagine it. I'd never even thought of such a thing.

" 'Could you take us to such a home?' I asked our host and translator. I wanted to see this with my own eyes.

"After the church service, we stopped at a small store and bought some flour, sugar, and oil—traditional gifts when visiting a home. I was traveling with another woman, Karen. We had to walk down, down, down a steep earthen path to a mud hut that had no windows. It was owned by a widow. She'd been a widow since 1973. She was raising four children. They were her grandchildren. The mothers of these children, her two daughters, had gone to Nairobi to try to earn a living, most likely as barmaids or prostitutes.

"The only piece of furniture in the house was a single chair. There was no bed, no blankets, just a few rags, a pot for cooking, and a pile of sticks for the fire, which I could see they usually made inside the house. There were some large stones and ashes on the earthen floor.

"When I walked into the house, I saw three young children sitting on the red dirt floor like little mushrooms. They didn't move.

They didn't react to me at all—didn't get up and run, didn't laugh or cry, didn't do anything. They just sat there. Now usually when African children see a white person for the first time, it's pretty scary. Usually they cry. We look too pale, and it's frightening to them. But these children didn't react.

"'Karen!' I called. 'Come here and look at these children. What's wrong with them?' I asked her. Karen had been to Africa fourteen times, so she had more experience than I did.

"'Oh, Kathryn,' she said, 'they're starving. They don't have the energy to react.'

"The widow was holding one child in her arms. It looked like an infant, but this child was eighteen months old. The three children sitting on the floor were six, four, and three. They looked much younger. The three-year-old had not yet learned to walk. He didn't have enough energy to spare.

"There was nothing to eat in the house, except for the food we had just brought. I had never seen anything like it. We left the widow all the food we had with us—some granola bars and some vitamin drinks Karen had with her. But it wouldn't last long.

"Karen and I returned to our hotel room in Nairobi and sat on our two comfy beds wondering what we could do for this widow. How could we help her? If we gave her a hundred dollars, even two hundred, they would last only a while. Then they'd be gone. What if we gave her chickens? Could she feed them and eat the eggs?

"Then I thought of something: We'd buy her a lactating goat! That way she could milk the goat and give the children the milk. I remembered reading about tribes in Africa that lived mainly off cows' milk. But a goat is easier to take care of and feed than a cow.

"We had to leave for Ethiopia, but we gave our hostess the thirty dollars for a goat. Later we heard that the day she brought the goat to the widow, she arrived at the funeral of one of the children. I don't know which one. When the widow saw the goat, she thanked Jesus—not the woman, not the Americans. She thanked Jesus for seeing her need and answering her prayers.

"Since then, I can never just spend thirty dollars without thinking, *Maybe I can buy a goat with this money. It could be the difference between life and death for someone.* I could eat out. Or I could buy a goat. I've bought many goats for families in Africa since then.

"After Kenya, Karen and I flew to Ethiopia. In the capital, Addis Ababa, eighty percent of the three million inhabitants live in slums. We visited different churches in the capital and ministries serving street children or widows with AIDS. While there, we bought bottled drinking water—you certainly wouldn't want to drink out of the tap—and threw away the bottles at our hotel. Our host saw this and told us not to throw away the bottles because on Thursday, we'd be driving through the countryside to a town two hours' drive away. In the countryside, there are a lot of shepherds, and these empty water bottles—bottles like the ones we throw into recycling bins—would be 'big presents' for the shepherds. They have nothing to carry their water in while they're out with their herds of goats or cattle all day.

"So we saved our plastic water bottles. I even came across a conference at the guesthouse where we were staying, and asked the leader whether I could have all the water bottles that were left behind on the tables. By the time we went to the countryside, I had four large garbage bags of plastic water bottles. To us at home, they'd be trash. In Ethiopia, I was excited to have collected so many 'presents.'

"But giving out these water bottles could be a problem. A friend of mine who'd spent time in Africa described giving out colored pencils to schoolchildren. The children started a big fight over the pencils. It got so bad that my friend gave the pencils to the teacher and told her to give them out at another time. I didn't know how we'd give out these water bottles without starting a riot. But as we were driving through the countryside, I got an idea. Whenever we saw a shepherd, we'd roll down the windows of our van, take a water bottle in our hand and wave it out the window, catching the shepherd's attention, then hurl the bottle as far as we could toward the shepherd.

If there was more than one shepherd, we'd throw more than one bottle. When the shepherds saw us, they would drop what they were doing and run toward the bottles. They would pick them up, wave back to us, jump up and down holding the bottles up in the air. They were so excited about an empty plastic bottle—trash to us in America. A big treasure to them in Ethiopia.

"On my previous trip to Haiti, I came with my whole family. My daughter Alexandra got to meet the girl that she sponsors. I came across them as they were talking through a translator.

" 'What would you like me to bring or send you next time?' Alexandra asked her sponsored child.

"Oh-oh, I thought. Here it comes, that request for an iPod or something ridiculously expensive.

" 'Pencils,' said the girl. 'I need pencils for school.'

"It was not at all what I expected to hear.

"On this trip, I met a new preschool girl that I'm sponsoring. I brought her a gallon-sized bag with some toys and granola bars and a few other things, like soap. I expected her to focus on the stuffed animals, but she honed in on the granola bar and tried to tear open the packaging. I helped her. She stuffed that granola bar into her mouth like a person who hadn't eaten in a long time. Then I realized that it was before lunch on a Monday, and she hadn't had her school meal. Obviously she hadn't eaten at home. And I'm not sure that she ate the day before either, based on the way she ate that granola bar.

"Many Americans say, 'I'm not rich.' But you are!

"Did you know that if you own a car, you're wealthier than ninety-two percent of the people on earth[*]? You're in the top eight percent of the world's wealthy.

"In the Bible, there is only one correct response to having wealth and abundance: sharing.

---

[*] *Serving with Eyes Wide Open*, Livermore, David A., p. 23

"Turn to Deuteronomy 15:10. It says, *Give generously to them and do so without a grudging heart; then because of this the Lord your God will bless you in all your work and in everything you put your hand to.*

"God promises to bless you in all you do if you give to the poor.

"When my son was fourteen, I went with him on a youth mission trip to Mexico where they built homes for the destitute on a landfill. There was an active part of the garbage dump where the garbage trucks emptied trash and the poor came to scrounge for clothing, food, plastic bottles to sell to recyclers, and metal to resell. We took a bus of youth to the dump to distribute lemonade—and for them to see what life is like at the other end of the spectrum. I still remember the stench. The flies. The black smoke. And the people. They were surprisingly friendly and thankful for the lemonade.

"When we got back on the bus, the youth were strangely quiet. The leaders urged them to share what was on their minds.

"One of the girls said, 'It's only by the grace of God you weren't born here.'

"A young man stood up and said, 'I don't ever want to hear you complain that for Christmas you didn't get that iPod or cell phone you wanted. Be thankful if all you get is a pair of socks!'

"Another girl stood up. 'I don't want to go home. People back home are so materialistic. These people here are happy with garbage!'

"Have you considered that this material blessing, this wealth you have, is a test? That God is testing you? What will you do with it—spend it on yourself or share with the needy?

"Turn to 1 John 3:17. *If anyone has material possessions and sees a brother or sister in need but has no pity on them, how can the love of God be in that person?*

"Someday God will call us to give an account of our lives and everything God entrusted us with. Did we use these things for God's glory—or our own glory and pleasure?

"The burden on my heart and what I struggle with is this: James 4:17 says, *Anyone then who knows the good he ought to do and doesn't do it, sins.* God has so richly blessed me. Am I doing enough?

"I pray that God give each of us the wisdom to know the good we ought to do and the strength to do it."

Some distance from the main asphalt road, our tap-tap jounced along earthen roads and splashed right through a shallow river. Lynn and a Haitian builder and I were on a quest to visit and photograph newly built plywood homes for the families of sponsored children. On this ride, I had a glimpse of the interior of Haiti. We rode past tangles of green growth and trees with curiously wide root systems; by ramshackle hovels of corrugated metal and wood and cloth; past a man sitting outside at a treadle sewing machine; through fields of dust-covered tarps and tents labeled "US Aid," "Canada," and "Red Cross of China"; and by numerous voodoo temples recognizable by the brightly colored paintings of saints and serpents on their outside walls. I recalled we were in the voodoo capital of Haiti.

After locating several new plywood houses, meeting and photographing the owners by their homes, and exploring a few possible sites for future houses, the tap-tap deposited us by the boys' orphanage where our team was busy working.

In the afternoon after the school by the orphanage let out, many of the uniformed schoolchildren surrounded our team members. Some played with Jean's long blonde hair; others grabbed a shovel and filled a wheelbarrow with gravel, imitating what our team was doing. In the midst of this activity, a lanky buck-toothed boy about ten years old came up to our group. He wore bright yellow crocs and a tattered black tee shirt that was not long enough to cover him fully. He had no shorts. He hung back shyly, but eventually took a spade and took a turn shoveling gravel into a wheelbarrow. The school-children taunted him, pointing to his nakedness. My heart broke for the boy, one of the fifty percent of Haitian children not in school and living in abject poverty.

When I pointed out the child to Lynn, she said, "We just can't take them all. There are so many more like him. The pastor has picked out children from the poorest of the poor in this area to attend school, but there are many more that we just can't take."

In the midst of the shoveling, sweating, pushing wheelbarrows, and playing with schoolchildren, Pastor Al, one of our team members from Minnesota, approached me.

"Your devotional inspired me to sponsor another child," he told me. Praise God!

Saturday, 22 October 2011
Miami Airport

I have made the Sovereign Lord my refuge; I will tell of all your deeds.

– Psalm 73:28 (NIV)

Back in the U.S.A. I went from a place of tarp huts and garbage-strewn streets, the smell of diesel and charcoal, and where many people eat once a day to an airport with flawless fruit tarts where an ice cream cone costs as much as the one-day salary of an educated Haitian ($5).

Speak up for the poor keeps going through my mind. Proverbs 31:8-9 says, *Speak up for those who cannot speak for themselves, for the rights of all who are destitute. Speak up and judge fairly; defend the rights of the poor and needy.*

Many of those around me have not seen what I've seen. Not just those at this fancy airport, but back home. Once again, God has placed a burden on my heart to speak up for the poor and to somehow convey to my fellow Americans how excessively rich we are materially—and how that often obstructs us spiritually.

Monday, 24 October 2011

What good will it be for a man if he gains the whole world, yet forfeits his soul?

– Matthew 16:26 (NIV)

As I sat in a chair hooked up to the IV getting yet another dose of Herceptin, I could hear the conversation of the oncology nurses at the desk in front of me. They were chatting about puppies. One nurse showed off photos of her pup as if it were her precious grandchild. Talk then turned to grooming—at a doggie salon, of course. Shampoo, cut, nails trimmed. I listened with a sickening feeling.

It's always so hard to hear this sort of thing after returning from a mission trip to Haiti or Africa. Our society has lost its common sense as to the place of animals in our lives. Children, like the Haitian boy in the yellow crocs, go hungry and unclothed while America's canine Dollies are going to the doggie spas to get their pawdicures and massages. I recalled a Rotary Club meeting where I had given a talk about my post-earthquake relief trip to Haiti. I had just shown photos of people living in dismal conditions under cardboard and sheets, sleeping on cinder blocks in a field of mud. In a dramatic change of topic, one businessman told the others that he'd just sent his dog to summer dog camp. I'd never heard of such a thing. Summer camp—for dogs?! I was seized with a mixture of fury and sadness; I wanted to scream and cry at the same time. It's madness! We've become so obsessed with our canine companions that they live with us, sleep in our beds, vacation with us—and go off to summer camps? As a foreign visitor once pointed out, "You Americans take more walks with your dogs than you do with your children."

Granted, unlike me, these people haven't put faces and names to the impersonal statistics. Their hearts haven't been softened toward the world's poor. Oh, how I wish I could take them all with me on my next trip to Haiti!

November

Friday, 11 November 2011

Call to Me, and I will answer you, and show you great and mighty things, which you do not know.

– Jeremiah 33:3 (NKJV)

The day started out like many others recently, humdrum and tinged with sadness. The trees have been stripped of their summer garb and stand uncomfortably bare against skies, skies that have assumed their winter colorlessness. November is here. Winter looms ahead like a gray challenge.

When, Lord, is it over? How much longer do You want me to journal? I have wondered since the summer. *When can I stop thinking about cancer and put it behind me? When can I stop writing? And how will I know when to stop?*

When the Lord orchestrates something, only He can see the beginning and the end. For me to see His great and mighty works, I must be obedient to His leading. I never would have journaled through cancer if He hadn't told me. I never could have guessed what He had planned for me.

Last week Nadia called to inform me that the man who had prophesied to her co-worker is coming to Rochester to lead a service tonight. Nadia and I arranged to meet at the church, Faith Temple.

I learned from the church website that the visiting preacher was Ted Shuttersworth, and from his website that he was an evangelist who holds crusades. An evangelist? I hoped to meet someone with the gift of prophesy who would have a word from God for me, not an evangelist preaching the gospel and calling people to repent. I so wanted to hear that my cancer would not return, that I could put this episode of my life behind me. I had hoped against hope that this preacher would have a special message just for me. I had imagined that after the service when people were mingling about I'd go up to him, and he'd look at me and tell me that God says that I am healed and my cancer will not return.

But that's not what happened at all.

Although I've heard evangelists on the radio, I've never heard a nationally known evangelist in person, so I was curious. This event sounded too good to keep to myself, so I suggested to Tad that we go with our children, and to Nadia that she bring her family, too. I also proposed that we take Igor with us.

We hadn't been to this church before, so we came early. With a nationally known guest, perhaps it would be hard to find a seat. After we walked into the sanctuary and saw the instruments on the stage and the size of the speakers, we took seats about two-thirds of the way back as far from the front speakers as we could get without sitting right under the back speakers that hung from the balcony. Six to eight hundred people slowly filled the sanctuary. We didn't know anyone there.

Tad is a musician of classical hymns. When the service started, the music was painfully loud and unrefined. I knew that listening to this worship music was as agonizing for Tad as watching a slideshow of poorly composed photos would be for me. After a while, Tad leaned across Larissa and Nadia toward me. "Kathryn, I'm going to leave. I just can't take this."

"I'd like to hear the preacher," I told Tad, "so I'll get a ride home with Nadia."

But Tad didn't leave. He later told me than when he prayed about leaving, God told him to stay put.

After a long period of raucous worship, Brother Ted Shuttlesworth began a sermon. Brother Ted is not at all soft-spoken. He whoops and shouts "Hallelujah!" and "Amen!" He also has a lovely, strong singing voice; he interspersed his preaching with songs.

He spoke for over an hour—an hour of Bible teaching and captivating personal stories. Then he walked away from the podium, down from the stage, and as he continued to preach, he strode up the center aisle to a woman in a magenta sweatshirt sitting three rows in front of us. He said to her, "When I was preaching, Jesus told me, 'Go tell her, her blood is completely healed'—no matter what the doctor told you!"

That's all he said, no explanation. The woman nodded, so she must have understood what he meant.

Then Brother Ted walked a few more paces toward the back of the church, microphone in hand, and came up to Tad. "Where you folks from? Where you from, Brother?" he asked.

"Rochester," Tad replied. He never says 'Ukraine' even though I'm convinced that Brother Ted knew Tad is from another country.

"Right here in New York," Brother Ted repeated for the audience to hear.

"Is this your daughter?" he motioned to Larissa.

"Yes."

"Wife down here somewhere?"

I raised my hand just a little bit. I was sitting two seats away from Tad.

"Where's the wife? Could you com—" He started talking to me, then turned to address Tad. "Would it be all right if I prayed for your wife?"

Tad nodded. (He later told me that it meant a lot that Brother Ted asked his permission.)

"Please come here, little lady."

I made my way over Nadia, Larissa, Tad, and Igor, and stood out in the aisle.

"God bless you," he said, then turned to Tad. "Your precious husband. Is this your son?" He nodded toward Igor, who had the aisle seat.

"Sort of. He's like our adopted son," I tried to explain, but the congregation couldn't hear what I was saying.

"Just some boy you picked up off the street," Brother Ted teased, and turned to Igor and shook his hand.

Then he got serious. "When I pray for you, the Lord's going to heal you perfectly. You believe that?"

"Yes," I said.

"When I was preaching, I saw the Lord, He spoke to me about this" (he pointed to the woman in magenta), "then I felt the anointing go right down this row—some of you felt it while I was preaching—but then I noticed the anointing rested and abided and remained on you" —he glanced up at the clock overhead—"at five after nine. That's fifteen minutes ago. And I'm gonna tell you this: the Lord takes the death sentence off your life! He extends your life on the earth. Amen?"

My heart was pounding at this point, and I could hardly believe what was happening: he wasn't privately telling me a message from God; he'd singled me out of the crowd right in front of everyone. I nodded my head and said, "Amen" as tears filled my eyes.

"You got a bad report, but God gives you a good report."

"Thank you, praise God," I said quietly.

"You believe it?"

"Yes, I do," I nodded as everyone in the sanctuary watched.

"You receive it. Then everything changes from this night forward. Amen?"

People were clapping. Brother Ted looked at Tad. Tad nodded and said, "Amen."

I made a movement to go back in my row and sit back down, but Brother Ted took my hand and directed me to stand in front of him.

"I'm not done with you yet. I'm going to lay hands on you like Jesus said to do. Jesus said you shall lay hands on the sick, and they *shall* recover! I come here tonight for miracles. And you got it!"

Then he placed his right hand on my forehead and kind of pushed me.

"Sssshhhhhhu! I curse every cell that is out of alignment with the Word of God, and I command healing in her body, and blood, and the marrow of your bones. In the name of Jesus, you shall live and not die. HALLELUJAH!!" (He shouted Hallelujah so loudly that I jumped.) "Whosoever heareth these sayings of mine, Jesus said, and doeth them... I did my part. He said lay hands on the sick. Then it says the sick shall recover. When you leave tonight, get out of here and recover!" He patted my arm as I turned to go back to my seat. "Hallelujah!" he said once more as he turned toward the front of the church. People clapped, he walked back up the aisle.

The entire episode took two minutes. I'll remember it the rest of my life. God not only answered my wish, He did so in front of hundreds.

Epilogue

"The LORD's right hand is lifted high; the LORD's right hand has done mighty things!" I will not die but live, and will proclaim what the LORD has done.

— Psalm 118:16-17 (NIV)

The following Monday I went to my oncologist and told her that I wanted to stop treatment immediately. I hesitated, then decided to tell her about the Friday service. Dr. Smith listened politely, but I could tell that she didn't believe in that sort of thing.

"Some patients feel that as long as they're under treatment, they're doing something to prevent cancer. They go through a period of grieving and depression when they stop treatment. Somehow I don't think that you're going to be like that," said Dr. Smith.

I smiled. "No, I'm sure I won't!"

On Thursday, I met with my surgeon and set up a time to remove the mediport from my chest. She performed that minor surgery in her office two days before Thanksgiving Day. What a day of giving thanks we had!

I still remember Tatiana's prayer, "Thank you for loving her enough to trust her with this illness." God entrusted me with cancer for a reason. It's not a journey I'd wish on anyone, nor one that I care to repeat. But I grew and learned from it—learned to rely more on God, and understood what treasures the people in my life are. I also discovered how to be more attuned to His soft voice.

Each cancer journey is different. Not everyone is as fortunate as I was. I did not have to spend weeks or months in hospitals. And I was blessed because at the end of my cancer journey I was healed. I even declined seeing my oncologist after my first follow-up visit because, as I was told months before, there were no blood tests she could do, nothing that she could monitor for a recurrence of cancer. I saw no point in these doctor visits.

Two years later, a friend invited me to join a faith-based cancer support group. I resisted. Wasn't my cancer journey over? I didn't even go to a support group when I had cancer; why should I go to one after I'm well? I decided to attend just once to please Liz. I have been attending these meetings ever since—and really enjoying the camaraderie. Those going through cancer need to hear the survivor stories. They need the sympathetic ear of someone who truly understands. And on some level, I need to belong to this group, too. After all, *cancer* and *Kathryn* have been used in the same sentence for a while now.

Two-and-a-half years after I was healed, I woke up one June morning and realized that the ache in my left hip, which I'd attributed to arthritis for over a year, had magnified into an excruciating burning pain for several days. Why was the pain on just one side? Why hadn't I checked out this "arthritis" sooner? Hadn't the nurse practitioner warned me of relentless pain in my hip? I had taken Advil, but… As quickly as the thought entered my mind—*could it be bone cancer?*— I plummeted into depths of worry. Fear engulfed me. Once you have cancer, the fear of it returning is always lurking under the surface. I had thought it was miles underground.

"Mom, God told you that you're healed," Larissa reminded me. But I was inconsolable.

God is indeed faithful. Despite my unbelief, the bone pain was not from cancer. However, the fright spurred me from my stupor.

That experience catapulted me into even greater ventures with God. He next led me on a wild and wonderful journey that I hadn't dreamed possible. I am currently transcribing it from last summer's journals.

March 2016
Rochester, New York

Appendix

E-mails sent out as mass mailings:

Date: Mon, Jan 3, 2011 5:07 pm
Subject: MRI news

Just got a call from the same doctor who did the biopsy. He examined the MRI results and said that it's good news: the lump apparently has not spread. It's fairly big—2.3 cm (almost one inch) in diameter—but surgery and radiation should take care of it. He thinks that I will not need chemotherapy. For the scientific, the doctor categorized the cancer cell as a "nuclear grade 3." His best guess was that the lump grew this big in 6–7 months, so I can stop beating myself up for not going for a mammogram last January.

Thanks so much for your support and prayers!
Kathryn

Sent: Sun, Feb 13, 2011 9:06 pm
Subject: update from Kathryn

Sorry for the mass mailing. I've had a lot of people inquire about my health, so instead of typing individual responses that get briefer with each note, I decided to send out this longer, but impersonal note. If you have already heard some of this, I apologize.

On December 29, I was diagnosed with breast cancer. I had found the lump myself after reading Elizabeth Edwards' obituary and how she had found her own golf ball-sized lump. How could she have a lump that large and not know it? I wondered. I found the answer when taking a bath about a week later. The lump I found was almost an inch in diameter.

When I went for a mammogram, I was informed that 80% of lumps are benign. However, my lump did look "suspicious," said that doctor, so he took a core needle biopsy. He called me the next evening with results.

"Unfortunately…" he began, and I barely heard what came next. I did register that I had to schedule an MRI and find a surgeon and schedule an appointment with him/her. Since I was going to Haiti on January 8, I knew that I had to make all the arrangements for surgery before I left.

During that one phone call, the course of my life took a radical turn. I had just stepped off the leisurely sidewalk of life onto a bullet train that someone else was driving. Since then, my doctor appointments are scheduled for me and the course of my treatment is predetermined by others.

Although initially I thought I would just need a lumpectomy, mine was an aggressive cancer, and by my surgery on January 26, four weeks after the mammogram and initial diagnosis, the lump had grown from the initial 2.3 cm to 2.9 cm. I had a mastectomy. And although the lymph nodes taken out during surgery were free of cancer, the size of the lump and the aggressiveness of the cancer warrant chemotherapy. The cancer was considered a Stage 2 simply because of the size of the lump.

For the scientific minded, the cancer was a nuclear grade 3 (out of 3), mitotic count 2 (out of 3), and glandular/tubular differentiation: score 3 (out of 3). The overall grade: Grade 3 (score 8 - 9) out of 9. In other words, it was quite aggressive; I got close to a perfect score!

The cancer is estrogen and progesterone receptor negative (not affected by female hormones; female hormones don't make it grow), but HER2/neu positive 3+ (out of 3). I felt like I got bonus points on this one. HER2/neu is a growth-promoting protein. HER2/neu positive cancers tend to grow and spread more aggressively than other breast cancers.

Thus chemotherapy was highly recommended. Not just the regular four months, but an entire year! I'm to get three different chemicals. I'll be getting Herceptin, an antibody that targets HER2/neu-sensitive cells, weekly for 18 weeks, then once every three weeks for the remainder of a year. The other concoction of two chemicals, which usually makes hair fall out, will be administered six times, once every three weeks. Thus the first four months, I'll be getting chemo treatments at least weekly, sometimes twice per week. I counted up a total of 35 treatments, thus this coming Wednesday, I'm going for minor surgery to have a mediport installed. This is a device, installed under my skin on my chest, with a catheter that connects the port into a large vein. The port has a septum into which chemotherapy drugs can be injected and from which blood can be drawn. If I were to get an IV instead, my veins might be permanently damaged by that many treatments.

Cancer is a disease that affects your mind as much as your body. The more I learned about my cancer, the more frightened I became. Aggressiveness of the cancer, survival statistics, where it tends to return and how soon—the information became a bit overwhelming and depressing. It affects my mood at times. Even seeing diagrams of the port and how it'll be installed makes me queasy. Reading all the possible side effects of chemotherapy makes me feel weak in the knees. I want to be educated, but in some ways it's better not to know too much. It won't help me, but might affect my mood and outlook negatively. These days, when I hear that someone died of cancer, I cringe. It's close to home.

This Wednesday, I'm having the mediport installed at Rochester General Hospital. It's an outpatient procedure. I will be starting chemotherapy on March 1. I appreciate e-mails, phone calls, visits, and anything that keeps my mind off my illness and all those scary statistics, and I'm especially grateful for your prayers, both for my health and my mental state.

Thank you for your friendship and support. God bless you!
Kathryn

Contact information

To contact Kathryn, share your experiences, follow her blog, request a speaking engagement, or view photos from her mission trips, visit www.ventureswithgod.com.

CPSIA information can be obtained
at www.ICGtesting.com
Printed in the USA
LVHW111735300619
622770LV00038B/559/P

9 780997 398397